ATTITUDE

URBAN
EDUCATION
WITH AN
ATTITUDE

EDITED BY

Lauri Johnson
Mary E. Finn
Rebecca Lewis

state university of new york press

Cover photograph of the Buffalo skyline by Rebecca Lewis.

Photograph: Futures Academy students by staff; Shadow Boxes Jenner School by Mathias Schergen; CVCV students by Joel Malley; Center X teachers by staff; CAIC staff by Rebecca Lewis; Social Context of Education course by staff. Drawing of lawyer by Joseph Gilley. All work is used by permission.

We would like to thank Roger Bruce for his generous help in preparing the photographs for publication.

Published by
STATE UNIVERSITY OF NEW YORK PRESS
ALBANY

© 2005 State University of New York

For information, address
State University of New York Press
90 State Street, Suite 700, Albany, NY 12207

Production, Laurie Searl
Marketing, Anne M. Valentine

Library of Congress Cataloging-in-Publication Data

Urban education with an attitude / edited by Lauri Johnson, Mary E. Finn, and Rebecca Lewis
   p. cm.
   Includes bibliographical references and index.
   ISBN 0-7914-6379-6 (alk. paper) — ISBN 0-7914-6380-X (pbk. : alk. paper)
      1. Education, Urban—United States—Case studies.   2. Community education—United States—Case studies.   3. Popular education—United States—Case studies.   4. Teachers—Training of—United States—Case studies.   5. Curriculum change—United States—Case studies.   I. Johnson, Lauri.   II. Finn, Mary E.   III. Lewis, Rebecca, 1952–

LC5141.U73 2005
307'.9173'2—dc22   2004048160

10 9 8 7 6 5 4 3 2 1

For Matthew and Christopher,
who love the city and all its possibilities
Lauri

For Positive Patrick
Mary

Contents

Reforming Teacher Education
to Improve Urban Education

University Partnerships for Parent Empowerment

Preface

In times of social crisis, communities often turn to universities and colleges for help. As major repositories of intellectual capital, universities are also primary institutions of social power and, as such, it is understandable that communities would look to universities for help. This relationship suggests, however, the role and responsibilities of the university in society. I subscribe to the belief that great universities will be known for and distinguished by their ability to solve, or at least make meaningful contributions to, the solutions of our most pressing social problems.

Surely the challenges of K–12 education must count as some of the most serious facing our society today. In schools of education then, where we are preparing the professionals who must meet and manage these challenges, how can we *not* direct our research and our collective efforts toward developing and promoting both strategies and conceptual frames that address this need? Would a culinary institute be credible if its graduates could only cook breakfast in a microwave? Or a medical school whose graduates could not stand the sight of blood? The worth of the academic experience in schools of education is manifested in graduates who are equipped for the multidimensional complexities of the classroom.

The list of educational exigencies ranges from the realities of language, culture, and cognitive styles to the nature of pre-service teaching experiences, leadership in educational administration, school resources, socioeconomic access, and family systems. What is the role of graduate schools of education relative to the crisis in education? They are uniquely equipped to generate relevant theory and to translate research and theory into effective practice. Research and theory, informed by practice, provide powerful tools for understanding the nature of needed interventions as well as the means for delivering them.

This volume addresses the current crisis in urban education. It originated in the presentations made during "Urban Education Month," a series of lectures and workshops sponsored by the University at Buffalo Graduate School of Education's Urban Education Institute intended to facilitate a community-wide dialogue focusing on the challenges facing our K–12 system. This dialogue was held on campus and off, and included faculty, parents, and school district personnel, including teachers, school board members and superintendents. It was my belief then, as now, that schools of education must be encouraged and supported in their efforts to engage professional and lay stakeholders as mutual collaborators in order to fully understand and ultimately impact change. The dialogue was very successful in that each invited guest made substantive and noteworthy contributions to the understanding of the issues of urban education. As the Dean of the Graduate School of Education, I encouraged publication of this volume in the hope that others will continue this discussion until such time as tangible progress can be claimed by all.

Finally, the Graduate School of Education at the University at Buffalo has a commitment to urban education and a commitment to the urban community: it is where we live. While the distinction between urban, suburban, and rural are important and valid, in my view it is more a question of degree rather than kind. Therefore, if we can make a positive difference in the urban arena, we will have made a significant contribution to the whole.

Mary H. Gresham
Dean, Graduate School of Education
Vice President, Public Service and Urban Affairs
The State University of New York at Buffalo

Introduction: Linking Theory, Practice, and Community in Urban School Reform

Lauri Johnson, Mary E. Finn, and Rebecca Lewis

THIS BOOK PROFILES LOCAL AND NATIONAL efforts to transform urban education and reinvent urban teacher preparation through the development of democratic school-community relationships and community-based curricula. It is premised on our belief that authentic urban school reform requires educators to work collaboratively with parents, neighborhood activists, policy makers, and community development specialists to alter the power relationships between urban schools and the communities they serve, and to create relevant, student-centered curricula and teaching methods.

The current crisis in urban schooling is well recognized. Prevailing responses to this crisis have been to hold urban schools accountable by raising standards and instituting high-stakes assessments for students and teachers alike. These top-down reform proposals too often have centralized policy and curriculum decisions and resulted in an increased emphasis on "teaching to the test," a strategy that has not adequately addressed the academic needs of urban children and youth. We believe these reforms cannot bridge the long-standing cultural divide between the educational establishment and urban families and produce the schools that are needed to give all urban students a high quality education.

The chapters in this volume offer alternative responses to the crisis in urban education by making urban schools accountable to the communities they serve through policy initiatives that promote educational equity, community-based curricula, and teacher education and parent empowerment programs that emphasize democratic collaboration between universities, urban teachers, parents, and community members. The genesis of this volume originated in a series of programs organized by Mary Finn, Director of the Urban Education Institute at the University at Buffalo Graduate School of Education, during Urban Education Month in March 2001. This month-long focus was designed to engage urban teachers, parents, university faculty, and graduate students in the discussion of innovative approaches that link theory, practice, and community involvement in urban school reform, with the goal of offering, as Jeannie Oakes says in this volume, "some images and ideas that may embolden people . . . to *act* on their best dreams for American schooling" [emphasis ours].

Several of the chapters were talks by urban education scholars and practitioners from throughout the country presented during Urban Education Month. Other chapters in this book highlight efforts by faculty and graduate students at the University at Buffalo to link the university more closely with work in city schools and urban neighborhoods.

Buffalo, New York, is often described as a postindustrial "rust-belt" city. The current population of just under 300, 000 (down from a high of almost 600,000 in the late 1960s) represents a steady decline in the industrial base and a population shift to the first-ring and second-ring suburbs, with a resulting loss of property tax revenues to support public schools. There has also been a historic disconnect between the university community and the city schools. The Graduate School of Education is located on the North campus of the University at Buffalo that was built in the suburbs during the early 1970s, much to the dismay of many of the city's residents, who continue to believe that a downtown campus might have helped to anchor Buffalo's struggling neighborhoods.

In the fall of 1998, the new dean advocated a focus on urban education as a central mission of the Graduate School of Education and established an Urban Education committee co-chaired by Patrick Finn and Lauri Johnson to develop a strategic plan. The Buffalo-based projects profiled in this book represent some of the recent efforts to use university resources to serve city neighborhoods and act as a catalyst for urban school reform.

Through the voices of teacher educators, community activists, urban teachers, parents, and students, we aim to illustrate how the theory and practice of community engagement might be enacted in urban teaching and preparation programs. Too often, when teacher preparation programs link research and theory-based practice, the theory studied is devoid of the social, cultural, political, and physical contexts of urban schools. The authors of chapters in this volume focus on socially and culturally based theory, theory about equity and justice and the power relations that call for action to address the educational needs of urban students.

The notion of linking sociocultural and politically grounded theory to teacher education was first developed in the 1930s at Teachers College, Columbia University, where a program was established to provide educational practitioners with a broad, integrated, and progressive approach to teaching and learning, drawing on the traditionally separate fields of educational sociology, history, philosophy, anthropology and social psychology (Tozer, Anderson, & Armbruster, 1990). By the 1960s, teacher education students at many universities were encouraged to focus their professional development in the areas of subject-based curriculum and methods of instruction, where the theories that underlie the practice are more likely to be psychological than sociological, and more inclined to encourage support for the status quo than to challenge or change it.

In addition, the emergence of urban education as a field of study in the 1960s and early 1970s often took a deficit approach to urban students and their families rather than examining the structural inequities that created poor urban neighborhoods. The legacy of teacher preparation programs that are largely discipline-centered and aim to "fix" poor and working class students and their families remain with us today.

In short, traditional approaches to linking theory and practice in teacher education have not resulted in widespread equity and social justice *action* on the part of educators. We believe such action may be exactly what is required to create urban schools that excite and inspire. While the chapters in this volume offer diverse approaches to urban school reform, there is a single theme that resonates throughout the volume, and that is the necessity of honest, democratic collaboration with the immediate community in which the urban schools are situated. We believe it is perhaps the single most important imperative that the dominant, top-down trend in urban education reform has sadly neglected.

Patrick J. Finn, in *Literacy with an Attitude: Educating Working-Class Children in Their Own Self-Interest* (1999), argues that if we are to make significant progress in urban education, those most affected by the current conditions, the urban working class themselves, must take an active role. According to Finn, many parents sense their children are getting a lesser education, and while that angers them, they often feel isolated and dependent on the authority of the professional educators to do the right thing. To expect that the education establishment can implement the necessary reforms solely on their own initiative, however, is unrealistic.

In order to reform urban education, Finn urges us to study the work of Saul Alinsky, who used the labor organizer model to create a new public activist role, the "community organizer." Public engagement is the term most often used to describe the efforts of a community organizer. In his summary of the 1998 report by The Annenberg Institute on Public Engagement for Public Education, Finn provides a description of public engagement and its promise:

> There is a quiet revolution taking place in public education. It is the beginning of a fundamental shift in the kind of behavior Americans engage in on behalf of their children. It signals a change in the structures of power in education. It is referred to as public conversation, parent involvement, school/community partnerships, citizens' action, neighborhood improvement, community organizing, and even standards setting. It has the following characteristics: it focuses on improving teaching and learning; it brings to the table those who are typically excluded; and it facilitates training and dissemination of information that prepares communities to make tough decisions. (p. 196)

The chapters in this volume reflect the wide variety of ways public engagement might link teachers, parents, and community to the reform process and contribute to improving urban schools. They are organized around the following themes: Call to Action: Promoting Educational Equity; Linking Urban Schools to Their Communities; Reforming Teacher Education to Reform Urban Education; and University Partnerships for Parent Empowerment.

CALL TO ACTION: PROMOTING EDUCATIONAL EQUITY

Current solutions to improve student achievement in urban schools, such as higher standards, achievement testing, accountability, charter schools and vouchers, teacher-proof curricula, and school-business partnerships, are intended to satisfy demands by educators, parents, and community leaders who are frustrated with the level of urban students' learning. But the success of any reform is dependent on the extent to which the beneficiaries of the reform are involved in its development and implementation (e.g., see Fields and Feinberg, 2001). The chapters in this section argue that without democratic and participatory educational systems—from students and teachers involved in curriculum decision-making to parents and community members addressing the need for equitable funding and neighborhood development—education reform has little chance of ameliorating the social and economic forces that are widening the income gap in U.S. cities.

Pedro Noguera links the problems of schools to the culture of the larger society, questions education reforms that focus only on testing, standards and accountability, and vouchers, and argues that the urban school curriculum should connect students to their communities. Dennis Carlson challenges school reforms that "de-skill" classroom teachers through scripted curricula and emphasize cost efficiency, and argues that there is a relationship between the crises in urban schools and the way society and communities understand teachers' work. Michael A. Rebell describes the history of fiscal equity in education cases in the U.S., the shift from equity cases to adequacy cases, and the strategy of tying fiscal adequacy to standards-based reform, which was developed by the Campaign for Fiscal Equity in New York with input from focus groups of community members. Henry Louis Taylor Jr. argues that the necessary relationship between school reform and community development must be recognized if the structural inequities in urban areas are to be addressed.

LINKING URBAN SCHOOLS TO THEIR COMMUNITIES

Redressing power differences in the social and economic forces that impact urban education is vitally necessary but is not in itself sufficient to improve urban education. Educational structures have to change as well, from classroom to school to district. Curricula must become more community based. Textbooks should take a back seat to teachers and students exploring their worlds together, with teachers designing lessons that help students make connections between their community "funds of knowledge" (Moll, 1992) and "mainstream academic" knowledge. Experiential learning and the expressive arts, whether using traditional media or digital media, are pedagogical approaches too often ignored in test-driven education reform. This section highlights curriculum programs that are interdisciplinary, connect students to their neighborhood and the wider world, and use varied mediational tools to foster learning.

This emphasis on child-centered, experiential curricula that ground students' learning experiences in their local environment has a long tradition in progressive education (e.g., see Dewey, 1938). In recent years it has also been manifested in rural and environmental education through the notion of "place-based" or "place-conscious" education, which aims to "enlist teachers and students in the firsthand experience of local life and in the political process of understanding and shaping what happens there" (Gruenewald, 2003, p. 620). These chapters highlight examples of how "place-conscious" education that is centered on the strengths of urban schools and communities might be implemented.

Greg Farrell and Michael McCarthy describe Expeditionary Learning, a school reform effort that is based on experiential learning through the interdisciplinary, long-term study of a topic that meets content standards and often results in a project that connects the school to the larger community. Arnold Aprill describes ongoing arts partnership programs in thirty public schools in Chicago, which integrate the arts into the curriculum, provide professional development for classroom teachers, and connect the schools to the larger arts community of the city. Mathias Schergen, a Chicago art teacher, describes the creation of an art installation called the "Memory Museum," by students in a Chicago elementary school in response to the massive wave of gentrification and redevelopment taking place in their community. Suzanne Miller and Suzanne Borowicz report on City Voices, City Visions, a project that prepares teachers to use digital video technologies with their sixth- to twelfth-grade urban students.

REFORMING TEACHER EDUCATION TO
IMPROVE URBAN EDUCATION

While many colleges and universities have programs to prepare students to become teachers in urban schools, the number of teacher education programs that focus on social justice, equity, and community engagement remains far too small. Most teacher preparation programs offer few opportunities for students to learn the basics of parent and community involvement through their coursework and practicums or to gain an understanding of the strengths of the diverse communities that make up poor urban neighborhoods. This section includes three examples of teacher education approaches that recognize the need to prepare teachers who understand and appreciate the communities in which they teach, as well as the need for community involvement in authentic school reform.

Jeannie Oakes describes the teacher education program at UCLA's Center X, in which learning to teach means becoming a member of a community of practice within a school and also involves spending time in and making connections with the communities outside of schools, with an explicit commitment to social justice. Ann Marie Lauricella reports on a learning experience designed to expose pre-service teachers to the positive aspects of city life, through visits to urban neighborhoods led by local activists and community organizers. Dennis Shirley reflects on how a statewide school-university partnership in Massachusetts can serve as a source of community organizing for parent engagement and involve teacher education students in the real-life issues of urban schools.

UNIVERSITY PARTNERSHIPS FOR PARENT EMPOWERMENT

The academic community, particularly urban universities and their schools of education, has an obligation to address the current crisis in urban education. Just as public schools must connect with their local communities and include all participants in the educational endeavor if education reforms are to succeed, urban colleges and universities also must connect with local schools and their communities if they are to contribute to education reform that brings about greater social justice and equity. The chapters in this section are examples of programs and projects, created by university educators and their graduate students, that seek to increase parental and community involvement in urban schools. These programs are based on a model of sharing power so that all members of the learning community can contribute to the process.

Lauri Johnson gives an account of a university-community partnership that conducted a door-to-door survey of parents of Buffalo Public School children about the schools we have and the schools we need. This partnership jumpstarted other school reform projects in the school district. Gillian Richardson reports the results of her study of working-class parents' perspectives on the politics of literacy education. Patrick Finn, Lauri Johnson, and Mary Finn describe a series of workshops conducted in a poor and working-class Buffalo school designed to develop "powerful literacy" and empower parents as active partners in and advocates for their children's education.

FINAL NOTE

The voices of students, parents, and educators throughout this volume challenge us to reimagine urban education, to move from a view focused on the deficits of urban schools and neighborhoods to one in which urban students, parents, teachers, and community members are empowered to transform urban schools through their collective efforts. The authors acknowledge and applaud the benefits that can be derived from democratic and participatory educational systems that collectively develop curriculum linked to community needs, enlist multiple stakeholders in working for equitable funding and neighborhood development, and establish true partnerships between university teacher education programs and the urban communities that they serve. We invite you to join us in this effort to envision urban schools that challenge and inspire and serve as engines for social change in urban neighborhoods and the larger community—to practice urban education with an attitude.

REFERENCES

Dewey, J. (1938). *Experience and education.* New York: Macmillan.

Fields, A. B., & Feinberg, W. (2001). *Education and democratic theory: Finding a place for community participation in public school reform.* Albany: State University of New York Press.

Finn, P. (1999). *Literacy with an attitude: Educating working-class children in their own self-interest.* Albany: State University of New York Press.

Gruenewald, D. A. (2003). Foundations of place: A multidisciplinary framework for place-conscious education. *American Educational Research Journal, 40*(3), 619–654.

Moll, L. C. (1992). Funds of knowledge for teaching: Using a qualitative approach to connect homes and classrooms. *Theory into Practice, 31*(1), 132–141.

Tozer, S., Anderson, T. H., & Armbruster, B. (1990). Psychological and social foundations in teacher education: A thematic introduction. *Teachers College Record, 92*(3), 293–299.

Call to Action:

Promoting Educational Equity in Urban School Reform

1 The Racial Achievement Gap: How Can We Assure an Equity of Outcomes?

Pedro Noguera

Pedro Noguera is a Professor in The Steinhardt School of Education at New York University. His work has focused on the ways in which schools are influenced by social and economic conditions in the urban environment. In this chapter, he characterizes the problems of public education as questions of social inequality and political will, rather than lack of technical capacity. The problems of schools are tied to the culture of the larger society, but discussions of education reform tend to focus only on testing, standards and accountability, and vouchers. Noguera argues that these narrowly conceived reforms cannot address the current youth crisis and the disconnect between students and adults. Schools should focus instead on engaging students intellectually and creating lifelong learners, by creating a curriculum that is meaningful to students and connects them to the larger community.

WHAT IS NOW WIDELY RECOGNIZED as one of the leading issues facing our country is the plight of our schools and the state of education. Not only has the current administration made education its first domestic policy initiative, but articles related to education and schools are featured daily in the media. There is a clamor in the country for ways to improve our public schools. It is ironic in some ways, for this is truly a rich country. We are the only remaining superpower; we can do incredible things with respect to research and technology; we can generate wealth, producing hundreds of millionaires a year—but somehow the task of educating our children eludes us. Over and over on international tests, the United States ranks last among industrialized nations, particularly in the areas of math and science. We are a first-world nation by economic standards, but a third-world nation by educational standards.

Our problems in education are problems of social inequality. They are not problems of knowledge—we know how to educate young people. There are lots of examples of schools in this country that do it well, even for poor youth. It is not a question of not knowing—we know how to do this. It is also not a question of not having the money. It is a question of will—whether or not

The University Project, with Berkeley High School

Codirected by Pedro Noguera and the Vice Principal of Berkeley High School, the University Project was initiated in order to study some of the issues raised by the film, *School Colors*, particularly the gap in achievement that is manifest along racial and socioeconomic lines. At the time, Berkeley High School served approximately 3,000 students and had 180 teachers. The project was organized by a core group of five teachers, all of whom had credibility among their peers. Close to forty teachers were involved in teacher research. The project also involved ten graduate students who worked with Noguera, as well as other university faculty and resources.

One portion of the study followed the class of 2000 for four years, looking at a wide range of factors, including social patterns, class schedules, and after-school activities and interests. The study used shadowing (including teachers-as-researchers shadowing students) and focus groups with students as well as parents. The data collected in the research study became the basis for ongoing discussion within the school community. The project also helped develop a Parents Center, staffed by parents, and a student outreach committee, which conducted forums with students. Interviewed in 2001, Noguera observed, "While we didn't want to create conflict, we realized that reform is always going to be political. Who gets heard is a result of who has the loudest voice and who is the most organized. . . . Part of what we had to do was find ways to get the parents of kids who were not doing well to be more organized so they could be heard."

—Editor's interview with Pedro Noguera 3/21/01

we care enough to provide all students, regardless of race and class, with a good education. So far the answer is no. We don't have the will, but there are lots of poor countries that do have the will.

For the last four years, I have had the privilege of teaching in Barbados, a small underdeveloped country that has exemplary schools. Three years ago students in Barbados took the SATs, because a growing number of students are interested in applying to American universities. (In the past, most college students from Barbados went to Britain or Canada.) The average score was just above 1200, which is higher than the average score for all ethnic groups in this country. Why is it that in an underdeveloped country like Barbados, being poor and black is not an obstacle to achieving at high levels?

It is not just Barbados that manages to do this. I have been to Curacao, which is a Dutch colony. There, somehow, it is possible for all students to learn to speak four languages fluently: Spanish, Dutch, English, and Papamiento. In this country we treat speaking a language other than English as though it were a liability, as though it somehow makes someone less than intelligent, and our schools work to ensure that students are not bilingual. We think that English only is the way to go. We are one of the few countries in the world that takes pride in the fact that we speak only one language.

And then there is Cuba. I hate to use Cuba as an example because Americans tend to think that anything Cuba does must be bad—but Cuba has done extraordinary things in education since the revolution in 1959. When you remember that most of the educated people in Cuba left the island after the revolution, what they have accomplished in education is truly extraordinary. At the time of the revolution there were 3,000 doctors in Cuba; today there are 60,000. UNESCO recently gave a test of basic skills to fourteen Latin American nations; Cuba outperformed all the other countries by a wide margin—the next country, Argentina, scored twenty points lower. Cuba shows that speaking Spanish isn't a liability for achieving at high levels. Moreover, Cuba shows that material incentives are not necessary to produce highly educated people—today, doctors earn less than cab drivers in Cuba. In our country, however, material reward is the primary incentive used to motivate students to learn.

What makes it so difficult to educate students at high levels? Again, the answer is largely political rather than an issue of technical capacity—we know how to do this. Richard Rothstein, a columnist for *The New York Times*, recently wrote that achievement levels could be raised by ignoring schools altogether but doing two things. First, focus on lead abatement. We know that exposure to lead in the environment results in lowered ability in children. We know that children in the inner city are more likely to be exposed to lead paint, lead in the soil, and lead in the air than other children. If we focused on removing lead from the environment, we could boost achievement ten points on the Stanford 9.

Secondly, he argues, there is evidence that about 25 percent of the youth in the inner city have at least one cavity that has been untreated because they don't have dental care. As anyone who has ever suffered from tooth decay knows, it can be hard to focus on anything if your teeth hurt. If we made sure that every child had access to dental care, we probably would see an increase in achievement. If we also provided for the large numbers of children who are labeled as slow readers because they never have had their eyes tested and they need glasses, we might see another increase in achievement.

Many of our educational difficulties have nothing to do with education at all, but with the fact that as a society, we don't care that much about poor children. We allow poor children to go to school hungry, to go to school with bad teeth, to live in homes with lead exposure, to have poor nutrition when they are in utero. We wring our hands and engage in acts of seeming to care about education, of seeming to want to improve schools, yet we are unwilling to address issues that we know are vital to any serious effort to educate students. Any teacher can tell you that a child who hasn't eaten has trouble sitting still in class; a child who hasn't slept in a warm home has trouble concentrating in school; a child who is abused often acts out. What happens outside of school affects what happens in school, but we pretend we can focus on education in the narrowest way, without addressing these other issues.

Three narrowly focused reforms dominate current policy discussions: testing, standards and accountability, and vouchers. Perhaps the primary reform of the day is testing—we are going to test students to death. I'm not against testing; it is a valuable way to measure what has been learned. Instead of relying exclusively on standardized tests, however, our assessments should also demonstrate what students can do with what they have learned. But first, students have to learn something, and we are responsible for providing students with knowledge that can be tested. The most valuable form of testing, I would argue, is diagnostic testing.

The second reform of the day is standards and accountability. The newspaper in Buffalo lists schools according to the results of their achievement on tests—California and Massachusetts do the same thing, and we all know the rankings before they come out. It would be surprising—and newsworthy—if affluent students from suburban schools were at the bottom and poor students from inner city schools were at the top. We know that we could just as easily list schools by the percentage of students on free and reduced lunch and have identical rankings. Knowing the race and class makeup of the school predicts the academic outcomes. We do provide all children with access to school in this country—public education remains the only social entitlement in this country—but we get unequal education. The quality of teaching varies, the salaries of the teachers vary, the quality of facilities varies, and the quality of materials varies. I once worked with a school in West Oakland where students had no access to scientific lab equipment—it was locked in storage. The reason given was that the students could not be trusted not to break it.

We engage in acts of holding schools publicly accountable on the presumption that the measures of accountability are equitable. We require all students to learn the same things and judge them by the same standards even when we haven't ensured that they have an equal chance to reach those standards. We don't focus on the conditions under which students learn even as we rank schools—as though public humiliation is enough to get schools to improve. I see no evidence that it works. Compton, California, and the state of Florida both implemented a strategy of affixing letter grades to the school buildings. In Compton, the school system was taken over by the state, and the primary innovation was to put letter grades on buildings. In these places, getting an "F" on the door does nothing towards getting new resources or help or a plan to improve, but it is demoralizing for the students who walk through those doors. This makes a mockery of educational reform.

Some of what we do in the name of reform has a debilitating effect on public education because it undermines public confidence in our ability to educate. For example, a voucher is not going to get poor children into an elite private school—such schools are elite precisely because they keep poor children out. As public confidence in education is diminished, the market, privatization, and vouchers are proposed as the solution even though there is no evidence that this strategy works. The market and privatization of services for poor people hasn't proved to be an effective way to provide people with what they need. In housing, the voucher program is called Section 8. These vouchers provide access to a subsidy, but people with Section 8 vouchers are confined largely to the inner cities because people in the suburbs are not interested in renting to them. The power of a voucher does not include access in housing or in education—access to vouchers does not guarantee access to good schools.

Rather than turn our backs on public education, we need to focus on the serious business of trying to make the schools we have work. This country was the first country to develop a system of public education, long before any other Western European country. We did it without leadership from the federal government, as towns and villages in Massachusetts and across the country independently recognized the need for common schools to educate children. As first conceived, the common school did not serve everyone, but the idea of who should be included has expanded over time. Education has been a more democratic institution than any other in that every series of democratic rights—whether civil rights or women's rights or disability rights—has been achieved in education before it has been achieved in any other sector in our society. We should be proud of our history in public education and the democratic promise of our schools. We haven't always achieved that promise, but our schools have been far more democratic and far more receptive to demands for access than other institutions in our society.

To turn our backs on our schools is crazy, particularly because we have a youth crisis on our hands. All the signs point to it. Mass shootings in schools are no longer isolated phenomena. Such incidents occur regularly and follow a distinct pattern. They are occurring in suburban communities, with predominantly white, middle-class students who are distressed and alienated, who have no connection to adults. The theme that is most common in all these incidents is that the adults had no idea that there was a problem or that a student was at a breaking point. Students were aware that something was going on, but the adults were clueless.

A vice-principal at a high school in East Oakland told me that once, when the school was getting ready for a homecoming game, the students had designed T-shirts with the number 28 across the front and fire across the top. He assumed it referred to a player from another team. The day of the game he saw the cheerleaders practicing a routine with toy machine guns, and he forbid the use of the toys. During the half-time performance, the cheerleaders carried a toy coffin with the number 28 to the center of the football field and set it on fire. It turned out that the students from the other school belonged to the 28th Street gang. Although this vice-principal prides himself on knowing lots of students, talking to them, and trying to nurture them, he had no clue that gang rivalry was involved in the football game. That situation is not uncommon—it is not uncommon to be in schools where the adults are so disconnected from the students that major incidents are occurring among the students and no adult knows. Fights can brew for days, but often the adults find out only when a fight is in progress.

In order to address the threat of violence in schools, we need to invest heavily in counselors, social workers, and other adults who spend time talking to students. The disconnect between students and adults is so great that it is not surprising that we have a youth crisis. Margaret Mead warned us fifty years ago that any society that becomes disconnected across the generations is in trouble. When she came back from Samoa, she saw that we were allowing our youth to socialize themselves. We are now seeing the consequences in youth who are cut off from adults and have only their peers to turn to when they face a crisis or a personal dilemma. If that is not a reason to invest heavily in our schools, to create safe schools through nurturing relationships, then we really don't get it.

On one recent weekend there was a teen shooting in San Diego, and a fourteen-year-old in Florida was given a life sentence for killing a six-year-old child. You would have to be blind not to see that our youth are crying out for help. Our schools are in the best position to provide that help, but we haven't quite figured out that testing is not going to get us there. We need something more than testing if we are going to create conditions that lead not just to academic engagement but also to the development of young people who feel connected, responsible, and healthy, and who are able to make a contribution to society and their communities.

I am not against all testing. Since the emphasis on testing, there has been a change in the levels of complacency in the schools I visit. I used to see schools where kids showed up and bells rang but nobody learned; today, people are trying to make sure test scores go up (public humiliation works to a certain degree). But to narrow the value of education to improved test scores misses the point of the purpose of education. We are asking the wrong questions. Instead of asking how to raise achievement—which becomes how to raise test scores, which becomes how to teach to the test—we need to ask how to create schools that engage students intellectually and produce lifelong learners. That is a different question.

Most children want to learn. I taught for three years at a continuation high school—an Orwellian term in California for a last chance school for students with disciplinary problems. There was a truce between the teachers and students: you don't bother me and I won't bother you. I came to that school after working for two years as deputy to the mayor in Berkeley, California. When I was in that position, the principal of the continuation school came to me one day with a student he wanted me to encourage to run for student body president. John had a gold ring on every finger, gold teeth, and a big gold chain. My first thought was that John already had a job that kept him in gold and he didn't need to be student president. However, as I spoke to John, I found him to be very bright, articulate, and charismatic, and I realized the principal was trying to co-opt the local drug dealer, who clearly had a lot of influence among the students at his school. I was so taken with what the principal was doing, and with John himself, that I left the mayor's office and went to teach at that school. The district had assigned this principal to the school as punishment, hoping it would force him to retire, but he was reborn by the challenge. Convinced he could create a good school out of this dumping ground for bad teachers and bad students, he recruited people like me to come and work with him.

Over the next three years, we worked to transform the school, in part by figuring out what we could do within the classroom that would be so compelling that it would convince students that they should attend school—and actually learn something. I taught a course in African American history. A gay white man who wanted to teach art and music at this school asked me for advice about dealing with the students. I told him that if he was genuine, the students would see it and respond. They didn't see it at first and they gave him a hard time. Finally he realized the students were really into hip-hop music, so he used hip-hop as a strategy to teach poetry. Soon he had them writing and publishing their poetry, and then selling books of poetry. Then he had them making art and producing African masks and selling their artwork. The students said, "He might be weird, but he's a good teacher." The students are not prejudiced—most of the young people I know are not prejudiced—if you are genuine, they will accept you regardless of your race, sexual orientation, or class background. If you care about them, they respond.

Students at that high school told me that they look for three things in teachers. They look first for people who care. We forget sometimes how basic that is, but all students respond to teachers who care for them. Second, they respect teachers who are strict and hold students accountable. Third, they like teachers who teach them something. When they found a teacher who was caring, strict, and challenging, they responded really well. Some of these students had criminal records or missed more days than they attended, but when they got excited, they produced incredible things. These students had high cognitive ability but didn't have the literacy and math skills needed for school. Our challenge was to teach those skills by drawing on the knowledge they brought with them from outside of school in order to create a bridge to school knowledge. Whether they are at-risk or high achievers, all young people need a caring relationship with adults. They need to feel that the people who teach them also care about them; they need to be challenged; they need to become intrinsically motivated learners. The challenge we face as educators is how to stimulate the desire to learn, how to help students become self-motivated to learn. If we asked those questions, we would have very different schools and classrooms, and we would have higher achievement as well. Caring does not come at the expense of high achievement.

We don't have to eliminate testing, but we do have to create a curriculum that is meaningful to students and to create classrooms that excite and stimulate students. It is important to remember that when the adults are learning, the children will learn. In how many schools have the teachers stopped learning? Is it surprising that bored teachers cannot inspire anyone? It is hard to be inspired by someone who hates what they do, someone who has been doing the same lesson plan year after year, someone who feels no passion for the subject they are teaching. Students deserve teachers who are able to excite them and make the material come alive. I became a teacher because I know that education has a unique power to transform people, to inspire people to see beyond the limited situation they are in, and to imagine new possibilities. That is the power of education. We need to think about designing schools that unleash that potential. That is the challenge, not how to raise test scores.

How do we create schools that excite and inspire? Instead of focusing on rescuing a few talented students from inner city schools, instead of thinking of education as a question of individual achievement by which one escapes poverty, we should be designing education that provides people with the knowledge and skills to improve the communities they are in. What would that look like? What if we designed a curriculum around the problems young people face in their community, so they could figure out how to solve them? That would be a democratic education; it is not what we provide now. We need to think creatively about how our schools can become access points for our communities, how we can use education as a means to change and improve our communities, to improve people's lives—we need to think differently about the students and about the community. The community should not be seen as a problem but as a resource. The school has the potential to play a role in the redevelopment and revitalization of our inner city communities. That is what we need to do.

Universities also have a role to play, starting with the schools of education. If there is a crisis in education and schools of education are not actively trying to help, the justification for their existence is called into question. Too often, we university educators tend to see the work of schools and the work of teachers as less important. We don't want to work with schools—we want to talk about schools. We don't want to work with teachers to figure out how to educate students—we want to theorize and talk about what might be possible under ideal circumstances. The University of Chicago has shut down its school of education. Berkeley almost closed its education school fifteen years ago because it was not operating as a professional school and working with the public schools. Although the need to be accountable, relevant, and useful starts with the school of education, the whole university has a responsibility. What does this university do for the people of Buffalo? Is it a resource? Is it an asset? Is it involved in helping to address the problems of Buffalo? I hope the answer is yes. When a public university is not involved in serving the pressing needs of the public, it raises questions about the university's claim on public resources.

It's easy to point the finger at public schools and tell them to get it together. We also have to ask what we are doing to help. How can we use our resources and privilege to help those whose work is much more difficult? It is hard to figure out how to create schools that inspire, that excite—but it is the most important work we can do. The future of our country hinges upon the future of our young people, which will be determined by what we provide for them in the way of schools. Right now we are doing a bad job. Are we going to sit back and accept this as inevitable, or are we going to seize the moment and ask what we can do to make a difference in our schools and in our communities? If we ask ourselves that question, we ought to be able to come up with the beginnings to some answers—not miraculous solutions, but small solutions that start to make a difference.[1]

NOTE

1. This paper originated as a presentation given during Urban Education Month, organized by the Urban Education Institute at the University of Buffalo Graduate School of Education, and co-sponsored by the Buffalo Board of Education and the Buffalo Teacher Center in March 2001.

SELECTED READINGS BY PEDRO NOGUERA

Noguera, P. A. (1994). More democracy not less: Confronting the challenge of privatization in public education. *Journal of Negro Education, 63*(2), 237–250.

Noguera, P. A. (1995). Preventing and producing violence: A critical analysis of responses to school violence. *Harvard Educational Review, 65*(2), 189–212.

Noguera, P. A. (2001). Racial politics and the elusive quest for excellence and equity in education. *Education and Urban Society, 34*(1), 18–41.

Noguera, P. A. (2003). *City schools and the American dream: Reclaiming the promise of public education.* New York: Teachers College Press.

Noguera, P. A. (2003). The trouble with Black boys: The role and influence of environmental and cultural factors on the academic performance of African American males. *Urban Education, 38*(4), 431–459.

2 Things to Come: Teachers' Work and Urban School Reform

Dennis Carlson

Dennis Carlson, Professor of Educational Leadership and Director of the Center for Education and Cultural Studies at Miami University of Ohio, describes school reforms that promise progress through de-skilling and re-skilling classroom teachers. He argues that promoters of these reforms do not trust teachers to be competent educational decision-makers and that there is a relationship between the crisis in urban schools and the way we look at teachers' work.

THESE DAYS, MANY STATE AND LOCAL school officials are occupied by discussions of how much progress is being made in winning the "war" against chronic underachievement among poor black, white, and Latino youth in urban schools, but in this chapter I suggest that we should question the idea of progress and what constitutes progress. Test scores, we are told, are still too low, but they are rising as a result of wave after wave of school reform initiatives. Progress is being made, we are told, in holding students (and teachers) more accountable and in raising standards, again for both students and teachers. Progress is being made, we are told, in moving beyond the "old" teacher unionism to a "new" unionism based on shared decision-making and collegiality, with teachers assuming professional status and sharing power with administrators.

So the current reform discourse in urban education seems to be working to address the crisis of student underachievement and teacher demoralization. At least that is what those who speak such a discourse would have us believe. Still, beneath the facade of progress lies a system still in crisis, and anyone who has spent time in urban schools serving those marginalized by class and race knows that. Furthermore, they know that the reform discourse that has brought about all of this supposed progress is part of the problem much more than it is part of the solution to what ails urban education. And they know that teachers have born the brunt of this progress. My interest, then, is in both questioning the dominant reform discourse of progress in urban education and raising the question of what it might mean to make progress in a way that empowers urban school teachers and leads to the democratic renewal of public

> What is all this progress? What is the good of this progress? . . .
> We must measure and compute, we must collect and sort and
> count. We must sacrifice ourselves . . . What is it, this progress?
>
> H. G. Wells, *Things to Come* (1935)

education and public life. To make progress in this sense, we will need to challenge dominant reform discourses of progress.

One of my favorite science fiction novels about progress is H. G. Wells' *Things to Come* (1935), which was made into a movie in 1936. Wells offers us a vision of the future as it looks in the year 2059. Humanity is about to make its giant leap to the moon in a rocket. While this is a significant achievement, Wells suggests the project to send men to the moon provided a pragmatic means of creating a type of top-down, organizational society, run by scientist-technicians and a managerial elite—so that progress no longer had a democratic meaning, only a technical one. Right before the launch of the moon rocket there is a revolt against this new technical-managerial system of control and domination. An anonymous worker cries out, "What is all this progress? What is the good of this progress? . . . We must measure and compute, we must collect and sort and count. We must sacrifice ourselves. . . . What is it, this progress?" (p. 118).

I think we need to ask, along these lines, what has progress been all about in urban schools? Whose interests have been served? Who has been made to sacrifice themselves in the name of progress? Teachers have long been the sacrificial lambs in urban school reform in a dual sense. They have been blamed for systemic problems, and they have been made to sacrifice more and more of their autonomy, their academic freedom, their agency within the system. But over the past two decades of reform, since *A Nation at Risk*, the 1983 report of President Reagan's Commission on Excellence in Education, this sacrificial quality of teachers' work has been accentuated.

The shift to a discourse and practice of high-stakes testing provides a good case in point. In the 1980s I was at Rutgers University on the Newark campus, involved in a teacher education program, and in my visits to the schools of Newark and the surrounding urban districts I could see the impact of the institutionalization of a state high school graduation exam in 1985, the first such high-stakes test in the nation. I could see how teachers were pressured to "align" their teaching strategies to the state-mandated "Madeleine Hunter" lesson format, and "align" the curriculum to the test. I saw schools and classrooms being reorganized into test-preparation sites, where teaching to the test was not only condoned by state officials but also actively encouraged. And I saw many good teachers leave the system during all of this because they were demoralized.

In my study of an urban teachers union in New Jersey, published as *Teachers and Crisis: Urban School Reform and Teachers' Work Culture* (1992), I documented some of this. What I found truly amazing was that state officials, in their "war" against the crisis in urban schools, kept declaring that they were making progress, that test scores were rising, although they certainly were not high enough yet. The "real" crisis was being papered over. Of course, high-stakes testing has only become more hegemonic over the past decade, and it has increasingly been tied to new school reorganization models that promise to bring up test scores. Teachers are expected to "buy into" a collective, unified school "vision" and "mission" and become "stakeholders" in school reform. While some reform models, such as the Coalition of Essential Schools, may make serious efforts to empower teachers and reorganize their work in ways that allows them to be effective, many if not most reform models adopted in urban schools continue to treat teachers as sacrificial lambs.

Let me give an example. Currently, I work with teachers in a master's degree program in curriculum and teacher leadership at Miami University of Ohio. I often ask the teachers to talk about how school reform models are impacting their working lives, and the most common complaint I hear is that their working lives are being further intensified, that all of this leads to more teacher burn-out and stress. An elementary school teacher from Hamilton, Ohio, a rust-belt city north of Cincinnati, recently led a class discussion about instituting the "Success for All" reform model in her school. Success for All is a popular reform model in urban schools, based on the idea that every staff member in the school assume responsibility for ensuring that every student succeed, with success defined as moving up to grade level in standardized achievement tests. The teacher observed that when her school adopted the program, the teachers agreed to increase the number of after-school meetings from three to nine each month, thereby also agreeing (under intense pressure) to set aside contract language. The physical education, music, and art teachers were asked to volunteer to give up their prep periods to tutor students identified as needing remediation.

I asked the teacher what the effect of all the reform was, whether it had indeed raised test scores as promised. No, she said. But then, so far the school had only implemented the Success for All reading curriculum. That, the principal had decided, was not enough. So more reform was on the way in the form of Success for All math, which would mean more meetings. Then, there was talk of adding Success for All science and social studies. Success for All is a highly scripted curriculum, and to make sure everyone was on script, teachers had agreed to be monitored at random by a staff person hired specially for this purpose. One result was that many experienced teachers were transferring out of Success for All schools in the district, and those who stayed were demoralized by the standardized curriculum, the constant monitoring, and the general intensification of their working lives, which left little time for reflection. Is this progress? What constitutes progress, and who does the sacrificing?

Before I point to some of the ways we may begin to rethink progress in urban schools consistent with a democratic progressive discourse, I want to return to the theme of looking into the future, to point to some things to come if currently dominant reform discourses continue to set the conceptual parameters for thinking about progress. I want to organize my thoughts around a brief discussion of two commission reports published in 1994, each of which I think has done much to both anticipate and shape the course of urban school reform in the intervening years. While I focus upon how these two reports represent the "problem" of teachers' work and the need to reorganize teachers' work, I do not want to separate what is happening to teachers' work culture from what is happening to the culture of the urban school, or from broad shifts that are reshaping the cultural terrain and landscape. These shifts, and this reorganization of teachers' work, have continued under both Republican and Democratic leadership. What we are facing, then, is a dominant discourse on school reform that has remained largely unchanged over the past two decades and that continues to point us toward things to come.

One of these commission reports I want to discuss is the Brookings Institute's *Making Schools Work* (1994). This is a neoconservative discourse on reform, and one thing that separates neoconservatives from neoliberals is that they continue to voice support for some form of voucher system of public education, based on a free market metaphor. This market metaphor provided the discursive framework for the 1990 Brookings Institute study by John Chubb and Terry Moe, titled *Politics, Markets, and America's Schools*, and it continues to be an important metaphor in *Making Schools Work*. For example, that report suggests that when states take over urban school districts that are failing to raise test scores, "the most useful interventions will probably help the students of poorly performing districts to help themselves, through school choice programs or voucher systems" (p. xxiv). Nevertheless, what is new in *Making Schools Work* is that the free market metaphor is no longer the central, governing metaphor in the text used to construct "truths" about what is wrong with urban schools and how to make them "work" again. The privatization of public education is no longer the primary objective of reform. The report takes for granted the continued existence of public schools into the foreseeable future. The shift, then, is toward a corporate management discourse of reform organized around the metaphor of the "cost-effective" school.

What, then, are the attributes of a cost-effective school? According to *Making Schools Work*, public schools will not receive significantly more funding in the coming years, and they actually will have to make do with less. Thus, the cost-effective school is one that that is organized to get the most out of each dollar invested in the school by taxpayers, and "efficient use of resources" is presented as the first indicator of whether or not a school is "working." This certainly has a populist appeal to it, and it is linked to the claim that "more and more people concerned with the high cost and seemingly low return of additional spending in the educational system are joining those with traditional concerns about performance and equity to urge immediate reform" (p. 2).

Notice here that an attempt is made to appeal to a broad-based constituency, including progressives concerned about equity. According to the report, if schools serving socioeconomically disadvantaged groups were run more cost-effectively, they would serve students better and that would help them get ahead. Now there is just enough truth in this appeal to make it a very effective legitimating device in defense of further budget cuts, which impact most adversely on urban schools. It provides us with a way of abandoning historic commitments to quality public education and to backing up that commitment with adequate funding.

This is where teachers come in. A major recommendation of the report is, believe it or not, that ways be found of lowering the exorbitant labor costs in public education. The largest single component of the educational budget is teacher salaries, the report notes, so this is the logical place to cut costs. But how? One way to lower labor costs, according to *Making Schools Work* is to increase class size since "studies show that reducing class size usually has no general effect on student performance." This means that calls for "smaller classes and commensurately more teachers" must be rejected, for they would raise labor costs dramatically (p. xx). So much for the accumulated wisdom that points to the importance of lowering the teacher-student ratio, and rather dramatically in some cases.

But such wisdom surely is based on the conviction that teaching must be personalized, that it cannot be reduced to a standardized transmission of curriculum. Obviously this is not a conviction shared by the authors of *Making Schools Work*. Larger classes are to be made possible, according to the report, through more use of new computer technologies. It notes that "Computers can replace teachers in certain tasks, such as drill-and-practice activities." Furthermore, "television and radio broadcasts, combined with correspondence materials, can provide high-quality education at relatively low costs" (p. 113). The clear implication here is that a virtual school could even be established, with students communicating with teachers via class websites and chat rooms, and with instructional videos downloaded for personal viewing.

This is, I am afraid, very close to becoming a reality. In Cincinnati, Ohio, for example, the school district has recently established a virtual high school in which students can do almost everything online, either from home computers or in school district computer centers. This not only requires fewer teachers but also means that more use can be made of part-time teacher aides and instructional assistants. This, the report says, will mean taking on the power of teacher unions to block change. Among other things, the union movement will need to endorse more performance incentives and merit pay systems and largely abandon the idea of tenure for teachers entering the system. According to the report, "New teachers are likely to be more receptive to these changes because they will not regard the new policies as violations of past understandings or intrusions on their accustomed routine" (p. 7).

This is another way of saying that if teachers do not get used to certain contract rights and the academic freedom and security afforded by tenure, they will not miss it. To me, this means teacher unions will need to be very careful not to let bureaucratic elites dismantle the very limited contract rights they have. The "new unionism" that is much talked about these days could find itself in the position of being continuously expected to set the contract language aside and be "flexible." But this contract language currently is one of the few things that stand in the way of the further disempowerment of teachers through more reform. Progressives need to resist the promise of progress represented in the image of the "cost-effective school."

They also need to resist the promise of progress represented in another influential commission report published in 1994, *Prisoners of Time*, the report of the National Education Commission on Time and Learning. That commission, established under the Bush administration in 1991, included a select group of school board members, superintendents, and principals, along with representatives of the Business Roundtable and the Hudson Institute—both major neoconservative think tanks in education. Social efficiency educators have long been obsessed with time wastage, and certainly we find this concern already in the work ethic of Benjamin Franklin and his obsessive scheduling of his own day so that no waking moment was not put to good use.

In contemporary education, we find this obsessiveness in discourses of time management and "time on task." In this case, the concern is that there is just not enough time in the school day to cram everything we have tried to cram into it, and that teachers are not able to be effective as a consequence. There are three basic responses the report calls for to deal with this problem. First, distinguish between "academic" and "nonacademic" uses of school time and eliminate everything from the latter category so that during the academic day instruction can focus on the basics, "the common core all students should master." Second, lengthen the school day and year so that "nonacademic" curriculum and activities can be offered after the regular school day, as extracurricular. Third, reorganize teachers' work so that teachers are better paid and have more time for meetings and professional development during the school day—which means teaching fewer classes.

Before I say a bit more about these recommendations, let me say that this vision of a school that has become the master rather than the prisoner of time makes a good deal of sense, so I do not mean to merely refute it. Indeed, I want to argue that many of the ideas and metaphors embraced by the *Prisoners of Time* report are worthy of support by progressives, with one provision—and that is a big one. They are worthy of support only when they are framed and given meaning within the context of a progressive discourse on the democratic renewal of public education and public life. So long as they take on meaning within a neoconservative or neoliberal reform discourse that is deployed by bureaucratic state and corporate managerial bureaucratic elites, you can pretty well be assured that they will not serve to empower urban teachers or transform urban schooling.

This means that it is more important to ask which discourse is producing these "truths" about the way schools should change or are changing than it is to try to evaluate these "truths" independently. For example, in some contexts, voucher plans and charter schools may make a lot of sense, if they are tied to a democratic decentralization of power to teachers, students, parents, and local community groups, and if they can be used to open up space for progressive forms of culturally relevant and student-centered instruction. Within neoconservative and neoliberal reform discourses, however, voucher systems and charter schools take on meaning within a policy that creates more inequality—inequality among teachers and inequality among students.

Let me then return to the major recommendations of the *Prisoners of Time* report to explore what they mean within the context of the currently dominant or hegemonic reform discourse and also what they might mean in a more democratic discourse on the reimagination and renewal of public education. The first recommendation, as I said, is that schools eliminate the use of "academic time" (regular school hours time) for "nonacademic" purposes during the regular school day. And just what are nonacademic purposes? According to the report, they are anything that is not related to the "common core all students should master," which includes English and language arts, mathematics, science, civics, history, geography, the arts, and foreign language. Everything else is to be relegated to the realm of the extracurricular, something that can be offered through school clubs and activities after the regular school day. This includes physical education, family life education, band and orchestra, yearbook and school newspaper classes, classes and programs for unwed teenage mothers, and driver's education.

There certainly is some good sense to the idea that the school day should not be cluttered with a lot of classes and programs in which students are not learning much and in which the curriculum is not challenging. On the other hand, many of these "nonacademic" classes play an important role in motivating young people, in helping them contribute to community and engage in dialogue and common activity with other young people. As Lois Weis would say, many of these "nonacademic" classes are "safe spaces" where youth marginalized by class, race, and other markers of difference can engage in the kind of work that leads to self-affirming identities. So the piece-by-piece elimination of such spaces over the past decade is a serious cause for alarm and one that impacts dramatically on urban schools.

What else constitutes "nonacademic" purposes that need to be eliminated from the school day? According to the report, core academic learning is being sacrificed to make room for "education about personal safety, consumer affairs, AIDS, conservation and energy, family life, [and] driver's training" (p. 15). Now, this is an interesting grouping of topics, and to relegate them to the realm of the "nonacademic," as if they were not central to the school's mission of teaching core academic subjects, is political. What gets valued as "academic" is instruction that is directly related to the skill needs of a "world class" work force that can compete with Japan and Germany, skill needs that supposedly can be and should be measured by more standardized testing on a more regular basis. Everything else gets jettisoned from the curriculum and the schedule. In response to such reform agendas, which certainly are being pushed with increasing regularity by state officials these days, I think progressives will need to rupture or trouble the borders that separate the academic from the nonacademic more than erect them ever higher. Popular culture, for example, plays an increasingly central role in youth identity formation, and discussion or use of popular culture—for example hip-hop culture and rap music—needs to be part of the curriculum. Yet efforts to do so are currently stymied by the neoconservative and neoliberal attempts to erect rigid borders between the academic and the nonacademic.

A second major recommendation of *Prisoners of Time* has to do with expanding the role of the public school as a site for the supervision and surveillance of youth. The report observes that in many communities, particularly in "troubled" urban environments, children are growing up "without the family and community support" they need to do well in school. The crisis of child care, the report says, "can no longer be ignored." Finally, schools in high-poverty urban communities are increasingly being called upon to offer a wide variety of services—"immunizations, health screening, nutrition, and mental health, among other things" (p. 34)—and unless they stay open on a longer year-round basis, they cannot meet these needs. This too makes some sense from a progressive standpoint. Rather than assuming a less important role, public schools need to assume a more important role as community centers, as sites in which a wide array of services and activities are going on, year-round and all day. It needs to be a much more open institution in this regard.

But when this recommendation to expand the role of public schools in "troubled" urban neighborhoods is articulated within a neoconservative reform discourse, as it is in *Prisoners of Time*, it becomes part of a movement to bring the growing urban underclass under a more inclusive surveillance, part of a paternalistic discourse of the more cost-effective management of "troubled" urban youth. This is very close to the vision of things to come represented by Richard Herrnstein and Charles Murray in their influential book *The Bell Curve* (1996), in which they foresee urban neighborhoods turned into reservations for the underclass, with the state coordinating their every need and keeping them under the gaze of power through a coordinated network of social services. Ironically, those on the political right now hold out the vision of a welfare state form of public education—which perhaps suggests that liberalism never was so much about empowering the poor as managing them.

A third set of recommendations in *Prisoners of Time* has to do with the professionalization of teachers' work. What is interesting here is just how much neoconservatives have been able to effectively co-opt the language of teacher professionalization. The report holds up Germany and Japan as examples of nations who treat their teachers like professionals. Teacher preparation takes up to six years, and there are rigorous examinations prior to certification. Furthermore, Japanese teachers may have larger classes (thirty-five to forty students, compared to an average of twenty-three in the U.S.), but they typically are only in front of the class in an instructional role four hours per day. Time spent outside the classroom involves meetings to plan and evaluate students, along with staff development. Similarly, in Germany teachers are in front of classes only about twenty-one hours a week (p. 27).

This all sounds very good, but what does it mean in terms of specific changes in American schools? The only way to make it work, it becomes clear, is by rather dramatically reducing the number of teachers in the system. Thus, the professionalization of teaching means constructing a relatively small (by today's standards) cadre of highly educated and high-paid teachers who assume broad responsibilities for managing individualized educational plans. This professionalization, according to the report, is thus consistent, and in fact dependent upon, "the widespread and systematic use of a cadre of well-prepared, full-time, substitute teachers" (p. 36). Substitute teachers and teacher aides would monitor much of the instruction in these retooled schools, which would now be much more computer-based and individualized. The role of the teacher is thus increasingly one of "designing instructional programs for their students" (p. 37). The report sees a future ahead in which "telecommunication technologies make it possible for students to move at their own pace" through an instructional program tailor-made for them.

The future that lies ahead for us, if this dominant reform discourse has its way, is one in which the schools become more cost-effective in preparing young people to become "world class" workers, using new technologies to deliver a prescriptive package of skill programs to students, with a relatively small and privileged group of teachers monitoring the process, who have been transformed into professional technicians of knowledge, who know more about how to assemble information from the "information superhighway" into programmed instructional units than they do about how to engage young people in dialogue and in the critical reading of texts.

The future imagined by both neoconservatives and neoliberals is also one that finds urban schools working more closely with a whole array of social welfare agencies and juvenile and adult courts to keep "troubled" youth under a more totalizing gaze. It is a future that represents the school as an agent of control and supervision more than critical inquiry or empowerment. The vision of progress offered by *Making Schools Work* and *Prisoners of Time* is ultimately one that would have us abandon any pretense that public schools should be about challenging inequalities and empowering the marginalized and silenced, about inducting young people into a diverse democratic public life as active makers of meaning and community.

What kind of progress will prevail in the years ahead? Whose progress will prevail? So long as dominant reform discourse in urban education is not seriously challenged, I think the things coming down the pike will not be kind to teachers or their students. Indeed, collective bargaining rights will be slowly eroded and then eliminated entirely if current trends continue. What progressives can offer in response, I think, is a different vision of progress, one that is not so narrowly tied to the interests of global capital, that uses a language of equity, social justice, human freedom, and communities of difference to reconstruct public schools and public life, that helps those who have been disempowered and silenced find a voice and affirm empowering identities, that is actively engaged in challenging racism, classism, sexism, homophobia, and other markers of marginality and "outsider" status. Within the context of such a democratic vision of progress, there is room for considerable disagreement as to how to proceed, and certainly there are no utopias waiting for us anymore.

Progressives will need to be pragmatic and adapt to the changing cultural and technological landscape, and teachers will need to be prepared to move outside of many of the entrenched ways of thinking associated with the collective bargaining mentality, and to become more adept at using the new technologies. Schools as we know them now are relics of an early twentieth-century corporate state reform initiative—and they are about to be transformed. The only question is whose vision of things to come will be realized. Progressives can still shape the direction of that transformation, I believe, but only within the context of a broader counterdiscourse on American public life that has not coalesced at this historical juncture. There are some encouraging signs, however, that such a discourse and movement may be in the process of constituting itself as discontent with high-stakes testing grows in urban school districts and among those most disempowered by dominant reform discourses of progress.[1]

NOTE

1. This paper originated as a presentation given during Urban Education Month, organized by the Urban Education Institute at the University of Buffalo Graduate School of Education in March 2001.

REFERENCES

Carlson, D. L. (1992). *Teachers and crisis: Urban school reform and teachers' work culture.* New York: Routledge. [Winner of the 1995 "Critics' Choice" Award, American Educational Studies Association.]

Chubb, J. E., & Moe, T. M. (1990). *Politics, markets, and America's schools.* Washington, D. C.: Brookings Institution.

Hanushek, E. (1994). *Making schools work: Improving performance and controlling costs.* Washington, D.C.: Brookings Institution.

Herrnstein, R., & Murray, C. (1996). *The bell curve: Intelligence and class structure in American life*. New York: Free Press.

National Education Commission on Time and Learning. (1994). *Prisoners of time*. Washington, D.C.: U.S. Government Printing Office.

Wells, H. G. (1935). *Things to come*. Boston: Gregg Press.

OTHER RESOURCES

Assessment Reform Network: www.fairtest.org
National Coalition of Education Activists: www.nceaonline.org

SELECTED READINGS BY DENNIS CARLSON

Carlson, D. (1997). *Making progress: Education and culture in new times*. New York: Teachers College Press.

Carlson, D., & Apple, M. (1998). *Power, knowledge, and pedagogy: The meaning of democratic education in unsettling times*. Boulder: Westview Press.

Oldenski, T., & Carlson, D. (2002). *Educational yearning: The journey of the spirit and democratic education*. New York: Peter Lang.

Dimitriadis, G., & Carlson, D. (2003). *Promises to keep: Cultural studies, democratic education, and public life*. New York: Routledge.

3 Court-Ordered Reform of New York State School Aid

Michael A. Rebell

Michael A. Rebell is Executive Director and Counsel of the Campaign for Fiscal Equity (CFE), a nonprofit coalition of parents, school boards, concerned citizens, and advocacy groups. Since 1993, CFE has been working to change the way New York State funds its schools, promote dialogue and input on education and school funding reform, and conduct policy research on student access to a sound basic education. In this chapter, Rebell describes the history of fiscal equity and education adequacy cases in the U.S., focusing on the case brought by CFE, which was one of the first to tie the issue of fiscal adequacy explicitly to standards-based reform by defining the sound, basic education guaranteed in the state constitution as high-level cognitive skills. In January 2001 the New York Supreme Court ruled in favor of the plaintiffs. Governor George Pataki successfully appealed that ruling, but the New York Court of Appeals, the state's highest court, reinstated most of the New York Supreme Court's findings and ordered the state to substantially reform its system for funding education by July 30, 2004.

IN AN HISTORIC DECISION ISSUED January 10, 2001, Justice Leland DeGrasse of New York Supreme Court declared that

> New York State has over the course of many years consistently violated the State Constitution by failing to provide the opportunity for a sound basic education to New York City public school students.

The case brought by the Campaign for Fiscal Equity against the state of New York is one of a number of cases of fiscal equity or adequacy reform over the past few decades that are tied historically to the promise of *Brown v. the Board of Education*. Nineteen years after *Brown*, civil rights advances for fiscal equity in education were halted in *Rodriguez v. San Antonio*. In that case, the U.S. Supreme Court offered two major doctrinal justifications for not providing relief to the plaintiffs, even though the court acknowledged that the factual record was overwhelming regarding the clear inequities in Texas and the need

New York State School Funding Facts

* New York State has the largest gap in spending per student between the wealthiest and the poorest districts.

* In 1996–1997, the average school district in the state spent $9,321 per pupil.

* Local tax revenues provide the majority of school funding in the state.

* Districts with the highest property wealth spent almost twice what those with the lowest property wealth spent ($12,209 versus $6,462).

* Low wealth districts tax themselves at a rate of $15.35 per $1,000 of full property value and generate an average of $1,351 per pupil.

* High-property wealth districts tax themselves at a rate of only $11.00 per $1,000 of full property value and generate an average of $10,206 per pupil.

From the Campaign for Fiscal Equity Web site

for action. The first major doctrinal point was that poverty was not a suspect class for equal protection purposes. The second was that although education is enormously important, it is not a "fundamental interest" under the federal constitution. In holding that education is primarily a responsibility of the states, the federal courts refused to get involved.

The Supreme Court's decision also reflected an underlying concern regarding the ability of the courts to bring about effective reform in areas that involve complex educational policy. The court was aware of the problems district courts had encountered in trying to desegregate schools since *Brown v. the Board of Education* and questioned whether the courts could devise remedies for complex education problems:

As Justice Powell wrote in the majority decision in Rodriguez:

> This case also involves the most persistent and difficult questions of
> educational policy, another area in which this court's lack of special-
> ized knowledge and experience counsels against premature interfer-
> ence with the informed judgment made at state and local levels. On
> even the most basic questions in the area, the scholars and educational
> experts are divided. Equally unsettled is the controversy as to the
> proper goals as to the system of public education. In such circum-
> stances, the judiciary is well advised to refrain from imposing on the
> states inflexible constitutional restraints that could circumscribe or
> handicap the continued research and experimentation so vital to
> finding even partial solutions to educational problems and to keeping
> abreast of ever-changing conditions.

In essence, the court seemed reluctant to hold that the current system of
public education was unconstitutional, in that there was no clear consensus on
the part of scholars and practitioners regarding remedies or goals. Therefore,
the federal court decided to leave it to the states.

Since 1973, there has been fiscal equity or adequacy litigation in forty-
four states. When I started out in civil rights work in the 1970s, conventional
wisdom held that federal judges were more sympathetic to civil rights issues
and that the procedures in federal courts were more geared to providing relief.
From a civil rights advocacy point of view, you wanted to stay out of the state
courts. But in the areas of fiscal equity in education, the state courts have been
actively involved in developing constitutional doctrine more expansively than
in any other area.

The fiscal equity cases that have been brought since 1973 can be analyzed
in terms of three waves. In the mid to late 1970s, immediately after *Rodriguez*,
there were very strong decisions in favor of the plaintiffs. State courts seemed
to have little trouble finding that the public education systems in a number of
states—including California, Connecticut, New Jersey, West Virginia—were unconstitutional. Consequently, people began filing in other states, including the
1978 *Levittown* case in New York, in which a group of poor districts in Long
Island, with the intervention of the five big cities, won a tremendous victory. The
second wave occurred during the 1980s, when defendants won two-thirds of the
cases, including the ultimate outcome of the *Levittown* case in the court of
appeals in 1982. The 1978 verdict was reversed—even as the court admitted the
inequities in the education finance system, it refused to get involved.

From 1989 to the present there has been a third wave, in which plaintiffs
have won about 70 percent of the cases. While the number of cases is too small
to have statistical significance, it seems there is a clear pattern having to do
with the question of remedies. In the early cases, the remedies ordered by the
courts often were not implemented successfully, which may explain why many

courts in the 1980s became reluctant to rule in favor of the plaintiffs. In California, for example, the *Serrano* ruling resulted in significantly reduced comparative spending on education because the case got tied to Proposition 13, which put a ceiling on property taxes. It is ironic that what was from the plaintiff's point of view the first great state court decision, filled with wonderful rhetoric, has in many ways impeded rather than advanced educational opportunities in California. In West Virginia the state court issued an order that was about three hundred pages long, detailing and prescribing every aspect of the education system, but the legislature challenged the court by ignoring the order, and the court backed off. In New Jersey as well, the legislature resisted the court's orders, but the court did not back off and there was continuing confrontation between the courts and the legislature for years thereafter.

If the difficulty of finding workable remedies was the concern, what happened in 1989 to swing the pendulum back the other way? One explanation is that the national standards-based reform movement took off in that year. What do standards have to do with fiscal inequities? From the point of view of a court interested in the problem of how to put together a workable remedy, the standards-based reform movement offered clear guidelines: provide sufficient resources to give kids the opportunity to meet the specific standards that the state has said they need to meet. Standards-based reform has provided the judiciary with a clear framework.

There also has been an interesting doctrinal shift since 1989 from equity cases to adequacy cases. In the third wave of cases, most of the decisions in favor of the plaintiffs—including the CFE case—are based not on constitutional equal protection doctrines of equity, but on clauses in state constitutions that seem to guarantee some basic level of education for all students, whether it is called "thorough and efficient education," "ample education," or "sound basic education." Almost all the state constitutions include language, derived from the eighteenth- and nineteenth-century common school movement, that describes the kind of education to which kids are entitled.

Article 11 of the New York State constitution, for example, says the legislature shall establish "a system of free common schools in which all the students in the state can be educated." In the *Levittown* case, the court of appeals said that "a system in which students can be educated" means "a sound basic education." The issue in *Levittown* was that some students were getting only the minimal in education, while others were getting much more. With the shift to adequacy, the argument is that some kids are not getting even the minimal sound basic education, which forces the court to look more deeply at the meaning of sound basic education. In New York, the Court of Appeals has now defined sound basic education in terms of the skills students need for "competitive employment" and "for meaningful civic participation in contemporary society," including the skills needed to function "capably and knowledgably" as voters and jurors. Responding to the intermediate appeals court's attempt to equate sound basic education with middle-school level reading and math skills, the Court of Appeals also held that the constitution requires students to be provided the opportunity for a "meaningful high school education."

The CFE case and a recent decision in North Carolina are the first two cases that explicitly analyze state standards in regard to their development of constitutional adequacy standards. Over the course of our seven-month trial, CFE brought to the court's attention the history of the national standards-based reform movement and described the development of the Regents' learning standards in New York in great detail. We knew we had to argue for an emphasis on the "sound" part of the definition because whether one emphasizes "sound" or "basic" in "sound basic education" determines whether a substantive or a minimal standard is created.

In the first CFE decision in 1995, the Court of Appeals had refused to dismiss the case and held that adequacy is not the same as equity. The court offered a tentative definition of a sound basic education and sent the case back for a trial, expecting to see the case again on appeal, at which time it would reconsider the preliminary definition. Obviously, the definition became key. On the one hand, the court defined a sound basic education as providing kids with the skills they need to be civic participants capable of voting and serving on a jury, which pushes the definition toward high-level skills. On the other hand, in discussing the resources needed, the court used such language as "minimally adequate."

Early in the trial, Judge DeGrasse was very helpful in establishing the context for how to define the level of skills needed by voters and jurors. Fortuitously, there was a recess for election day on November 2. The next day, the judge asked the experts from both sides to show whether New York State high school graduates were capable of understanding the charter referendum that had been on the ballot. He also asked us to look at juror questionnaires and other juror documents. On our side, Linda Darling-Hammond analyzed the ballot initiative and identified the conceptual and reading skills needed to understand it. She then compared that list of skills to the old Regents' competency tests (which are at about sixth- to eighth-grade levels in math and reading) and to current Regents' standards, demonstrating that the current state standards are a good match for the skills needed to be voters and jurors. In his ruling, the judge strongly affirmed that constitutionally a sound basic education should provide the following high-level cognitive skills:

> An engaged, capable voter needs the intellectual tools to evaluate complex issues such as campaign finance reform, tax policy, and global warming, to name a few. Ballot propositions in New York City, such as the charter reform proposal that was on the ballot in November, 1999, can require a close reading and a familiarity with the structure of local government.

He talked similarly about jury service and the ability to analyze evidence.

What did the defense say about all this? The state argued that sound basic education as a constitutional matter requires only a sixth- to eighth-grade level of education, even if that means you do not possess the cognitive skills to be a capable voter or juror. Basing much of their case on public opinion polls and on social science data regarding actual voting behavior, their expert witness reported that 75 percent of the American people base their voting decisions on information from television and radio news, and that 99 percent of voters have made up their minds before entering the voting booth. Consequently, they argued, the ability to read firsthand the ballot proposition is irrelevant to actual voting practices. That is an astounding position for the state of New York—that our kids don't really need to know how to read what is on a ballot proposition.

The state not only hired expert witnesses at taxpayer expense, but they also hired attorneys. Dennis Vacco, the attorney general at the time, felt the three hundred to four hundred lawyers in his office could not handle this case, so he retained a private law firm. Apparently, he couldn't find a competent law firm in New York, so he went out of state and paid $11 million to a firm from Atlanta, Georgia. Although outside counsel is often accepted without question, in this case we objected and asked for justification. The state submitted affidavits stating that the firm was recognized nationally as expert in education law and since the stakes were so high, New York had to get the best. While this is a firm of first-class lawyers, they were not really experienced in fiscal equity or adequacy cases, but in fighting school desegregation. The current attorney general, Eliot Spitzer, decided not to use the private firm on the appeal level.

In sum, we tied the issue of fiscal adequacy to standards-based reform and argued for a definition of sound, basic education as high-level cognitive skills. Although the Court of Appeals held that standards issued by the state board of regents cannot per se define the constitutional standards, the court's close analysis of the standards strongly influenced their understanding and formulation of the specific skills that were held to be part of the constitutional requirement.

In the first CFE decision, the Court of Appeals also had held that to provide a sound basic education requires certain resources. Judge DeGrasse restated and expanded that court's list of four resources to the following seven items, which were also implicitly approved by the appeals court:

1. Sufficient numbers of qualified teachers, principals and other personnel.

2. Appropriate class sizes.

3. Adequate and accessible school buildings with sufficient space to ensure appropriate class size and implementation of a sound curriculum.

4. Sufficient and up-to-date books, supplies, libraries, educational technology and laboratories.

5. Suitable curricula, including an expanded platform of programs to help at risk students by giving them "more time on task."

6. Adequate resources for students with extraordinary needs.

7. A safe orderly environment.

In order to provide the opportunity for a sound, basic education, one that gives kids a fair chance to reach the level of skills needed to be a voter and juror, public education must provide all these resources. Indeed, the Regents themselves have proclaimed that virtually all kids can meet their challenging standards if they are given sufficient resources and support. While not every kid is going to come out of school with high-level cognitive skills, the education system should be organized to offer that opportunity in a meaningful way. This is not pie in the sky—it is taking the state at its word. It can be done, but it takes resources.

The remedial order issued by the Court of Appeals included three basic principles to guide the restructuring of the school finance system:

1. Ascertain the actual cost of providing a sound basic education.

2. Reform the current system of financing school funding to ensure that every school has the resources necessary to provide the opportunity for a sound basic education.

3. Ensure a system of accountability to measure whether the reforms actually provide the opportunity for a sound basic education.

Although technically these guidelines apply only to New York City because the evidence in the case focused only on the city's schools, the judges apparently expected that the state would in fact need to consider reforms to the entire state education finance system, and both the governor and the legislative leaders have indicated that in fact that is their intent. The guidelines give a lot of discretion and flexibility to the legislature and the governor but also identify the major areas where the court expects serious reform action. The last principle, accountability, is particularly significant. Although the state education department has an accountability system in place, it is mainly a top-down process of regulations tied to high-stakes testing. We think there has to be a new focus on accountability, one that builds from the ground up and engages the community.

CFE takes public engagement very seriously. After the decision from the Court of Appeals, we asked people across the state to deliberate together about what a sound basic education should be. At the trial, we presented to the court an expanded definition of sound basic education that was derived from the statewide consensus. Engaged public interest will be critical to efforts to construct a new funding system as well, and CFE has already begun a series of state-wide forums that allow us to turn again to the people of New York to find out what the building blocks of that new system should be.

NOTE

1. This paper originated as a presentation given during Urban Education Month, organized by the Urban Education Institute at the University at Buffalo Graduate School of Education, in March 2001. It was substantially revised after the June 2003 New York Court of Appeals decision.

OTHER RESOURCES

Internet:
ACCESS (Advocacy Center for Children's Educational Success with Standards) is a national initiative of CFE that seeks to strengthen the links between public school finance litigation, public engagement, and the standards-based reform movement: www.accessednetwork.org.
Campaign for Fiscal Equity (includes education advocacy links): www.cfequity.org

SELECTED READINGS BY MICHAEL A. REBELL

Rebell, M. A. (1999). Fiscal equity litigation and the democratic imperative. *Equity and Excellence in Education, 32*(3), 5–18.

Rebell, M. A. (2002). Education adequacy, democracy, and the courts. In T. Ready, C. Edley, and C. Snow (Eds.), *Achieving high educational standards for all: Conference summary* (pp. 218–267). Washington, D.C.: National Academy Press.

Rebell, M. A. (forthcoming). Adequacy litigations: A new path to equity. In J. Petrovich & A. S. Wells (Eds.), *Bringing equity back: Research for a new era in American educational policy.*

Rebell, M. A., & Hughes, R. L. (1996). Special educational inclusion and the courts: A proposal for a new remedial approach. *Journal of Law and Education, 25*(4), 523–574.

Rebell, M. A., & Metzler, J. (2002). Rapid response, radical reform: The story of school finance litigation in Vermont. *Journal of Law and Education, 31*(3), 167–190.

4 Connecting Community Development and Urban School Reform

Henry Louis Taylor Jr.

Henry Louis Taylor Jr., Professor and Director of the Center for Urban Studies in the University at Buffalo School of Architecture and Planning, describes how both the community development and the urban school reform movements have failed to implement the structural changes necessary to improve the lives of residents of distressed urban neighborhoods. He argues that linking the two movements may be the only way either can succeed in addressing the structural inequities that are a barrier to turning urban neighborhoods into places "where people will have the best that humanity and technology have to offer." Taylor describes the model for such a linkage currently being designed by the Center for Urban Studies in collaboration with one Buffalo public school.

THIS CHAPTER MAKES THE CASE for building a bridge to link together the community development and the educational reform movements in distressed urban communities, and it discusses the barriers that must be removed before policy makers, practitioners, and activists create a new model of community development and school reform. It is divided into three parts. The first part discusses the structural limits of the community development movement and why it failed to incorporate school reform into its approach to neighborhood revitalization; the second part discusses efforts to forge a new model of community development. The final segment makes the case for connecting the community development neighborhood movement with the school reform movement.

THE STRUCTURAL LIMITS OF THE
COMMUNITY DEVELOPMENT MOVEMENT

The community development movement has not produced a model capable of transforming distressed urban neighborhoods into great places to live, work, and raise a family (Cummings, 1998; Lemann, 1993). This failure comes at a time when distressed neighborhoods have emerged as the place where structural racism and social class inequality are most sharply reflected in the United

Students from Futures Academy clean up a vacant lot near their school.

States (HUD, 1999; Taylor, 2001). In 1965, when the Black scholar, Kenneth Clark, referred to Harlem as a *Dark Ghetto* (1965), he was talking about the emergence of distressed urban neighborhoods as the new epicenter of structural racism and social class inequality. William Julius Wilson's *Truly Disadvantaged* (1987), Massey and Denton's *American Apartheid* (1993), and Paul A. Jargowsky's *Poverty and Place* (1997) confirmed that the socioeconomic problems facing blacks and people of color were intensifying. Public policy decisions, budgetary priorities at all levels of government, triage central city planning and development, low wages, unemployment, poverty, and bad schools have combined to create a Hadrian's Wall that forces blacks, Latinos, and poor whites to live in the most undesirable neighborhoods in the metropolis. In this distressed residential environment, institutionalized socioeconomic problems not only are self-perpetuating, but they also spawn other socioeconomic problems that continually produce havoc in the lives of residents.

The goal of the community development movement was to break this cycle of distress by fostering a fundamental transformation of these troubled communities and by altering the life chances of the individuals and families living in them. The movement not only has failed to achieve this goal, but also has fragmented into a series of disjointed, uncoordinated activities in which the sum is much less than the parts. Rather than becoming a comprehensive movement for radical change, community development has degenerated into a series of discrete activities, such as enterprise zones, community development corporations, neighborhood housing services, community economic development, community-building initiatives, social capital efforts, faith-based movements, and comprehensive community initiatives. Such a splintered movement cannot possibly radically transform distressed neighborhoods. It is helpless in the face of the powerful economic, political, and social forces that continually reproduce distressed communities populated by people of color and poor whites (Katz, 2002).

The lack of a coherent national urban policy has combined with structural forces to fragment the community development movement. Federal policy makers do not appear to understand that a comprehensive, coordinated approach is needed to regenerate distressed urban neighborhoods. So they have established a plethora of federal agencies that administer housing, labor, health, education, and business programs for residents of distressed communities, which work in near total isolation from one another.

For example, the Department of Housing and Urban Development (HUD) sponsors such programs as the Community Development Block Grant, housing subsidies, and aid to the homeless. Three other cabinet agencies—departments of Labor, Education, and Health and Human Services—help residents of distressed neighborhoods enter the labor market by training them, educating their children, and strengthening their families. The Small Business Administration and targeted minority business programs are run by the Commerce Department. Not only is there little communication between these agencies, but also even within them, there is little communication and discussion across departmental lines.[1] This same style of work is also found in local government and in distressed neighborhoods, where community organizations are established along sectorial lines, and they rarely communicate, coordinate, or collaborate across organizational and institutional boundaries.

Summarizing the failure of the community development movement, Bruce Katz (2000), of the Brookings Institute, said, "Over the past few decades, national urban policy has been reduced to a small set of micro initiatives and marginal investments. . . . The buzz words—'empowerment zones,' 'community renewal'—come and go but the end effect remains the same" (p. 4). The community revitalization movement has brought benefits to some inner city neighborhoods and has done good things, but few initiatives have fundamentally transformed neighborhoods or changed the trajectory of older inner city places. *No harm, (no real money), no foul* has become the community development credo (Katz, 2000; Medoff & Sklar, 1994).

THE SCHOOL REFORM MOVEMENT

At the same time, after the triumph of the civil rights movement, school reform efforts were separated from the movement to transform distressed neighborhoods. During the Jim Crow era, school segregation was viewed as the citadel of racism in the United States. If school segregation unraveled, then the citadel of racism would soon come crumbling down. In *Plessy v. Ferguson* (1896), the Supreme Court held that separate schools for black and white students were legal. This separate but equal doctrine became the foundation upon which the edifice of post-slavery racism was based. In a series of legal battles, starting with *Missouri ex el. Gaines v. Canada* (1938), blacks launched a series of legal attacks against the separate but equal doctrine (Logan & Cohen, 1970). In the post-World War II era, school desegregation became the major civil rights issue and this battle culminated on May 17, 1954, when the Supreme Court announced its decision in the case of *Brown v. Board of Education of Topeka*. This landmark decision by the Supreme Court reversed *Plessy v. Ferguson* and made possible the high tide of the civil rights movement (Logan & Cohen, 1970).

The battle against school segregation was also a fight for quality education. Trapped in inferior public schools, blacks knew they would never have an opportunity to achieve equity in the United States. During the early 1960s, the civil rights movement shifted northward and increasingly focused on neighborhood development. Community control became the battle cry of the neighborhood movement and throughout the decade a new type of organizational thrust gradually emerged. One of the driving forces behind this new grassroots organizational movement was Saul Alinsky and his Industrial Areas Foundation, which built organizations in Buffalo and Rochester, New York, and in a number of other cities across the nation (Ecklein & Lauffer, 1972; Taylor, 1986; Wilson, 2000).

In this early period, school reform was connected to the community control movement. The most celebrated fight over community control of schools was the Oceanhill-Brownsville conflict, which took place in Brooklyn, New York. Through community control, parents and activists, religious leaders, and politicians succeeded in wrestling control of neighborhood schools from predominantly white educators who were perceived as indifferent and unsympathetic to the needs of the community and its children (Noguera, 2001). Nevertheless, in the end the school reform movement separated from the community development movement.

Over time, the school reform movement also became a fragmented, apolitical process, in which reformers seemed to believe they could ignore distressed neighborhoods in their quest to develop high performing public schools. In the post-civil rights era, the single characteristic of school reform, regardless of the particular reform trend, has been its staggeringly introspective quality (Shirley, 1997). This idea of introspective schools was the theme stressed by Jonathan Kozol in *Savage Inequalities* (1991). Simply put, educational reformers preferred to believe great schools with highly motivated students, who excelled academically, could be developed without altering the conditions of life found in distressed neighborhoods.

Consequently, school reform became a building-centered movement informed by a belief that urban schools could function effectively, and the academic gap closed, without simultaneously transforming the conditions of life inside the distressed, underdeveloped neighborhoods where people of color and poor white populations lived. The fragmented, disjointed approach to community development and school reform has not worked. Despite an array of programs developed since 1960 to improve schools and communities, no one has devised a viable model for turning them into great places to live, work, raise a family, and get a good education.

TOWARD A NEW MODEL OF COMMUNITY DEVELOPMENT

The community development and school reform movements have not produced a viable model for educating students of color and radically reconstructing their neighborhoods because neither movement has challenged the structural forces that continually reproduce distressed neighborhoods and the people living in them. Without attacking these structural barriers, the community development and school reform movements cannot uproot the causes of distress and underdevelopment in urban neighborhoods (Harvey, 1985).

Jean Anyon (1997) makes a similar point from a teacher educator's perspective. She gives a "deep structural diagnosis of educational problems" in Newark, New Jersey, and calls for the dismantling of structural barriers to quality education. Anyon argues the ultimate goal of educational reform ought to be the elimination of the effects of destructive ghettoization of cities and their poorer residents and the reduction of the political and economic isolation that produces such ghettoization (p. 164). In essence, like political scientist David L. Imbroscio (1997), she believes that reconstructing city politics so that distressed community residents are politically empowered is part of the key to meaningful urban reform. For Anyon, "small victories," such as school restructuring or new pedagogical techniques, no matter how satisfying, will not change educational outcomes unless they are linked to long-range strategies to eradicate poverty and end racial isolation (p. 165). It is highly unlikely that inner city educational reform will take place unless it is linked to the economic and political redevelopment of the urban region (p. 167).

The point is that structural relationships, spawned by race-connected practices and social class inequalities, are the determinants of socioeconomic outcomes and conditions of life in distressed communities. Consequently, unless these structural barriers are identified, attacked, and removed, the problems of urban distress and underdevelopment will persist and become increasingly complex and difficult to solve with the passage of time. As long as such distressed communities exist, educational reform will fail unless it is made an integral part of the battle to transform and redevelop such neighborhoods and the regions of which they are a part.

Education must be linked to social change and explicitly involve administrators, teachers, students, and their schools in the struggle for the radical reconstruction of the communities in which they live. This notion is built on the ideas espoused by Paulo Freire (1970) more than thirty years ago: in order to break the cycle of education designed in part to continually reproduce the class structure and racial hierarchy, and to turn education into a liberating force, it must expand the students' consciousness and make them see the connection between advanced knowledge and their ability to transform and create a better world.

The first step is to merge the separate components of the community development movement into one comprehensive, highly integrated initiative designed to transform distressed neighborhoods and the metropolitan regions of which they are a part (Taylor, 2000). This view is based on the belief that metropolitan regions are composed of an interactive, functional network of neighborhoods and that distressed communities are complex places that usually include a resident community and a wealth-producing community, such as businesses, offices, factories, and public institutions like universities and hospitals. In many central cities and localities, distressed communities have wealth-producing institutions that contribute significantly to regional growth and development, but seldom do they contribute significantly to the growth and development of inner city resident communities.

Educational reform has not normally been part of neighborhood planning efforts, but in a comprehensive approach to planning, school reform is an integral part of the community development process, which involves all elements of the community—including schools—in planning and development. The idea is to wed the school to the neighborhood by involving it, along with residents, in redeveloping the community. This happens in two highly interrelated ways. First, a representative from the schools is designated to work with other neighborhood residents and professional planners on the development of a redevelopment strategy for the community. Second, students also are part of the neighborhood planning and community development process, in order to show them that knowing and learning can be used to refashion and shape the environments in which they live (Forsyth, 2002; Vazquez-Castillo, 2002). This goes to the core of school reform. How do you motivate children in distressed neighborhoods? What incentives make them want to learn, grow, and develop? How do you make them believe that education is important? How do you make them want to learn?

In Buffalo we are developing a model of community development based on four interrelated components: social development (which includes education, health, recreation, culture, civic participation, and leadership training); physical development; economic development; and safety and security. While a range of activities flowing from these areas is critical to the community development process, to develop initiatives in all four areas is beyond the capacities of any single organization. To build one super-organization, with the ability to plan and implement programs in each sector also is unrealistic. Instead, a plethora of groups, organizations, and institutions—inside and outside the neighborhood—needs to be involved in developing and implementing programs. The goal is to develop a comprehensive neighborhood initiative with a highly effective system of coordination, communication, and collaboration across components and within components. A coordinating committee with the authority and power to oversee this development would lead such a community initiative. By "coordinating committee," I am referring to a democratically based organization that guides the neighborhood-based community development movement. Building such a coordinating committee is an issue of neighborhood governance (Fredrickson, 1973). In the United States, most communities are not organized to develop, implement, and sustain a comprehensive development strategy. Inner city communities are highly organized. Most inner city communities can boast of numerous churches, mosques, block clubs, community development corporations, and varied community-based organizations. These organizations deliver important services, but they are not responsible for the redevelopment of the community. Moreover, they are not built around the democratic principles of community participation (Hamilton, 1973). That is, most community organizations do not profess to be democratic institutions that are representative of the wide spectrum of community residents. Yet this is precisely the type of organization needed to carry out comprehensive community development. The early history of the neighborhood movement and, most recently, the experiences of the Dudley Street Initiatives have provided compelling evidence that the struggle to radically reconstruct inner city neighborhoods must be led by democratic organizations. Since such organizations normally do not exist in neighborhoods, we have to build them (Cunningham & Kotler, 1983; Imbroscio, 1997).

A detailed discussion of this comprehensive community initiative is beyond the scope of this chapter, but before turning to the discussion of education reform in the final segment, I do want to discuss briefly the need for community-based leadership and describe aspects of the design and planning process for the physical renovation of urban neighborhoods. Although I will make a few comments about educational reform in this section, I will reserve most of the commentary on education for the final segment of the chapter.

COMMUNITY LEADERSHIP AND POLITICAL POWER

You cannot radically transform distressed communities without struggle and political battles. Power yields nothing without demand. The business, civic, and political elites that control poor urban areas, for the most part, have no real interest in turning distressed communities into places where people will have the best that humanity and technology have to offer (Catlin, 1993).

In most urban places, the redevelopment of distressed neighborhoods is not a high priority. City leaders normally use a system of triage planning and development in making resource allocation decisions. Typically, these leaders want to invest in big economic development projects, provide the private sector with massive tax abatements, and build or improve roads that will facilitate economic growth and development (Lucy, 1988). In the United States, the political economy of capitalism counterposes economic development to social development (including education). Economic development is seen as an end within itself rather than as an engine that drives social development (Hudson, Miller, & Feder, 1994). In this city-building model, by the time policy makers get to the distressed neighborhood agenda, most of the resources have been exhausted (Taylor & Cole, 2001b). Consequently, city leaders and officials want to control and placate the residents of distressed communities, but do not want to radically reconstruct the neighborhoods.

This is why community leadership is so important. It will take a fight to transform distressed neighborhoods, and only those with a vested interest can be trusted to lead it. This is also why political engagement is so important. Politicians do not listen to people who are politically inactive and do not control blocks of votes. Residents cannot change their communities without political allies. So they must become a political force capable of swinging elections, helping people get elected, and even fielding their own candidates.

Given these dynamics, it seems naive to believe that elected officials or business elites can lead the movement to radically reconstruct distressed communities. Where would African Americans be today if business leaders, college presidents, and politicians had led the civil rights movement? The point is that their interests and the interests of the residents are simply not the same. The two groups can and should work together, and the relationship does not have to be a contentious one. But the movement to radically reconstruct distressed neighborhoods must be led by neighborhood residents.

Community leadership is also important because distressed neighborhoods must be recreated from the inside out. The goal of community development is not only to regenerate the physical environment, but also to transform people, so their lives are informed by a new set of values, beliefs, and attitudes (Perez, 1999). Individual self-realization, interconnectedness with other neighborhood residents, and a spiritual transformation can happen only if residents are deeply immersed in the redevelopment process. Thus, if radical reconstruction of distressed communities is to be a truly empowering and transformative experience, neighborhood residents must lead it.

Neighborhood governance and democratic institution building must also be part of this process. Distressed communities must construct a new organizational framework before they will have the capacity to lead and control a comprehensive community development initiative. In most neighborhoods, existing community organizations and groups work in virtual isolation from one another. A community organized this way cannot successfully remove the barriers to development. To launch a successful comprehensive community initiative, distressed neighborhoods need to be led by a federated governance organization that can construct a framework capable of uniting diverse organizations, groups, and individuals.

The distressed and underperforming schools found in inner city neighborhoods are caused by a variety of structural and attitudinal factors, including housing market dynamics, a dual labor market, and triage planning and development. Intervention in this situation requires a multifaceted and multilevel strategy, which is carried out by a highly organized community (Byrum, 1992). Such unity of purpose will happen only if a new type of organization is built. An organization of this type would not only include residents, but also stakeholders and other individuals and groups concerned with the community's development. The key is bringing this diverse group together under the leadership of neighborhood residents. Such an organization would have the capacity to carry out a wide range of public and private actions and formulate and implement a unified development strategy (Vidal, 1998).

PHYSICAL DEVELOPMENT

The process of physically transforming a distressed community involves more than constructing affordable housing. We begin by establishing a "visioning" process that encourages residents to articulate their dreams of the type of community they want to build. In this process, we follow the credo of the great architect and planner, Daniel Burnham: "Make no little plans, they have not magic to stir men's blood" (Hines, 1974, xvii). So we dare residents to dream big dreams, and we tell them that they must be prepared to fight to make their dreams come true. The process also represents the first stage in the community-organizing process, providing a framework for uniting the community behind the movement to radically reconstruct the community.

After the design, planning, and community-building process, the second step is to devise a strategy to finance the redevelopment. Unless the total cost of recreating and rebuilding a particular neighborhood is calculated and an adequate finance package obtained, the community development process will fail. Given these conditions, the Center for Urban Studies has developed *Turning Point Scenarios* (Taylor & Cole, 2001a) to guide our strategic planning activities, based on the belief that investments in an inner city neighborhood must rise above a *turning point threshold* before that neighborhood can be transformed (Galster, Quercia, & Cortes, 2000; Gladwell, 2000). If the money spent on housing rehabilitation and construction, infrastructure development (streets, sidewalks, and curbs), landscaping and streetscaping, workforce development, educational development, and service delivery does not rise above this threshold, the conditions of life in that neighborhood will remain basically the same.

In order to secure the financing for a comprehensive redevelopment project in Buffalo, the Center for Urban Studies explored the ways that the city finances corporate economic development projects, which involve much more sophisticated development strategies than those normally used in developing distressed neighborhoods. We developed a finance strategy, based on the utilization of tax increment financing and gap financing, to be carried out in partnership with the Erie County Industrial Development Agency (Johnson & Man, 2001).

LINKING COMMUNITY DEVELOPMENT TO SCHOOL REFORM

Education is key to the forward advancement of all people of color. It is the foundation upon which the community development movement must be built. Therefore, linking school reform to the community development process must become a top priority in the community development movement. This will not be easy. Denying blacks and people of color a quality education has been the primary method used to lock them in the nation's economic basement and maintain their subordinate status in American society. Black scholar Carter G. Woodson, more than anyone else, understood this role of the American education system. Woodson argued that blacks had never been truly educated; they had simply been informed about things in the world and brainwashed to keep them subordinate to whites. In his classic book *The Miseducation of the Negro* (1933/1998), Woodson noted:

> When you control a man's thinking, you do not have to worry about his actions. You do not have to tell him not to stand here or yonder. He will find his "proper place" and will stay in it. You do not need to send him to the back door. He will go without being told. In fact, if there is no back door, he will cut one for his special benefit. His education makes it necessary. (p. xiii)

Without the proper education, Woodson continues, one can easily "learn to follow the line of least resistance rather than battle against the odds for what real history has shown to be the right course" (p. xiii). African Americans have been battling for a decent education for a very long time—in the slave quarters, in sharecropper's huts, and in segregated rural and urban schools during the Jim Crow era, blacks fought for a decent education. And with the epoch-making 1954 Supreme Court decision, they thought their dream had come true, but it was a dream deferred.

White political regimes had no intention of providing blacks with an education that would allow them to compete with whites in the labor market. Many higher paid white workers responded to the myopic 1954 Supreme Court decision by moving to prosperous suburbs, beyond the legal reach of forced busing, recreating de facto racial segregation. There, they built a new public school system, deliberately segregated along racial and class lines.

As the quality of urban public education declined, many of the whites who remained in the city lost faith in public schools and sent their children to private institutions. In time, middle-class blacks and Latinos followed their lead. The departure of middle-class children from central city public schools led to the growing concentration of low-income children of color and poor whites, who have come to dominate the system. Race and class combined to produce a new crisis in pubic education (Educational Choice Committee, 2001).

This analysis tells us three things about the educational crisis in public schools. First, the crisis is really a problem of educating blacks, Latinos, and poor whites who live in a third world setting, especially those who are members of racial groups that have never been provided with the same educational opportunities as most whites (Berube, 1983). Second, low-performing schools are one symptom of the malady of distressed, underdeveloped urban places, another facet of the urban predicament, which includes poverty, unemployment, bad housing, blighted and unkempt physical environments, and an endless struggle to raise children, earn a living, and make ends meet. Third, these neighborhoods are characterized by years of betrayals and broken promises that have produced a culture of civic withdrawal, cynicism, and hopelessness. Neighborhood life and culture significantly influence the education and learning process, which means it is impossible to educate students successfully in these communities without simultaneously fighting to transform the neighborhoods in which they live.

Yet for the most part, the school reform movement has been driven by a building-centered approach to education that assumes urban schools can function effectively without any transformation of the conditions of life in the distressed communities where their students live. A growing number of progressive educators, scholars, and practitioners, however, are calling for building bridges to link the community development movement to the school reform movement.

An evolving "community school" movement represents a first step in linking school reform to community development. Although models of community schools vary, most conceptualize the school as the center of neighborhood life and culture; they try to bridge the gap between schools and community by transforming schools into places that not only teach children, but also function as community hubs. In a number of places the community school model has begun to include community organizing, mobilizing residents to take on a number of community development tasks. For example, in *Community Organizing for Urban School Reform* (1997), educator Dennis Shirley outlines a series of case studies of Texas schools where citizens have fought to reform their schools and link them to the community development process. Ira Harkavy, at the University of Pennsylvania, also has been deeply involved in a school reform movement that ties the school and community groups to a range of community development activities.

These and other efforts around the country are truly encouraging, although they have not articulated a progressive philosophy of education. In the typical community school model, students in distressed neighborhoods are taught that the purpose of education is getting a good job and escaping the ghetto. This "Harriet Tubman" approach teaches students that once they escape the ghetto, they should return and help someone else get out. Students learn that the formula for achieving happiness is Good Job + Money + Material Possessions = Happiness. They are taught to place the individual over the group, that competition is everything, and that democracy involves voting, free speech, and belonging to a volunteer organization.

For the most part, these students know nothing about their history and have little or no understanding of the economic, social, and political forces shaping their daily realities. In the current community schools approach, linking education to community is focused on academic success and making the immediate neighborhood better. While this method of schooling might create better students, it will not break the cycle of miseducation that Carter G. Woodson talked about.

To achieve Woodson's objective, we must create a more radicalized approach to education. In the model of community development and school reform we are creating in Buffalo, we seek to teach students that the purpose of education is not only to earn a living, but also to create a world worth living in, that the formula for happiness is Education + Health + Recreation and Culture + Participation in Civic Life = Happiness. We want students to believe that people should be placed over economic profits, that the group is more important than the individual, that collaborating and cooperating is more important than competing, that family and community are important, and that elders should be revered.

We also want students to learn that real democracy involves participating in the development of one's neighborhood, city, and region, and that people should fight to influence the types of policies, programs, and budgetary decisions that shape the development of society. We want them to learn that democracy is not just voting; it is being able to determine who runs for office. Most important, we want students to understand the history of their people, their country, and the neighborhood and community in which they live. Children educated in this holistic manner, we believe, will not only be excellent students, but also will be civically conscious and socially involved citizens who have no trouble finding jobs and opportunities in a competitive labor market.

THE FUTURES ACADEMY INITIATIVE

In Buffalo, we are beginning to implement the ideas outlined above by partnering with Futures Academy, a Buffalo Pre-K though Eighth Grade Magnet/neighborhood public school. The idea is to involve not only the students, but also the teachers in the community-building process. At the same time, we want to involve neighborhood residents in all aspects of the development of Futures; we want Futures to become their school. Moreover, as teachers become more involved in the community development effort, they will see more opportunities to integrate community-building activities into the curriculum.

We have already started engaging students and teachers in the community planning and development process. A teacher from Futures has been appointed to serve as the main liaison between the school and the planning and community development process; the students have designed a community garden; and community residents have joined the struggle to keep Futures as a magnet school.

Involving students in the planning and development process was based on the simple idea that the neighborhood context matters in the education of inner city children. It is difficult to help students understand the power of knowledge to shape the world and make it a better place, when they live in dilapidated and rundown communities. A group of university students in the UB Department of Urban and Regional Planning worked with seventh and eighth graders, whose first assignment was to take pictures of places they liked and disliked in the neighborhood. We wanted students to begin thinking about the community as a place and, within this framework, to identify things they liked and disliked about the community. In informal conversations, the students were asked to explain why they liked certain places and disliked others. For example, one student took a picture of a boarded up building and vacant lot, containing an abandoned car and rubbish:

> I don't like this picture because of the busted up cars because the way the windows are bust out. If someone was to run they could fall and cut themselves. The house, I really don't care what you make out of it because the church is right next to the house and we wouldn't get to play because we would be distracting the church.

This and other analyses by the children gave us insight into their views of the neighborhood and how life and culture in the community affects them; they helped us to understand the neighborhood as a place and influenced the neighborhood redevelopment plan (Center for Urban Studies, 2002).

This process encouraged the students to think critically about their neighborhood and to imagine what could be done to improve it. By linking academic activities, such as critical thinking and writing, to the process of understanding neighborhood and community development, we hope to bolster the students' desire to learn. Also, by incorporating their ideas into the actual plans, we hope to show them that their ideas matter and that it is possible to make positive change. This activity incorporates Carter G. Woodson's notion of *high strivings* and Paulo Freire's (1994) *pedagogy of hope*. By showing the students that their knowledge can be used to change their community, they may begin to view education as a useful problem-solving tool rather than as a vehicle of escape and flight to the good life (Woodson, 1998).

In another significant activity, the students have designed a community garden, which will transform a trash-filled vacant lot into a symbol of cooperation, pride, and determination. Futures Academy faces a series of city-owned vacant lots and an abandoned building. Everyday, children walk to school past dilapidated housing and vacant lots, a symbolic environment that says *you are a worthless person and no one cares about your existence.* The last thing they see before entering the school building is a vacant lot overflowing with trash and rubbish. By involving students in the transformation of this vacant lot, we hope to demonstrate yet another way that knowledge can be used as a force in societal transformation. The students not only designed the garden, but also planned the type of activities that should take place there. They wanted a space that could be used for quiet meditation and play. Construction of the garden began in the spring of 2002. The students are also developing a plan to maintain the garden, as well as a plan to conduct a yearly clean up of the community immediately adjacent to the school.

A third project has involved a group of seventh and eighth graders, who are working on a Sym-City design simulation with the help of two graduate students in the Department of Urban and Regional Planning and two teachers at Futures. The students are designing a city and developing a strategy for financing its operation. Through this process of engaging students, teachers, and the principal in the battle to regenerate the neighborhood and through the process of engaging the residents in the fight to build the school and educate the children, step by step, we are building a bridge to link community building and school reform.

This project is still in its infancy and much work remains to be done, including enlisting the involvement of the University at Buffalo Graduate School of Education, getting more teachers at Futures involved in developing a problems-oriented approach to teaching, and developing assessments to measure the effectiveness of our efforts. Moreover, we plan to develop a technology and neighborhood-planning center across from the school, which would be a laboratory setting where students can learn to use mathematics, computers, and technology in the community-building process. Teachers and students will participate in the activities required to secure funds to renovate the structure to support the program activities. We hope to construct a venue where the needs of parents, students, and community residents can be met in an environment of mutual assistance and benefit. The ultimate goal is to create an exciting community learning environment for knowledge acquisition and application to problem solving.

NOTE

1. This insight is derived from conversations with local HUD officials about the problems of coordinating various activities related to comprehensive development. Also, in my interactions with local government over a range of development projects, I have found the lack of communication to be an ongoing problem and issue.

REFERENCES

Anyon, J. (1997). *Ghetto schooling: A political economy of urban educational reform.* New York: Teachers College Press.

Berube, M. R. (1983). *Education and poverty: Effective schooling in the United States and Cuba.* Westport: Greenwood Press.

Byrum, O. E. (1992). *Old problems in new times: Urban strategies for the 1990s.* Chicago: Planners Press.

Catlin, R. A. (1993). *Racial politics and urban planning: Gary, Indiana, 1980–1989.* Lexington: University Press of Kentucky.

Center for Urban Studies (2002). *Fruit Belt redevelopment plan: A preliminary study.* Buffalo: Author.

Clark, K. B. (1965). *Dark ghetto: Dilemmas of social power.* Middletown: Wesleyan University Press.

Cummings, S. (1998). *Left behind in Rosedale: Race relations and the collapse of community institutions.* Boulder: Westview Press.

Cunningham, J. V., & Kotler, M. (1983). *Building neighborhood organizations: A guidebook sponsored by the National Association of Neighborhoods.* Notre Dame: University of Notre Dame Press.

Ecklein, J. L., & Lauffer, A. (1972). *Community organizers and social planners.* New York: John Wiley and Sons.

Educational Choice Committee. (2001). *Buffalo Public Schools: Compilation of demographics and other pertinent information about the Buffalo Public Schools.* Buffalo: Author.

Forsyth, A. (2002). Involving youth in planning: The progressive challenge. *Planners Network,* Winter. Retrieved on December 8, 2003. *http://www.plannersnetwork.org/htm/pub/archives/151/forsyth.htm*

Fredrickson, G. (1973). *Neighborhood control in the 1970s: Politics, administration, and citizen participation.* New York: Chandler.

Freire, P. (1970). *Pedagogy of the oppressed.* New York: Seabury Press.

Freire, P. (1994). *Pedagogy of hope: Reliving Pedagogy of the Oppressed.* New York: Continuum.

Galster, G. C., Quercia, R. G., & Cortes, A. (2000). Identifying neighborhood thresholds: An empirical investigation. *Housing Policy Debate, 11(3),* 701–732.

Gladwell, M. (2000). *The tipping point: How little things can make a big difference.* Boston: Little, Brown.

Hamilton, C. V. (1973). Neighborhood control and urban governance. In G. Frederickson (Ed.), *Neighborhood control in the 1970s: Politics, administration, and citizen participation* (pp. 249–258). New York: Chandler.

Harvey, D. (1985). *Consciousness and the urban experience: Studies in the history and theory of capitalist urbanization.* Baltimore: Johns Hopkins University.

Hines, T. S. (1974). *Burnham of Chicago: Architect and planner.* Chicago: University of Chicago Press.

Hudson, M., Miller G. J., & Feder, K. (1994). *A philosophy for a fair society.* London: Shepheard-Walwyn.

Imbroscio, D. L. (1997). *Reconstructing city politics: Alternative economic development and urban regimes.* Thousand Oaks: Sage.

Jargowsky, P. A. (1997). *Poverty and place: Ghettos, barrios, and the American city.* New York: Russell Sage Foundation.

Johnson, C. L., & Man, J. Y. (2001). *Tax increment financing and economic development: Uses, structures, and impact.* Albany: State University of New York Press.

Katz, B. (2000). Enough of the small stuff. Toward a new urban agenda. *The Brookings Review, 18*(3), 4–9.

Kozol, J. (1991). *Savage inequalities: Children in America's schools.* New York: Crown.

Lemann, N. (1993, January 9). The myth of community development. *The New York Times Magazine,* pp. 28–31.

Logan, R. W., & Cohen, I. S. (1970). *The American Negro: Old world background and new world experience.* Boston: Houghton Mifflin.

Lucy, W. (1988). *Close to power: Setting priorities with elected officials.* Chicago: Planners Press.

Massey, D.. & Denton, N. (1993). *American apartheid: Segregation and the making of the underclass.* Cambridge: Harvard University Press.

Medoff, P., & Sklar, H. (1994). *Streets of hope: The fall and rise of an urban neighborhood.* Boston: South End Press.

Noguera, P. (2001). Transforming urban schools through investments in the social capital of parents. In S. Saegert, J. P. Thompson, & M. R. Warren (Eds), *Social capital and poor communities* (pp. 189–212). New York: Russell Sage Foundation.

Perez, L. A. Jr. (1999). *On becoming Cuban: Identity, nationality, and culture.* New York: ECCO Press.

Shirley, D. (1997). *Community organizing for urban school reform.* Austin: University of Texas Press.

Taylor, H. L., Jr. (1986). Build, unity, independence, liberty, dignity (BUILD). In P. M. Melvin (Ed.), *American community organizations: A historical dictionary* (pp. 22–24). Westport: Greenwood Press.

Taylor, H. L., Jr. (2000). Creating the metropolis in black and white: Black suburbanization and the planning movement in Cincinnati, 1900–1950. In H. L. Taylor Jr. (Ed.), *Historical roots of the urban crisis: African Americans in the industrial city, 1900–1950* (pp. 51–71). New York: Garland Publishing.

Taylor, H. L., Jr. (2001). *Rethinking community development and neighborhood revitalization.* Keynote Address, Fourth Annual Philadelphia Higher Education Network for Neighborhood Development, Philadelphia, Pennsylvania.

Taylor, H. L., Jr., & Cole, S. (2001a). *The turning point: A strategic plan and action agenda for the Fruit Belt/Medical Corridor.* Buffalo: Center for Urban Studies.

Taylor, H. L., Jr., & Cole, S. (November 2001b). *Structural racism and efforts to radically reconstruct the inner city built environment.* Paper presented at the 43rd Annual Conference, Association of Collegiate Schools of Planning, Cleveland, Ohio. [Winner of the ACSP Fannie Mae Foundation Award, Best Action Research Paper, 2001.]

U.S. Department of Housing and Urban Development. (1999). *Now is the time: Places left behind in the new economy.* Washington, D.C.: Author.

Vazquez–Castillo, M. T. (2002). Townview, Texas: A high school adoption program. *Planners Network,* Winter. Retrieved on December 8, 2003. http://www.planners network.org/htm/pub/archives/151/vasquez.htm.

Vidal, A. (1998). *Community organizing: Building social capital as a development strategy.* Thousand Oaks: Sage.

William, W. J. (1987). *The truly disadvantaged: The inner city, the underclass, and public policy.* Chicago: University of Chicago Press.

Wilson, B. M. (2000). *Race and place in Birmingham: The civil rights and neighborhood movements.* New York: Rowman & Littlefield.

Woodson, C. G. (1998/1933). *The miseducation of the Negro.* Trenton, NJ: African World Press.

Linking Urban Schools
to Their Communities

5 Creating Small Urban Schools: Expeditionary Learning as School Reform

Greg Farrell and Michael J. McCarthy

Greg Farrell is President of Expeditionary Learning/Outward Bound. Michael McCarthy is the principal of a small Expeditionary Learning school in Portland, Maine. In this chapter, Farrell describes the origins and development of Expeditionary Learning, which is based on the philosophy of educator Kurt Hahn, who started Outward Bound and emphasizes teamwork and practical problem solving. McCarthy describes the curriculum, culture, and experiential instructional practices at King Middle School, where students learn to work together in teams, rise to seemingly impossible challenges, and use their knowledge in service to the community. Using an interdisciplinary, inquiry-based approach, the learning expeditions are planned to meet content standards and often result in a project that connects the school to the larger community. In the fall of 2003, Expeditionary Learning/Outward Bound received a $12.5 million grant from the Bill and Melinda Gates Foundation to establish twenty new Expeditionary Learning high schools across the country.

GREG FARRELL

THE EVOLUTION OF EXPEDITIONARY LEARNING as an idea or a design for changing schools grew out of an Outward Bound course I took in the early 1960s. I was interested in the course because I was stimulated by the language of the man who had founded it, a German Jew named Kurt Hahn, who ran a private boarding school in Bavaria. Hahn had grown up in Berlin but went to college in Oxford, where he was impressed with some of the thinking in progressive British schools at the time. He also had had personal experiences that made him reflect on the power of adventure and service for learning. Hahn was offered the opportunity to start a boarding school and created one that had the qualities of adventure, service, and craftsmanship he had come to admire. When he publicly challenged Hitler, he was jailed but was then released through the influence of friends in high places in England. Hahn made his way to Great Britain, where he started a school in Scotland, Gordonstoun, which was attended by Prince Phillip and, later, Prince Charles. As in his previous

Expeditionary Learning

The first Expeditionary Learning schools were established in the United States in 1993; there are now almost one hundred such schools in twenty-nine states. Expeditionary Learning works with whole schools to transform instructional practice and school culture so K–12 students can meet rigorous academic and character standards. It is based on five core practices:

1. *Learning Expeditions*: Learning expeditions are long-term, in-depth investigations of a topic that engage students through authentic projects, fieldwork, and service.

2. *Reflection and Critique*: Teachers model a culture of reflection, critique, revision, and collaboration.

3. *School Culture*: Expeditionary Learning promotes a strong culture of best effort, high expectations, community and collaboration, service, and diversity.

4. *School Structures*: Expeditionary Learning requires the reorganization of time, student grouping, and resources to support high-quality learning expeditions.

5. *School Review*: Schools engage in an annual review of school progress to reflect on their practice and plan for the future. A periodic peer review takes place every three years.

school, the ideas that later took shape in Outward Bound were part of the school.

Hahn had an interesting idea about competition—that one should never take unfair advantage. For example, an American track coach from Andover who knew about the Western Roll, a more efficient way of getting over the high jump, was not allowed to teach it to the Gordonstoun students because it would be taking unfair advantage of the other teams.

When I worked as assistant dean of admissions at an Ivy League college, I dealt with student applications from Hahn's school. The school's evaluation forms included interesting information, such as whether the student cleaned up after himself when on expedition and whether he did what he thought was right in the face of the ridicule of his peers. When I heard that Outward Bound was starting in this country, I took a course. I had been a high school English teacher, and throughout the course I kept thinking that school should be more like the Outward Bound course. We learned by doing; we learned things and applied them instantly. The experience was a series of anxieties resolved in positive ways, and you came away thinking you were capable of a great deal more than you had thought before and that the people around you were more capable than you had given them credit for. There was a loving spirit, based on getting everyone over the mountain, not on seeing who could get over first.

Right after the Outward Bound course, I took a job as director of the antipoverty agency in Trenton, New Jersey, which gave me my first opportunity to try out the idea that school should be more like the Outward Bound experience. On Outward Bound, there was very little instruction and a lot of application. We had the opportunity to make mistakes. As the course went on, the instructors stepped further and further back, and by the end the students were in charge of the course. The instructors were willing to let us make a twenty-mile mistake and learn from it. I thought we should teach French or English or math this way, by immersing people in situations where there is a little learning, then something to use it for, so there is a connection between the subject matter and real life.

For many years public school teachers have been attending Outward Bound courses and noticing what I noticed. I just came back from a sea kayaking course in Baja, Mexico, for principals from Expeditionary Learning schools from around the country. In our last gathering around the campfire, after kayaking six to eight hours a day for a week, we were asked to summarize the lessons for us as humans and teachers. One participant came up with this list, which is best appreciated if you imagine the physical hardships of sea kayaking.

1. Never be complacent. A lapse of attention, even for a moment, can have dire or at least unpleasant consequences.

2. Travel light; take care of what you have; things last a lot longer than you ever imagined.

3. Comfort is relative. We adjust to our surroundings, like sense of smell. Monday's dirty laundry might be the cleanest thing you have on Thursday. Or who would have guessed you could rejoice at finding a perfectly contoured shell or a velvet smooth stick?

4. Beauty has nothing to do with Madison Avenue or Hollywood.

5. You have absolutely no control over the circumstances around you. All you can control is how you will react. Plan carefully; read the signs; and adjust your course.

6. There is no such thing as standing still. If you are not active, you will drift off course.

7. To find your way, line up your short-term plans with your long-range goals.

8. Use your big muscles; go with your strength.

9. But use finesse over strength whenever you can.

10. Some effort on the right turns you right; some effort on the right turns you left. Know when to use your hands and when to use your feet.

Those are homely lessons from an intense week.

In 1993, a national organization, the New American Schools Development Corporation, was established to find and support the development and expansion of successful new models for improving our methods of schooling. We responded to their request for proposals. Our idea was to apply the philosophy and pedagogical practices of Outward Bound to the fundamentals of K–12 schooling—developing curriculum, instructional practices, scheduling, and the rest. Since we know that people learn best by doing, why do we make students sit still while adults talk at them? We should instead see how much of what schools have to teach and children have to learn could be embedded in projects that are interesting, engaging, and worthwhile. That is what Expeditionary Learning is all about.

We started our first schools in 1993–1994. Now there are almost one hundred schools in twenty-nine states, the District of Columbia, and Puerto Rico. Over half are elementary schools, about a quarter are middle schools, and the remaining quarter are high schools. They are mostly (70 percent) in low-income areas of big cities such as New York, Boston, Memphis, Cincinnati, and San Antonio. Some Expeditionary Learning schools are in small cities like Dubuque or Portland; some are on Indian reservations. Of the one hundred, roughly twenty are charter schools, which will likely be an increasing proportion of Expeditionary Learning schools. [Editor's Note: More public Expeditionary Learning Schools are in high poverty and urban areas because they are financed with Title I funds. Only one or two schools are in well-to-do suburbs (conversation with author 3/22/01)].

MICHAEL McCARTHY

I started my teaching career in a maximum-security prison. My student teaching internship was to teach twenty-six inmates in Concord State Prison in Concord, New Hampshire. It was there that I was fired with a passion for school reform. When you think about it, prison is the end point of some of the worst practices in public education. Some of those worst educational practices were taking place at King Middle School eight to ten years ago.

We are a school of six hundred students, grades six, seven, and eight. About 70 percent of our students come from single parent homes; 65 percent are on the federal free lunch program; and 24 percent are foreign-born students. We speak twenty-eight different languages. The reason is that Portland, Maine, is a refugee resettlement project for Catholic Charities. We receive refugees from wherever there is a revolution—Somalia and Sudan, for example. Many children come to us with no English and often have not been to school.

Although we are a small city, we face the same kinds of challenges that larger urban centers do. When I arrived in 1988, we were running two schools— a school for the "haves" and another for the "have-nots." We had special Chapter I classes, which set those students aside and gave them a dumbed-down curriculum. Special education stratifies and labels students. In 1998, we had seven different ability groupings: gifted, accelerated, middle, low, resource room, functional academics, and emotional. At that time only about 6 percent of the students were foreign born, mostly Vietnamese and Cambodian. We used to have 250 children enrolled in special education. That is now down to eighty students. Today we don't pull out at all for Chapter I and all of our special education is fully inclusive. We have one self-contained class; everyone else is taught together with high expectations for all. This has happened because we ensure that all learning styles are engaged. That is a snapshot of what our school looks like.

When I first arrived, this was a school with a lot of student-on-student violence, a lot of failure, a lot of grade retention, and low faculty morale— many teachers got in their cars at the sound of the bell. There were factions within the school. There was strong union resistance to change. The first year most people hated my guts. I had read about Outward Bound and thought it might be an approach that would bring about change. With a grant provided by Greg Farrell, we invited every member of the faculty to go on an Outward Bound course in the summer.

On that first trip we began to see how experiential learning works and to wonder what it would look like in the classroom. The next year fifteen people signed up; the following year, fifteen more. Expeditionary Learning has a cultural effect on the faculty, which is the group we began with. Those people were making the changes and were willing to take the risk. When the New American Schools' request for proposals came along, we became a test school.

After we studied the model of Expeditionary Learning and teams of teachers started practicing it, the students responded to it. Expeditionary Learning is a total school design based on the long-term study of a topic, using an interdisciplinary approach and an experiential model. It is very engaging.

An important part of Expeditionary Learning is reflection and critique. Students are asked to think about their learning and write about their learning; there are peer and faculty critiques, as well as public presentations of their work. Students are assessed traditionally, with report cards and grades, but they also build portfolios for every expedition as well as a portfolio that includes work and reflections on the work, which is presented to parents twice a year.

Faculty also engage in reflection and critique, meeting at the end of an expedition to talk about how it went. At the end of the year, all the teachers present their expeditions to the rest of the faculty and get feedback.

To address needed change in school culture, we spend a lot of time on professional development. The teachers meet for about a week each summer in order to plan their expeditions, which means that large chunks of curriculum are already organized when school begins in September. We also hold summer institutes. When you start an Expeditionary Learning school, on-site professional developers provide guidance through the first few years for twenty or thirty days during the school year.

Teachers have reported that Expeditionary Learning is more work but less stress because the students are responding and there is strong parent and community involvement. In a learning expedition, when you are going out in the field, you need parents. This is not asking parents to come sit in a meeting but rather to engage in a learning activity with the students. Before Expeditionary Learning, significant parental involvement was around 1 percent; after three years, that had risen to 30 percent; today the percentage is even higher.

A school structure and organization based on teaming is the cornerstone of Expeditionary Learning. At King, we are grouped into six teams of teachers, two at each grade level, organized in two houses, Windsor and York. In Windsor Six, for example, language arts, math, social studies, science, computer, and music teachers are part of the team. In an Expeditionary Learning school, the arts are essential, not an extracurricular activity. They are integrated into the academic course.

Another organizational structure in Expeditionary Learning is looping for grades six and seven. Parents appreciate that because they get to know the teachers. In middle school you often lose that familiarity with teachers. The flexible schedule is another structural element of Expeditionary Learning. We have a rotating six-day schedule. This doesn't mean that you have to go to school for six days, but that the teachers control time. There are only a few nonnegotiable blocks of time: portfolio time, lunch, and foreign language. Otherwise, each faculty team decides what to do—there are no bells, so there are not three minutes of chaos every forty-five minutes. Teachers can decide to go on a field experience, go to the park, or have math the whole day. The teachers define the time and can change it daily, which is empowering. They also have their own budget. They have control of time, budget, a phone, and computer. When we first started, the only drawback was that when parents called, we had a hard time knowing exactly where the students were at any particular time.

My favorite expedition is called "In the Zone." This was a study of the intertidal zone of Casco Bay, which is very close to the school. (This meant we didn't have to rent buses.) The science teacher decided to teach classification by having the students study the intertidal zone, explore the living ocean, find a piece of flora or fauna they were interested in, and create a page for a field guide that could be used by scientists who were studying intertidal zones. The final product was a field guide to the intertidal zone of Casco Bay. In the process of producing the guide, each student had to learn how to do electronic research and regular library research on the classification and habitat of the plant or animal. Every student, whether they were foreign born or had special needs, got to do a page. When the guide was completed, they sold it and gave the proceeds to the Friends of Casco Bay.

Expeditionary Learning recognizes that there are many ways of learning. While each expedition includes a lot of direct instruction, many different kinds of instruction are used in the course of an expedition. The students particularly enjoyed doing the field research on the shore in the Casco Bay expedition. Some did underwater photography. Those who did had to take a swimming test and learn how to put on a wet suit. They learned all these things with the purpose of learning about the intertidal zone, and the experience changed the meaning of school for them—and for us. "In the Zone" happened in the second year of the program and became a standard for quality of work from a wide range of fully included students. The students who created that first field guide have been through high school and are starting college; a surprising number of the girls have decided to major in science.

Another expedition, called "A Park Grows in Portland," also produced a field guide. Across the street from the school, we have a beautiful park that had a terrible reputation. The students got involved with a citizens group that was interested in making the park a better place. The guiding question for the expedition was: "What effect does a park have on a city?" The team of teachers and students studied the park. The students adopted a tree, learned about the history of the park, the impact of trees on our lives, and the life cycles of trees.

During the summers, the teachers plan learning goals and content standards that meet state standards—all of which are incorporated into an expedition. An expedition is not a series of interesting, fun projects; it is how we do school. Each expedition starts with a kickoff event to engage the students and to talk about the guiding questions. There is a total immersion in the expedition by all members of the faculty. Teachers think about what the children will need to learn in math or science, and design expeditions that will stimulate that learning. It may seem that Expeditionary Learning schools are loosely structured, but the planning and structures of the school almost have to be more well-defined than those of a traditional school.

Expeditionary Learning isn't very expensive. We use what is around us, from the natural environment to the politics of the city. In another expedition, called "Dream On," the students helped design an aquarium for Portland. Responding to a citizen group's desire to build an aquarium, the children became an architectural firm. They had business cards, wrote a business plan, wrote letters, and learned from architects how to measure and draw a full-size architectural rendering of a child-friendly aquarium. They visited the Boston aquarium, armed with clipboards and specific questions to be answered. They were invited to go behind the scenes to learn about the structure of the aquarium. They made architectural drawings and presented their plan to a jury of architects and an audience of two hundred people. They did a great job and got good feedback from the architects.

The expedition "Coming to America" is a study of immigration in the U.S. but through the eyes of our most recent immigrants. This expedition pairs a native-born student with a student who has recently come to this country. The native-born student writes the recent immigrant student's biography in order to capture his or her story about the experience of immigration. All the stories are gathered into a children's book. These collections are some of the most often checked-out books in the elementary school library. There is always a culminating event to a learning expedition, and for this expedition the final event brings together the collaborative biographers to read the stories.

Expeditionary Learning has resulted in improved scores on statewide tests. In the three years prior to Expeditionary Learning, the reading scores were 235 (on a scale of 100 to 400). Three years after we started Expeditionary Learning, they were up to 295. In science, scores rose from 260 to 275; in social studies, from 230 to 245. What these figures don't show is that in 1989, at the beginning of Expeditionary Learning, only 3 percent of the students who took the test were limited English proficient. In 1998, 22 percent of the students were limited English proficient. These scores are better than the state averages, but the story that is not told by the scores is the language factor. The state tests are open-ended, with a lot of reading—they are very difficult tests. With language factored in, these scores are really good. We credit that to Expeditionary Learning and getting the students involved in real-life learning.[1]

NOTE

1. This paper originated as the Herb and Anita Foster Lecture given during Urban Education Month, organized by the Urban Education Institute at the University at Buffalo Graduate School of Education in March 2001.

OTHER RESOURCES

Internet:
Expeditionary Learning: www.elob.org

Publications:
Bushweller, K. (1997). Expeditions in learning. *American School Board Journal, 184*(4), 30–33.

Cousins, E., & Mednick, A. (1999). *Service at the heart of learning: Teachers' writings.* Dubuque, IA: Kendall/Hunt.

Cousins, E., & Rogers, M. (1995). *Fieldwork: An expeditionary learning outward bound reader, Vol. 1.* Dubuque, IA: Kendall/Hunt.

Farrell, G. (2002). Expeditionary learning schools: Tenacity, leadership and school reform. In J. Murphy and A. Datnow (Eds.), *Leadership lessons from comprehensive school reforms* (pp. 21–36). Thousand Oaks, CA: Corwin Press.

Rugen, L., & Hartl, S. (1994). The lessons of learning expeditions. *Educational Leadership, 52*(3), 20–23.

Udall, D., & Rugen, L. (1997). From the inside out: The expeditionary learning process of teacher change. *Phi Delta Kappan, 78*(5), 404–408.

6 Why the Arts Matter in Our Schools

Arnold Aprill

Arnold Aprill is an award-winning theater director, producer, and playwright, and Executive Director of the Chicago Arts Partnerships in Education (CAPE), a network of public schools, arts organizations, and community organizations, working to increase the opportunities for integrating the arts into the overall educational program of the Chicago Public Schools. In this chapter, Aprill argues that the arts not only foster academic achievement, but also are central to educating students to be competent and responsible participants in a diverse democratic society.

As THE BASIS OF OUR ECONOMY SHIFTS from manufacturing to information, we are moving from people working in separate silos of service to people from different segments of the population who are concerned with lifelong learning and who work together holistically to meet the needs of young people. We need this diverse group of people at the education policy table in order to restore the arts to the educational process.

Why do the arts need to be brought back into our schools? Because schools need to create a social fabric that is inclusive of all learners, and the primary function of the arts in learning is to pull together learning from different knowledge bases. Unfortunately, the role of the arts in improving education has been limited by the segregation of arts learning from the rest of the culture. In many schools, art and music teachers are marginalized. In Chicago, for example, there is a half-time music *or* visual arts teacher for every 750 students. By contract, the job of the art or music teacher includes taking care of the students while the rest of the faculty plans curriculum. By contract, art and music teachers are structured *not* to be part of the pedagogy of the school.

Beginning in the fifties, art became a separate subject area, one that sometimes got marginalized and sometimes got included. Before that, the arts were included in a more integrated approach to teaching and learning. They were the glue that held together the educational process—not just music and visual art, but also dance and theater and media arts and literature. Culture is the medium in which all bases of knowledge have their life. Today we have structured our instruction so that art is a separate, often marginalized content area.

Chicago Arts Partnership in Education

CAPE works to improve education by forging partnerships between schools and arts organizations that make quality education a central part of the daily learning experience. It provides partnerships with funding and professional development opportunities for teachers, artists, and principals, and serves as a resource for curriculum development. CAPE is founded on the belief that collaborative partnerships can transform schools by improving the quality of arts learning through access to a community's arts resources; creating community-based arts experiences that recognize students as active citizens in their own neighborhoods; forging bonds between parents, schools, and communities that expand family-based learning opportunities both inside and outside school buildings; and connecting policy discussions at the local, state, and national level to innovative practice in arts and education. CAPE works to ensure that all students have equitable access to art in their lives and in their schools.

We need to put the arts back into schools because the arts are part of the way that all of education hangs together. The arts used to be a medium that held cultures together, not an activity just for a few weirdos or talented people. The arts used to be something that people participated in both as doers and as audience. Now we have the idea that the arts are something most people participate in only as audience rather than moving between doing and responding. We know from good teaching practice that learners need to be able to move between different roles: from observer, to inquirer, to creator, to performer, to reflector, roles that embody the five fundamental processes in a program developed at the Research Center for Learning Through Music at New England Conservatory, under the direction of Dr. Larry Scripp. It is the ability of the learner to engage a content area in different ways that gives them the flexibility and intellectual capacity to go deeply into a content area.

American culture used to be held together by music. John Phillip Souza bands would play in every gazebo in every town and everyone socialized around the music. Everyone was in choirs, and before there was recorded music, everyone was a music maker. One of the obsessions of underground cartoonist R. Crumb is collecting early music recordings. What blew his mind was that almost all these early recordings were brilliant and they were by musicians he had never heard of. It used to be normal for regular people to be virtuoso musicians. With the proliferation of recorded music, music is no longer something everyone does.

It used to be that every grade school teacher played piano. There was a piano in every classroom. Now basic art skills are not part of teacher pre-service. We need to reclaim the arts in schooling in order to reclaim democratic culture, which means including the artistic expressions of all cultures and all ethnicities and all classes. The arts have become associated with elite culture, but the real life of the arts is in all layers of culture and in all communities. The arts become a place where people can use their own voices and diverse voices can interact with each other—this is what the arts should be doing. It's time to reclaim the role the arts once played in agricultural and early industrial society.

The program of the Chicago Arts Partnership in Education (CAPE) aims to do just that. Our latest publication, *Renaissance in the Classroom*, documents that in an urban school system named by William Bennett as the worst in the country, students of different economic levels and ethnicities are doing cutting edge work. We are doing arts education that is the envy of suburban systems— not in one school with an eccentric, brilliant principal, but in thirty different Chicago Public Schools. We treat art as normal practice for normal students. Normal teachers can become colleagues with professional artists and arts teachers and form new professional communities that can become the basis of democratic culture and education.

That is a radical notion. People have been taught to fear each other across differences of race, of education, of class, and of occupation. Teachers and artists have been socialized to fear each other, even though both are interested in the development of our young people. The belief that art partners are predatory, outside artists and the enemies of authentic certified, in-school art teachers is based on the notion of a scarcity economy. The impulse to protect jobs is the result of a scarcity mentality. In fact, the in-school art teacher and the partnering outside artist serve different functions—the idea that there is one way for the arts to interface with the rest of the school is a lie. In fact, what we need is a much more complex interaction between schools and art in the community, education in the community, science in the community, and history in the community.

The purpose of an outside arts partnership is primarily to stimulate the classroom teacher, to provide professional development for teachers, not the delivery of services to students. The primary delivery of art and music to students is the job of the in-school art and music teacher. In Chicago, the thirty schools I've worked with have long-term partnerships between teachers and artists, not quickie residencies. In quickie residencies, artists don't learn how to become effective educators. They undermine the flow of instruction of the in-school curriculum and they undermine the in-school music and art specialists.

In our program, we build long-term relationships in which the artists and the teachers and the arts specialists all get professional development, in which the function of the outside artist is to provide professional development for the classroom teachers and to advocate for the in-school arts specialists. In our program, there is a coherent relationship developed over time around curriculum and the outside artist serves to connect the school to the larger arts community of the city. Schools learn that education can happen not just in the school building, but also outside; students begin to become responsible for their own learning and development. When a school begins to access the resources of the larger cultural community, it also learns to access its own resources and not count on the art teachers to do it all alone.

In Chicago, these long-term coherent partnerships have developed through people fighting and playing and laughing and revising. Teachers and artists have been working together for eight years—teachers have complete access to the cultural community and artists have complete access to the culture of the schools. Rather than eliminating in-school arts specialist jobs, the schools in our long-term partnerships understand and value the arts, and the number of arts specialists has skyrocketed. Despite the common belief that partnerships are the enemy of arts specialists, I think serious studies on the real impact on hiring would find that superficial partnerships result in the undermining of arts specialists while serious, rigorous partnerships result in an increase in the hiring of arts teachers.

The real issue is whether you can build an infrastructure in your community for serious engagement of the arts. Can you get the cultural community and the school system in your city to be collaborators and not just service providers? We have to get out of the model that the arts organizations are there to provide another nice drop-in program. Schools need to learn to treat the cultural community with much more respect, and that includes the arts teachers. The cultural community needs to treat the schools with more respect. They need to enter into a real dialogue rather than a service relationship.

In our schools where the arts have been integrated into the curriculum for eight years, test scores have gone up faster than scores in the rest of the district. This has been documented in a report called *Champions of Change*. It is true that test scores in the whole Chicago system are slowly creeping up, but that may have as much to do with the emphasis on test scores as with improving pedagogy. In some places, students who aren't doing well get pushed out of schools so the test scores will go up. It is scary when schools are encouraged not to improve instruction but to improve test scores. Nevertheless, I think test scores are really important—parents should be concerned if their students' test scores are in the basement. But the strategy for improving test scores has become "test prep," and I don't think that's how test scores really improve or how students learn more.

The purpose of testing should be to demonstrate that the students will be able to function as capable adults in the twenty-first century, but a lot of test prep is based on an industrial economy. Most test prep focuses on fragmented skills, when students need a wide range of integrated skills, including the ability to do math calculations and understand grammar. In our schools, test scores have increased, not because we are teaching to the tests, but because we are teaching beyond the tests. We start with the standardized course of study and then build an inquiry-based approach, with a diverse way of representing knowledge. We assume that students need real content knowledge in academic areas, but also that the knowledge should become the basis of interesting inquiry.

The skills students need for the twenty-first century include being able to do math and to read, and we are concerned about students who haven't acquired these skills. But there are other things they will need as well to be successful adults. The U.S. Department of Labor has identified the kinds of people who will be hired in the twenty-first century as people who can:

- plan with, negotiate with, and work well with diverse collaborators;

- imagine alternate solutions to a problem and choose between options;

- manage multiple diverse simultaneous projects;

- self monitor and adjust their work;

- organize space and time;

- convey information in diverse forms, which include the arts forms;

- synthesize information from diverse sources.

Those are the things students actually need to do to succeed in the twenty-first century. We believe that infusing the arts back into schools is one of the most effective ways for accomplishing those skills. Unfortunately, studies like the "Mozart effect" give a false impression that specific arts skills are directly applicable and measurable. The point is that everyone has the capacity to engage in a wide range of skills, and the arts require students to draw on skills they are not usually asked to draw on in school. The student who is a kinesthetic learner needs to have that validated, so she can draw on that in order to solve problems. The arts are one part of a broad palette of capacities that students must be able to access.

The linear idea that the arts will fix everything is not true. Education improves when there is translation and dialogue between different domains of knowledge. It is not that art is nice and will make the curriculum more entertaining—art is hard, and that is what makes it satisfying. Art is challenging. Art will increase self-esteem because self-esteem increases when people solve difficult problems, not when they solve simple problems. The arts should be at the table in dialogue with other domains of knowledge. Art doesn't fix everything, but art can be at the table in a way that convenes a useful discussion between communities. Because the arts have been so marginalized, however, arts education advocates often get whiney and beg to be recognized as a legitimate subject and to have a budget. We need to speak from a position of power, not one of marginalization or victimization.

Arts advocates need to reclaim their seat at the table and should help bring students to the table. Because the arts are sensory-based ways of representing cognition, they allow students to reclaim their voices. Because the arts are both intellectual and sensory, they are integrative and healing. It is important to bring arts back into the schools because the arts encourage the adults to respect the intelligence of their students and they put students in discourse with their peers.

The arts provide an arena in which people can have different subjectivities. Identical art products are not art—art is the aesthetic representation of diverse points of view. I believe that reclaiming the arts is profoundly connected to reclaiming democratic culture and to an honest respect for diversity. There is a lot of lip service given to diversity, in terms of holidays of famous people and foods of many lands. We tend to have very stereotypic images of cultural expression, but when engaged seriously, the arts open up the complexity of representation rather than shutting it down. A brilliant artist who works in our program, Indira Johnson, did an installation on different theologies' contributions to violence against women. Interestingly, she has been criticized by a group of Muslim women, who assumed that she is Hindu. She is Catholic.

I believe that the purpose of arts education partnerships is to frustrate teachers and to frustrate artists, to put them in serious enough contact/conflict with themselves that they have to drop their assumptions. The teacher who assumes that the arts aren't really important, or that her students can't do it, or that she has no talent is confronted by someone who says she is wrong. The artist who has been socialized to think of himself as an eccentric flake with no social responsibilities also gets confronted. The purpose of partnerships is creative frustration in the service of forcing the participants to grow and helping them understand each other's approach. Many teachers work structurally, while many artists work intuitively. Both need the gifts of the other's way of working.

According to the *Champions of Change* report, "There were seven different exemplary arts education initiatives of very different characters that were studied by seven very different research teams." Across these seven different studies—with different research teams, different methodologies, different cities, different student populations, and different teacher populations—there was an incredible consistency in the results. Across the various in-school, out-of-school, after-school, single-discipline, and multi-arts programs, the program directors and the researchers met regularly over three years and opened up a rich discourse. *Champions of Change* is a summary of these seven initiatives. They conclude: "The arts consistently reach students who are not otherwise being reached."

Another finding was that students get resocialized through the arts: "The arts transform the environment for learning. The arts provide learning opportunities for the adults who are in the lives of young people. The arts connect students to themselves and to each other. The arts connect learning experiences to the world of real work." A result that is of particular importance to me is that these initiatives reclaim the cultural resources of the city for the students and reclaim the importance of the arts specialist inside the school as a colleague with the rest of the faculty.

Finally, the arts provide students with diverse, connected opportunities to represent knowledge over time. What we know now about the development of higher order thinking skills and cognition is that the act of translating between different media encourages students to conceptualize. Students need to encounter Matisse in a lot of different ways before they can understand Matisse. It is translation that gives depth of meaning. The arts also create new kinds of discourse between young people and adults and can develop discussion across grades. Students can become mentors to each other as the arts become an arena in which the students can enact their capacities. We need to advocate not just for arts instruction but for all instruction, so a dialogue can develop between the arts and literature, science, and math. We should be colleagues together in our children's development, not competing factions.[1]

NOTE

1. This paper originated as a presentation given during Urban Education Month, organized by the Urban Education Institute at the University at Buffalo Graduate School of Education and co-sponsored by Canisius College and the Oishei Foundation in March 2001.

OTHER RESOURCES

Internet:
ArtsEdge: www.artsedge.kennedy-center.org
ArtsEdNet: www.artsednet.getty.edu
Arts Education Partnership (includes other arts education links): www.aep-arts.org
CAPE: www.capeweb.org
Gaining the Arts Advantage: www.pcah.gov/gaa

Publications:
Aprill, A. (2001). Toward a finer description of the connection between arts education and student achievement. *Arts Education Policy Review, 102*(5), 25.

Burnaford, G. E., & Aprill, A. (2001). *Renaissance in the classroom: Arts integration and meaningful learning.* Mahwah, NJ: Erlbaum Associates.

Champions of change: The impact of the arts on learning. (1999). Washington, D.C.: President's Committee on the Arts and the Humanities.

Dreeszen, C., Aprill, A., & Deasy, R. (1999). Learning partnerships: Improving learning in schools with arts partners in the community. Washington, D.C.: Arts Education Partnership.

Gaining the arts advantage: Lessons from school districts that value arts education. (1999). Washington, D.C.: President's Committee on the Arts and the Humanities.

7 Art: An Educational Link between School and Community

Mathias J. Schergen

Mathias "Spider" Schergen is an art educator at Jenner Academy of the Arts, a Chicago Public School located in the Cabrini Green Public Housing Community on the near-north side of Chicago. His role as art educator has afforded him many opportunities to explore the dynamics of expressive collaboration with students, parents, colleagues, administrators, community residents, and local arts organizations. His chapter describes two of these collaborative efforts and how they affected those who participated. It also reflects his firm belief that creativity is a process that provides meaning to every aspect of the educational experience, whether teaching or learning.

I CAME TO JENNER SCHOOL IN 1991 with four years of teaching experience and a desire to commit my energies to a single school site. I previously had been assigned in two half-time positions at schools on the far south side of Chicago, where I learned a lot about the management of students and materials in the art room. Working at two schools simultaneously allowed me to experience and gain insight into the dynamics that turn a school site into a unique school community. But the professional pull and tug of teaching in two different schools became an eventual hindrance to my practice and I requested an administrative transfer and left for the Jenner School.

Jenner could be described as a traditional "neighborhood school." Its enrollment represents families who have lived and were educated in the Cabrini Green Public Housing Community for generations. This is unique to most schools in the Chicago Public School System, where busing is provided and/or the surrounding community has transitioned to new residents. The ties that bind Jenner School and Cabrini Green are strengthened by extended family relationships that make students brother and sister, aunt and uncle, cousin and "Godcousin" to one another. School and community are woven in ways that make their strengths and weaknesses appear to be the same. That which affects the one affects the other. The death of a community elder can cause the

Shadow Boxes from the Jenner School, Chicago, Illinois

absence of twenty or thirty students, or a fight in school might provoke conflict between families in the community.

The successes and failures of my early years at Jenner grounded my educational practice in providing creative experiences that serve the needs of its students. As I entered my fourth year at the school, I noticed a shift in my curricular consciousness toward a greater awareness of the Cabrini Community. Families began using housing vouchers to relocate; cyclone fences were erected like encampments around long-standing vacant buildings, children were saying goodbye, and there was talk of a "new" Jenner School. Years of private planning sessions in city and corporate offices were coming to fruition. Facing a massive wave of gentrification and redevelopment on the near-north side, Cabrini Green and Jenner School braced themselves for an all-encompassing socioeconomic transition. By midyear I was hearing the dull thud of a wrecking ball against the high-rise building across the street from the art room windows. Children entering my room would often watch the daily demolition, recounting which of their family members once lived there or whether a certain slasher-film boogieman inhabited its apartments and hallways. As an art educator at this time and in this place, I sought ways to focus my curriculum on projects that would give visual voice to the sense of loss and hope these symbiotic communities were experiencing. By school's end the high-rise was level with the gravel surface around it.

That summer I attended my first Walloon Institute, directed by Harvey "Smokey" Daniels from National-Louis University (NLU) and funded by the Joyce Foundation. Jenner School's membership in the NLU-sponsored Best Practice Network provided me an opportunity to attend the Institute, where I was introduced to a diverse collection of parents, educators, and administrators who advocated Best Practice methods, community involvement, and an inclusive collegiality among all stakeholders in the school community.

As I entered my fifth year at Jenner, I felt energized by what I had experienced at the Institute and further committed to weaving art educational theory and practice into the relational fabric of Jenner School and the Cabrini Green Community. An opportunity to achieve this goal came by way of an invitation to participate in an exhibition titled "Spiritual Passports and Transformative Journeys." The exhibition, initiated by the DeWitt Wallace-funded Chicago Students at the Center Project (CSATC) and supported by artist and co-curator Cynthia Weiss, was part of a collaboration between the Chicago Art Partnerships in Education (CAPE) and the Illinois Art Gallery. The exhibition featured media performance, language, and visual art by students from schools in the Best Practice Network. Classroom teachers, art educators, artists, and curators were brought together to interpret the exhibition's theme in ways that would generate authentic curriculum at their respective sites. Together, we developed units of study using young adult literature, social studies, language arts, and fine arts.

Drawn to the idea of a "transformative journey" as metaphor for the changes transpiring in the school and community around me, I planned an art project where participants would construct individual shadow boxes to interpret their personal experience of change. The shadow boxes would then be arranged in a grid to represent the collective experience. In an attempt to replicate the inclusive approach of the Walloon Institute, not only students but also parents and teachers were invited to make shadow boxes. The project became a curricular focus for upper-grade students and part of the family history activities facilitated by Pete Lecki of the Parent Project (a community-based program, also an initiative of CSATC, that met weekly at Jenner School). Students also wrote poetry in writing workshops facilitated by Illinois Writing Project artist/writing consultant Lynette Emmons.

The individual shadow boxes were nine inches by eleven inches, constructed with one-by-two inch pine boards, backed with cardboard, then painted and filled with objects, images, and text. As the shadow boxes came to completion, students and adults began sharing them with one another at Parent Project meetings and informal visits to the art room. Well over 150 shadow boxes were made, far too many to spread across the gallery wall. We decided to construct four "shadow box walls" and connect them, with the boxes facing out. This structure not only served the original intent of representing the collective experience; it replicated the visual impact of the high rises at the south end of Cabrini (known as the "reds"). These buildings, designed with red bricks set into cream color concrete frames, are often used in media images of Cabrini Green. The shadow boxes were set into a cream color grid of two-by-fours, further replicating the "reds." We titled our three-dimensional shadow box tower "Landmark on the Journey."

The work was installed in the School of the Chicago Art Institute's Gallery II. "Landmark on the Journey" stood in the center of the space, surrounded by the student poetry on the walls. The combination of written and visual expression touched gallery visitors deeply. Field trips were organized throughout the exhibition to give students and parents from Jenner, as well as the other participating schools, an opportunity to serve as docents to one another and share their work in amiably structured critiques. Jenner School participants discussed their shadow boxes with student artists from Crown Academy, the school whose exhibit was composed as dream paintings in response to aboriginal art. The gallery was filled with a palpable sense of excitement as students, parents, educators, school administrators, and gallery curators mingled in the context of an exhibition opening. As I stood in the midst of the excitement, it occurred to me that a heady mix of authentic learning, integrated curriculum, and community involvement brought all of this about.

School opening in the autumn of 1999 brought us face to face with the architectural reality of the soon-to-be-completed new Jenner school, which was now a structure of brick with windows, doors, sidewalks, and a flagpole. The new school seemed destined to become a showpiece for the Chicago Board of Education and the affluent North Shore. It was announced that the old school was scheduled for demolition at the end of the school year. Children stood at the window with excited, anxious interest as they exchanged bits of current rumor and fact. There was going to be a swimming pool, but no one knew where, and an elevator large enough to carry us to the third floor so we wouldn't have to make the long climb. Computers, air conditioning, and a new playground were a given. Conversations became less directed when they turned to the topic of new students. Would kids from other Cabrini schools be allowed to transfer to Jenner? No, because that would cause too many fights. A more perplexing question was whether white kids would be attending the new Jenner. This is our school, was the initial response, then conversation trailed off into wonderment of what that would be like.

The day-to-day routine of school life was suddenly interrupted by gunshots on the west side of our school in front of the Cabrini 500 building during school hours. Seventh- and eighth-grade students, whose classroom windows faced the crime-infested high-rise, witnessed the incident. A typical flurry of news media attention ensued, prompting the Board of Education to decide to move the entire staff and student body to an abandoned school site, miles away, for safety. The decision seemed reasonable at face value, but its implications were unsettling to the families of Cabrini Green. Was it a plan to relocate the current Jenner population before the new school opened? This was not the first shooting witnessed by Cabrini children. Why all the fuss now? Community consensus was that the city should address the elimination of rampant criminal activity in the 500 building rather than relocate their children to another school.

Thankfully, the community's wisdom prevailed. The 500 building was closed and a parent patrol was formed to assure safe passage of students to and from school. This solution, however, also resulted in another drop in Jenner's enrollment, with more students saying goodbye as their families moved out of the 500 building. Soon another cyclone fence went up, creating another encampment. As the media spotlight and community activism dimmed, we refocused our attention on the inevitability of moving into the new Jenner and the demolition of the old Jenner.

Once again, I found myself reflecting on our circumstances and felt my art educative instincts stimulated by the gentle tension between looking to the future and reflecting on the past. Our success with the shadow box project, my continued involvement with the Parent Project, and the encouragement of the Best Practice network prompted another art educational project that would provide Jenner School and the Cabrini Community with an opportunity to express the transformative nature of their mutual experience. I was drawn to the notion that if objects, images, and text gained significance in the confines of a shadow box, how much more could be expressed if these elements were expanded and installed in the context of entire classroom space? This project was possible because there were several abandoned classrooms in our building, due to Jenner's low enrollment. Many of these rooms were filled with maps, books, manipulatives, and other assorted educational materials, untouched for years. I had been given access to such a room, across the hall from my classroom, to use as a storage area for art materials and assembly props, and as an additional studio space for large projects. It was a perfect space for a large installation piece. With the help of students, the room's contents were moved down the hall to another available room. We were now ready to begin the installation of a work in Room 307, titled "Memory Museum."

Installation is an art form that uses space as a medium for expression. This medium invites the viewer to actively participate in the work. The artists' intentions (in this case, Jenner students) are expressed through references to other interior spaces, the visual relationship of objects and an understanding of common experience. A well-crafted installation work provides enough selected sensory stimulus to engage the viewer in a personal process of exploration, observation, and interpretation. Whether an installation occupies an entire room or a corner, a closet, cabinet, drawer, an appliance box, or a shoebox, the space needs to be visually altered or decontextualized to separate it from its expected use. We accomplished this by whitewashing the room from floor to ceiling, including chalkboards, bulletin boards, cabinet fronts, windowsills,

and doorframe. After two coats of paint, new muslin curtains and the replace-
ment of the torn window shades, Room 307's pristine appearance was a stark
contrast to the poorly maintained, deteriorated classrooms throughout the rest
of the school. In the process of decontextualization, this clean, empty, and
visually neutral space gained the potential to add significance to any object
placed within it.

The first object placed in the Memory Museum was a letter signed by
Coretta Scott King and family, expressing gratitude for the condolences sent
from Jenner students at the passing of Dr. Martin Luther King Jr. in 1968. The
framed letter was anchored to a bulletin board and surrounded by photo-
graphic portraits of past and present students in Jenner School. A teacher's desk
and chair, student chairs, and a small wastebasket also were brought in and
whitewashed to blend with the walls. First-grade students were invited to draw
on the whitened chalkboards with ebony pencils and crayons.

Levels of interest with regard to the installation varied as the school year
unfolded. At one point, the Memory Museum served as a meeting place for
two artist-in-residence programs that facilitated the production of student
videos. A documentary about the construction of the new school, titled "The
Jenner Journal," was the first video, made under the direction of artist Kerry
Richardson with funding from the Illinois Arts Council. The second video,
under the direction of artist Sarah Strahan with Annenberg funding through
NLU's Center for City Schools, featured the voices and imagery of Jenner
students reflecting on their memories. The Memory Museum was further
blessed with the support and guidance of CAPE artist Cynthia Weiss and
Illinois Writing Project's Lynette Emmons, who worked independently with
core groups of students while I attended to regularly scheduled classes.

In March we took a field trip to Gallery 312 in Chicago to view an
exhibition of installation work by local artists. This experience gave us a
common conceptual springboard from which we could discuss ideas for the
Memory Museum. In the following week, students roamed the school with
Polaroid cameras, documenting objects and spaces they wanted to remember
from the "old" Jenner School. Then we began scavenging through vacant
classrooms for such artifacts as vintage educational materials, old textbooks,
science activity kits, maps, bookcases, forgotten graduation gowns, and anything else that wasn't bolted down. In time we realized the need to create
special divisions within the installation, so we began collecting cabinet and
closet doors, unscrewing them from their frames with the hinges attached. This
mismatched collection of doors was reassembled as a wall with numerous
recessed areas for displays and small-scale installations.

The installation began to take shape with a peculiar sense of organized
chaos. Displays were changed, objects painted, items added, and areas of interest
reorganized in ways that did not suit my aesthetic tastes. It often felt as though
the progress we made on one day was negated by what appeared to be an
arbitrary decision the next day because the children were naturally gifted with

an endless flow of ideas that remained inconsistent on a day-to-day basis. The installation continued in a state of aesthetic and conceptual flux until the very end. Eventually, every nook and cranny, every wall surface, cabinet, closet, and drawer were filled with the potential for visual exploration. What was once an empty whitewashed shell of a room became a highly embellished, deeply expressive, student-centered, collaborative installation dedicated to a school community in transition.

The Memory Museum officially opened its door for three days at the beginning of June 2000. Jenner students and staff visited the Museum in the mornings, while outside guests were invited in the afternoons. Community residents, Chicago Board of Education administrators, colleagues from the Best Practice Network, and news media outlets took the opportunity to visit and view the Memory Museum. Mary Schmich from the *Chicago Tribune* interviewed student artists and wrote an insightful column. Cable news Channel CLTV did a story, and public station WTTW Channel 11 produced an in-depth segment for their weekly Art Beat Chicago program.

This was a type of media attention Jenner School was not accustomed to receiving. Students were featured discussing their contributions to the Museum and answering questions about the future school. They were able to participate in a media image of their own making rather than being subject to the stereotypical images the media relies on when covering stories about Cabrini. Students also served as docents for guests visiting the Museum and set up the hospitality area. Guests were invited to make their own contributions to the Memory Museum by writing down their impressions of the installation and hiding them throughout. (When dismantling the Museum, I found bits of paper discreetly tucked in the most unusual places.)

One of the original concepts of the Memory Museum was that significant and historical items would be saved, but that the rest of the Museum would suffer the same fate as the old school building. As it happened, the artifacts, objects, and materials salvaged from the Memory Museum were subsequently reassembled to fit the needs of other installation sites. Gallery 400 at the University of Illinois, Chicago (UIC), hosted an exhibition of art produced by students under the direction of art educators brought together by Olivia Gude at UIC to explore the possibilities of using concepts and methods of contemporary art as a curricular foundation, in a program called Contemporary Community Curriculum.

In this gallery setting, not only were the art educational aspects of Memory Museum brought into sharper focus, but also Jenner's story and the creative voice of its students were brought to a new audience. From there, the Museum's contents were further simplified and installed in the street-level lobby at The Museum of Contemporary Art (MCA) in Chicago, where it was viewed and discussed for its conceptual and aesthetic qualities in the context of contemporary art history. Students who contributed to the Memory Museum were invited to visit the MCA and share their work with museum representatives, then tour the galleries with educational docents. In the end, the Memory Museum took on a life of its own, bigger and more expansive than anything we could have imagined at its inception.

It was profoundly ironic that at this high point of public recognition the Memory Museum's original site, Room 307, was exposed to the open air, its walls demolished by the thud of a wrecking ball. After the MCA exhibition and further simplification, the contents of the Memory Museum were packed in moving boxes and stored in my classroom. In the summer of 2001, I received a grant from the Chicago Neighborhood Art Partnership to build a large shadow box with students, which serves as the final installment of the Museum's contents and a testament to the old Jenner School, now a fenced-in area of weed and gravel. The shadow box hangs in the lobby outside the main office of the new school, a daily reminder that learning is an experience shared by school and community when they are partners on the same transformative journey.[1]

NOTE

1. This paper originated as a presentation given during Urban Education Month, organized by the Urban Education Institute at the University at Buffalo Graduate School of Education and co-sponsored by Canisius College and the Oishei Foundation in March 2001.

8 City Voices, City Visions: Digital Video as Literacy/Learning Supertool in Urban Classrooms

Suzanne M. Miller and Suzanne Borowicz

Suzanne Miller, Associate Professor and Project Coordinator for City Voices/ City Visions (CVCV), and Suzanne Borowicz, Graduate Assistant, in the Department of Learning and Instruction at the State University of New York at Buffalo, report on the CVCV digital video project. Since 2000, CVCV, a partnership between the University at Buffalo Graduate School of Education and the Buffalo Public Schools, has prepared middle and high school teachers in creative and purposeful uses of digital video technologies with their sixth- to twelfth-grade urban students.

HOW CAN DIGITAL VIDEO TRANSFORM URBAN TEACHING?

In 1997 A NATIONAL REPORT from the Educational Testing Service concluded that poor and minority students have less access than other students to computers, multimedia technology, and the Internet (see also Rohde, Shapiro et al., 2000). Moreover, even when poor and minority children are provided access to these more advanced technologies, they are often limited by teacher assignments to learning rote skills, thus becoming further disadvantaged for successful achievement and productive work. On the face of it, the failure to provide urban students access to new technologies for productive thinking and composing suggests inequity, a narrowing of life chances. Further, from a learning theory perspective, the development of higher psychological functions in students depends on access to and meaningful use of such cultural tools. In this view, human thought and action are shaped and defined by purposeful activity with mediational tools (Vygotsky, 1978; Wertsch, 1991)—which in the twenty-first century include not only the simplest of tools like pencil and paper, but also high-tech computer tools, such as digital video.

With its capacity for recording multiple modes of symbolic expression, digital video (DV) technology is in theory a tangible and potent mediator for constructing learning. Creating images to carry meanings and distill experience

City Voices, City Visions students working on a digital video

into visual concepts is central to what Eisner calls "visual learning"—a vital means of making sense of the world (1998, p. 71). Visualizing is a fundamental resource for understanding, with images often preceding language as a means of coming to understand. By combining the powerful tool of visualization with oral narration and music, digital video production can provide a three-in-one mediational tool for learners. In all, using digital video can provide access not only to new technologies, but also to learning tools that can promote powerful literacy and learning rather than the rote learning of domesticating literacy characteristic of poor urban schools (Anyon, 1997; Finn, 1999).

GOALS OF THE CITY VOICES, CITY VISIONS DIGITAL VIDEO PROJECT

Since its inception in 2000, the City Voices, City Visions (CVCV) project, a partnership of the University at Buffalo Graduate School of Education and the Buffalo Public Schools, has prepared over thirty teachers in the creative and purposeful uses of digital video technologies with their sixth- to twelfth-grade urban students.[1] In two-week summer institutes, these teachers learn how to engage students in creating digital video and written documentation of school-based and community experiences as part of a student-centered, inquiry-based, project-oriented curriculum. Using the Internet, hand-sized digital video cameras, and iMovie editing software as creative research tools, teachers engage students actively in strategic composing skills and encourage them to connect what they learn in school to what they know about the world outside. These activities help students develop composing strategies that assist them in achieving new higher-level state learning standards in literacy, social science, and other school subjects. Continued support of these teachers through bi-monthly reunions allows them to share their experiences and seek advice from other City Voices teachers and university participants.

Overall, the City Voices, City Visions digital video project has three key goals: (1) to provide ongoing professional development to prepare urban teachers as leaders in wise integration of digital video and information technologies into curricular activities; (2) to focus on helping urban students meet challenging subject-area learning standards by engaging in curriculum and community-based projects using these technologies; and (3) to archive the student- and teacher-produced digital video as curriculum and community resources for use in the professional development of present and future urban teachers. The ultimate aim of City Voices, City Visions is to foster student achievement by empowering them with digital video tools for analysis and visualization in thinking and understanding.

The urban and community focus of CVCV is an approach that has in the past proven a successful academic strategy to engage struggling learners to meet academic standards (e.g., Heath, 1983; Wigginton, 1991). The students' motivation for learning and using language more effectively in these projects was traced to the fact that they were engaged in purposeful learning and communicating their findings about their own community to a real audience. By integrating digital video and information technology into these kinds of projects, City Voices, City Visions brings to this innovative cultural journalism approach a new means of learning. During the annual CVCV Summer Institute, teachers learned to use digital video to engage students in curriculum projects linked to school and community, with the aim of both motivating student learning and developing teacher understanding of the urban community. For example, students and teachers have conducted video interviews of adults in the community and students in the school on current events (opinions about cloning), local politics (opinions on teacher layoffs), social issues (the homeless in Buffalo), subject-specific topics (Do you use math in your everyday life? What was your experience in the Vietnam War?), school history (How was our school different when you attended?), and literary themes linked to class reading (What are your dreams?).

Such projects also provide meaningful ways for students to meet learning standards. The New York State English Language Arts Standards, for instance, require that students learn to understand and process information, engage in critical analysis, respond to literary language and text, and learn through social interaction. All four standards were clearly met as Jeremy's students in small groups created poetry videos linking their interpretation of a selected poem to national and local issues, through school and community visuals and video, selecting music with the appropriate tone, and reading the text as a dramatic performance.

The NYS Social Studies Standards challenge both teachers and students to dig more deeply into key social ideas and issues locally, nationally, and globally. Shiarra's students created "The Ghosts of Black Rock," a history of their one-hundred-year-old school, beginning with attendance records for their grandparents, parents, cousins, aunts, and uncles they found in the basement of the school.

In Caitlin's class, students researched the history and current state of the football rivalry with another school, which they showed to great acclaim at the school pep rally. With the local community as the site of investigation, these teachers and students practiced and learned analytic skills by collecting and composing visual and written data on past and present conditions, documenting changes in area conditions, examining the changes in the roles and relationships of people and institutions, and constructing a sense of how the local school development can help them understand the corresponding development of Buffalo, New York state, and beyond. These academic competencies also contribute to advanced literacy skills and are vital if students are ever to understand social studies and history as more than a collection of disparate facts.

The City Voices, City Visions digital video and information technology projects offer a mirror in which teachers and students and, by extension, parents, community members, and others, can see themselves within the fabric of American history and culture. These projects can make similar contributions to learning academic standards in science, mathematics, and other school subjects by situating school learning in the local community, and simultaneously create transformative urban images for publication in the Buffalo schools and community.

In what follows we report the findings of an interview study of CVCV teachers from the first two years of the project in order to understand their perceptions about integrating DV activities into their teaching and student learning.[2] Then we move to their stories of student engagement with and achievement through curricular and community-based digital video production.

TEACHER PERCEPTIONS OF CVCV

Because the integration of DV computer technology in classroom curriculum is a relatively new phenomenon, the field of education needs a research-based framework to provide guidance and answers to emerging questions such as: How and why do teachers integrate DV activities into their teaching of academic subjects, if at all? When things go well, what does it look like? What are the influences on classrooms and student learning? The first step in our research was to understand teachers' perceptions of the digital technology and the potential of leading students toward literacy learning through DV activities. To that end, at the close of the second year of CVCV, an interview study was conducted of the fifteen teachers who had been involved in the program to that point. The teachers were asked to answer open-ended questions in an informal context. The interviews were filmed on the digital camera and recorded on an audio tape recorder.[3]

The findings suggest that teachers' conceptions of integrating the digital technology are varied and impact the way teachers approach DV. Teachers' beliefs about literacy and learning are a key element in their ability to integrate DV as a learning tool in their classroom. CVCV teachers who successfully integrated DV perceived literacy and learning as extending beyond a mechanical definition of student skills. That is, they understood "literacy" defined in its broadest sense, as language use, and perceived language use in its many forms as central to all learning. Much as Hobbs (1997) argues, these teachers seemed to believe that "Language must be appreciated as it exists in relationship to other forms of symbolic expression—including images, sounds, music and electronic forms of communication" (p. 7). These perceptions of literacy, language, and other forms of expression as central to both learning and communicating learning were evident among CVCV teachers who integrated digital video into their curriculum.

Further, though, these CVCV teachers perceived DV production as a social phenomenon that arises from active participation in a group, what Leontiev (1981) calls an "activity system." The findings of this study are congruent with the sociocultural perspective that student participation within these activity systems and the support they receive therein contribute not only to students' knowledge and skills, but to their values, beliefs, and their very being (Gutierrez & Stone, 2000; Lave & Wenger, 1991; Wells, 2000). Teachers' conceptions of literacy and learning influenced whether they viewed the digital technology as merely a technological toy or as a mediational tool.

IMPACT OF TEACHERS' NOTIONS OF DV AND LITERACY/LEARNING ON PEDAGOGICAL CHANGE

Teachers who held fast to the traditional notion of literacy as simply reading and writing used digital technology only peripherally. Teacher concerns about the reading and writing required for the state tests influenced this perception—that DV production was mainly an extracurricular activity. A few such teachers began DV clubs, disconnected from the curriculum. In class, these teachers filmed the students at work and then used the footage as an assessment tool. At times, the teacher and students viewed the raw film to assess whether the terms of a performance rubric had been fulfilled. At other times, the teacher edited the film, but only to weed out unnecessary footage in order to save time when the class was viewing the film. Although these uses of digital video aided teachers, DV did not become a student tool for composing learning as part of the curriculum.

Hal, a middle grades teacher, expressed his concerns about redefining literacy and letting go of the traditional paradigm this way:

> Well, I was torn, and I still am. . . . Are we, then, changing the focus of our course now? What is English? And I guess that's our part, to start redefining what we mean by English. Traditionally, it has meant literature and the study of literature and writing composition skills, speaking skills per se in a kind of frozen or academic way. I want to say, this equipment would allow those pursuits in a more naturalistic way as they would appear in the twenty-first century.

Even though Hal felt the potential of DV for his students, his conflict between the traditional and reenvisioned notions of literacy is apparent in his discourse. Not surprisingly, he had difficulties integrating digital video when he suspected it was outside the real focus of "English."

CVCV teachers who embraced a broad definition of literacy more successfully integrated digital video production with their students. The successful digital technology teachers, whether in English or Social Studies, were less concerned with the micro question of What is the curriculum standard?; they were more focused on the macro questions of What is education? What prompts student growth? What is a literate education, and how can I lead my students to it? They worked to transform their goals and activities. For instance, Frank, a CVCV social studies teacher in the middle grades, put it this way: "The goal for me is, ultimately, for [my students] to grow. I'm here to try to provide [my students] with an opportunity to show some growth. . . . if [they] pick up life skills, that's what I'm really interested in."

Classrooms of these teachers are often hotspots of activity, with students out of their seats, shooting footage, acting out skits, discussing issues, planning and storyboarding, researching in books and on the Internet, and clustering around computers in cooperative work groups, creating meaning out of their experiences. They describe their classrooms as being filled with excitement. Kyle, a high school social studies teacher, explained it this way:

> It's Christmas morning when you take the video equipment out. [The students] all want to touch it, and they all want to use it. . . . What you do with that excitement is a different story, but I think just having the video equipment is an immediate plus because it generates an excitement right away.

Our original view of the CVCV project—that the technology itself could usher in more active learning in urban classrooms—resonates with what Kyle said; he, however, also realized what we, too, learned quickly—it is "what you do with that excitement" that makes the difference. That is, we learned that it was the teaching, not the technology, that made the biggest difference.

The CVCV teachers who successfully integrated DV see their classrooms as places of transformation for their students as well as for themselves, where students are in control of their own learning. The teachers in these energy-charged classrooms describe themselves as "guides," "facilitators," "a third arm" in their students' learning events. Ramona, an elementary Spanish teacher, stated it best when she described her own surprise about the power of having student groups use the technology to write and perform skits and create DVs:

> I literally covered almost a whole marking period of lessons in that one [DV] project because I covered four or five verb forms, and it was just amazing. I'm not going to . . . give myself credit and say I planned it out perfectly. It just worked itself out. I just kind of went at it blind and then when I started panicking because we were four or five weeks into this, and each marking period is ten weeks, and taking five weeks of a marking period to what seemed like playing with the camera was like—okay, we have to stop here. But then when I realized how much I had covered, I hadn't lost out on anything. I had covered the material. I just wasn't lecturing. So it's great . . . and I'm learning.

Like Ramona, teachers integrating DV were willing to learn by getting out from behind their desks, trying it out, trusting students, and monitoring how DV can provide new teaching tools that prompt dynamic learning.

The look of the digital video classroom is certainly not one of silent yawning and uniform immobility. It is, rather, an active classroom where use of DV learning tools is the norm, and participants are authentically engaged in shared cooperative knowledge-making. It is twenty-first century literacy in action.

BUILDING BRIDGES: DV SUPERTOOLS
MEDIATING LITERACY/LEARNING

DV Bridges to Higher Achievement

While we have not directly collected data on achievement (the next stage of our research), teachers in CVCV classrooms that were involved in DV production reported specific ways that student achievement improved. Ramona told us an impressive story:

> Probably the best story is one of my students who has fought me for five years on learning or, you know, basically he's got it in him that "I can't do this. I don't know Spanish, I can't do this, I can't do this." . . . And he still struggled with it but . . . that he even wanted to do this [work on the video] was a big step for him and actually this year he's actually passed every marking period—65, 64, borderline, but he went from not even coming close to passing, to "Okay let me try this for the sake of I want to be a part of that scenario. I want to be a part of that video." . . . He's now in eighth grade. He'll be graduating.

Improved student motivation to achieve, arising from opportunities to produce DV as part of classroom learning, was a recurring theme in the teacher interviews. Wanda told us another story:

> One of my English 11 students was a reluctant student, reluctant reader, reluctant writer, special education. He did nothing. He didn't even bring a notebook to class. Once he saw the computer set up, because I had the iMac set up over there, [he] totally changed his philosophy and his outlook on education. Not only did he start bringing a notebook, he came up from a 50 to a 90 in English. He read *A Lesson Before Dying* from front to end. He even said, "This is the first time in my life I've ever read a book." He was so excited about it. And, of course, they don't understand that once you have the information it's easier to put info down on paper. And he did very well in finishing up with English 11 last year. . . . It was something different. It wasn't the same old read a book and take a test. It was different. Something that he could engage in and he was constantly thinking, rethinking, "Oh, what can I do here?" So I think it was the hands on and it's constant, you're always thinking about, "What transition can I use" or "Which clip should I use? What should I take out?" He was actively involved in learning so it made a big difference.

The DV excited this student's interest and prompted an engagement in the class, thinking about the class content and composing meaning from text—all of which seemed to be new for him. Not only did he pass the ELA graduation test—a six-hour writing test—Wanda told us that her students' scores on the ELA graduation test went up significantly during the first year that she used DV, compared to previous years.

These stories of upturn in achievement are compelling, but, we wondered, *how* does DV production actually promote such change? Was it, as both Wanda and Ramona suggest, that students simply engaged more with content, or was there something more? As we examined the interview data more closely, we found that teachers told revealing stories about the specifics of student engagement. Based on the findings of this finer-grained look at the interviews, we argue this key point: using digital video to compose meaning from content serves as a kind of supertool for building bridges to powerful literacy and learning. In what follows we present several undergirding elements that teachers perceived at work in DV activities.

EMPOWERING STUDENTS WITH VOICE, VISION, VISIBILITY

Over and over, teachers told stories of their students' new-found interest in literate activities born out of a new positive self-awareness and self-confidence.

Like the tiny stars that slowly appear in the night sky, these students seemed to step out of their unnoticed place in urban classrooms to shine. All the CVCV teachers, even those who were struggling with their own concepts of integrating digital technology, tell tales of student success, the "invisible" student becoming more assertive, the raising of student confidence and self-esteem. Their collective voices illustrate this phenomenon:

> [The digital video] could actually turn kids around in classes. Rather than sitting in the classroom and reading from a book or just listening to lectures, [students are] actively doing things that they like to do. They're relating. They're participating. They're giving their ideas. These ideas are being taken into consideration. They're not . . . just occupying space here. (Pearl)

> One particular young lady was very quiet in the beginning of the year, and she was the first person I taught how to do editing, and I could really see a big change in her. She speaks a little more often now. She asks questions in class. She volunteers to do extra things. I think . . . it empowers her. (Mary)

> [There's] one student in class, space cadet, unorganized, free spirit, often not here in the room, mentally he's daydreaming . . . but the [DV] work he does is great. He's great on camera. There's a few scenes actually . . . where [this student] is being interviewed, and you can see the difference. He's locked in. He's focused. He knows what he wants to do. (Frank)

The multi-sensory nature of the digital video seems to awaken something in students that traditional academic tools of books and paper do not. Anne told a story about a student mainstreamed in her high school English class, a student who struggled with traditional literacy tools:

> There's one boy in my class—very, very, very smart boy but has a lot of reading difficulties, a lot of writing difficulties and he did not think that he could do anything as far as English. He tries, he tries very hard but he never has success. . . . He's got a lot of things going for him outside the classroom. Inside the classroom he struggles. . . . But if you put him in something technical he could do well, very well. He was the master editor of the whole project. He was the one who made sure everyone was doing their project and doing it well and he's the one who's put every extra minute he had into it. And to be honest with you, without him the project

probably would not have gotten done. . . . He was up in my room every day working on his movie. I was the guide person for it and he produced it and then he went back and he felt that he had more success in that classroom.

Given access to these new tools, this mainstreamed student became the "technical guru" for the whole school, helping other students and teachers use these tools to produce iMovie videos to demonstrate their learning.

Even fairly successful students sometimes found that DV tools enabled their best meaning-making and learning. Kyle told the story of a student in his high school social studies class who

was doing the reading and the writing and kind of trudging along and surviving, and when the video came in he immediately found that that was his niche. And he found this other instrument to use to express himself in the classroom. And I don't know where he's going to go with it, but he's so skilled and he's so talented that this could be something that could provoke him to be a lifelong learner where he could go and extend upon his introduction to the video experience.

Finding this new "instrument to use to express himself" opened a new space for this student's learning. In fact, his learning elevated to a level of engagement that every teacher wants to see; he became what Kyle calls a "lifelong learner."

All of these students' natural curiosity and enthusiasm were roused out of dormancy with a new vigor for knowledge making (Vygotsky, 1978). With DV production, teachers saw both struggling and successful students become focused, confident students capable of meeting challenges. We have come to believe that digital video may appear to be one learning tool, but it is more. Its power comes from the fact that it is actually a tool kit, a supertool that combines multiple, intertwined mediators—dynamic visualization, constructed narration, and musical selection—as means for developing and expressing understanding.

DV BRIDGES TO SOCIAL AWARENESS AND RESPONSIBILITY

In addition to students' engagement and achievement transformations, CVCV teachers also observed a new social awareness and community building in their classrooms through the collaborative nature of digital video activities. Anne, a high school special education teacher, reports that the DV collaborations led to conflict-resolution skills in her students. She said:

[The students] did a lot of conflict resolution for themselves and a lot of behavior modification for each other because putting kids in a group [where they] don't necessarily want to work together doesn't always work. And I told them, 'You're stuck,' and there was no going back. So they had to figure out—okay, he writes better, and she reads better. So we'll have her read the material for us, so we'll all listen, and we're all going to take notes. This person's going to try and write it, and [he'll] bring it back, and we'll work on it. So everybody found what they were good at, and they were able to take pride in what they did. They were all willing to work together after awhile.

Similarly, Mary observed a dramatic turn-around in some of her students' attitudes and social behaviors. She related her story about the DV literature project on thematic commercials in her classes:

I have one particular class. It's a very large class. It has about thirty-six students in it. And at the beginning of the year, they had quite a few issues with working in groups. They did not like it. It's hard when you have thirty-six to put them in groups of four, so they really didn't care for it. But when we worked on thematic commercials and they had to work in groups to do their storyboards in order to write the dialogue to present a message from a novel we read, I really found that some of the students became close knit. They were supporting each other. They were encouraging each other as opposed to the beginning when they weren't so nice to one another. And that was because of the digital technology.

Dewey (1933) says that the normal source of social order is in such shared cooperative activity. The CVCV classrooms are spaces where students are engaged in joint activity around production. In this centered environment students' energies are turned to a productive, collective goal that creates the need and respect for interdependence and social support.

Some of the most dramatic stories of students' emerging social awareness and behavioral response in working with the DV came out of Frank's class-room. Frank teaches social studies in an elementary school where the student population represents a multitude of cultures, and where as many as forty different languages are spoken in any given school year. In this international setting, the school aims for students to learn to respect each other's customs and differences. At the same time, this is also a setting where students can potentially become isolated by their differences.

Frank developed a digital video project that involved students throughout the school from sixth through eighth grades. With this project Frank reported some dramatic results:

I think [the digital video] builds bridges. The kids that worked on the project from my homeroom—it's considered an honors class so . . . they travel as a class and they really don't have a lot of contact with the other classes. . . . In the film there are two students from another homeroom that are the main actors, the main characters in the film. So it forced my students to have to interact with those students, so it built those bridges that normally wouldn't be there.

Beyond that collective connection, Frank also told the personal story of Rowanda, the student who played the female lead in the video. During the course of the school year, Rowanda had been repeatedly suspended for a variety of offenses, usually stemming from her inability to control her angry impulses. Frank explains:

> We call it the suspension merry-go-round. Well, once Rowanda applied for the role, was given the role . . . I sat down with her and [the production team of students] and we said, "You have to get off this suspension merry-go-round." And since that time she hasn't been suspended. She's been able to control her temper. She's been able to manage her anger to a large degree, a great deal more than she was prior to that.

Working in the kind of community atmosphere that requires commitment to the other community members seems to have given Rowanda the impetus she needed to work through her own self-control. Where traditional mediational literacy tools failed to inspire Rowanda, the excitement of filming the digital video, combined with the importance of her role in the video, moved Rowanda toward self-regulating behavior for the remainder of the school year.

Another form of social awareness and responsibility occurred with the academically successful students. The video project presented a reason for Rowanda to work closely with Ming, an honor student. Because of the school structure, Rowanda and Ming might never have met. "In fact," Frank says, "Ming would probably avoid Rowanda, being that Ming is focused and dedicated to her studies and Rowanda has other things going on that would ultimately lead to her suspension." Not only did Rowanda benefit from the new integrated relationship, but Frank also saw positive growth in Ming. "She learned to be more patient. She learned to be more specific in what she asks [others] to do. Initially, she would have an idea [for the video project] and she would say, 'This is what I want.' And she would assume [the others] knew." Eventually, through commitment to this joint activity, Ming learned to explain her ideas and discuss them with the other students working on the video project.

This story adds the dimension of dialogic discourse (Bakhtin, 1981) to the growing number of critical mediators embedded within the classroom use of digital video. Within the dialogic experience of conversing across their many differences, students have many opportunities for intellectual and social growth.

DV Bridges to Active, Purposeful Reading and Writing

During our school visits we often asked students what they were doing as they worked on DV projects, in order to understand what meaning their activity had for them. In one high school, two boys were working on a video about the positive aspects of their school because they felt others thought their school was for "losers." As they explained the way they collaborated on their project, the process they detailed sounded very familiar. We said it sounded as though they were talking about writing. Both lit up and said, "Yes, exactly." We asked how, and they jointly constructed this argument:

Rick: Definitely opens up the creative part of your mind and gets you involved in art. All art is imaginative and a real strong image, or idea that you want to get out, an opinion or a belief. It is definitely thinking. It is all thinking.

Don: You have so much material and . . . you are definitely think-ing, about where to put fade ins, fade outs. It all comes together and you feel pretty good cause it all comes together and it looks pretty good. . . .

Rick: I see a lot of similarities. As a musician and a creative writer, when you write something down, you have an idea, and after you re-read it, you add more in, and that's what we do [with DV].

Don: Cause like when you sit down and write a story, you have certain ideas of what you want to write about. But then you'll hear a word or a phrase, and you're, like, I really like that phrase and you put it in a poem. . . . I see a lot of similarities to doing this and writing a song or something, because every-thing eventually has to come together, but it doesn't have to be at a certain point. You can always figure it out and it will always come together because it's all about creativity.

The student-initiated notion that video production draws on composing strat-egies similar to those they use in writing is an important one. Rick identifies the power in writing and DV production of a strong image and idea to focus reflection/revision; Don points out the process of selection needed to "figure it out" and bring coherence—"everything eventually has to come together." He adds the notion of selective attention in both creative processes, bringing in a phrase you hear to a poem or a new transition you learn to the DV; in his view, new texts emerge from this new way of seeing and attending.

This explicit student connection between video production and writing occurred in less elaborated forms in other interviews. Teachers suggested that video production engages students in thinking and creating meaning, which serves also as a bridge to later meaning-making through written language alone. Hal, an eighth-grade teacher, saw the potential of DV production to mediate language use: "I think it inspires students, motivates students to learn to use language to learn new things." Mary, a high school English teacher doing thematic commercials on a novel, explained how visuals serve as a bridge to writing: "They had to work in groups to do their storyboards in order to write the dialogue . . . in order to present a message from a novel we read." The images on the storyboard aided the writing of the dialogue, as a visual and dramatic means of generating language and ideas from their own envisioned experiences. Issues of planning, moving back and forth between visuals and text to represent them, selecting shots/music/text to communicate a focus/theme—all are essential components of writing, which students are immersed in during DV production. Further, though, all teachers consciously asked students to write as an ongoing part of video production, including text and narrations for storyboards, interview questions, skits, process journals, and after-film reflections and evaluations.

DV production seemed, also, to develop a new student stance toward reading. For example, Wanda explained how students began to envision what they read in anticipation of making a video:

> Well, when I worked with my English 11 students, they became much more involved in the literature, which had always been a problem for me in the past especially with this school because they're very reluctant to read. But once I introduced the video and the digital technology, they needed to have something to video tape, something to write about—so they would read. So that was a very good way *into* literature for me because not only were they reading, they were rereading, trying to find things that they could put into the video.

Adding the high-interest visualization tool, Wanda suggests, added a new purpose for reading which prompted, in fact, two important reading strategies—rereading and visualizing the text. DV production served as a bridge to these new reading strategies—by engaging students' minds in their own visual production of meaning rather than simply consuming it.

Tammy, a high school English teacher, elaborated this notion of DV mediating reading engagement and meaning-making, with an emphasis on providing students the means of saying what they were unwilling or unable to say in words:

> There were a lot of moments where I saw evidence of learning. In *The Watsons Go to Birmingham*, it dealt a lot with poverty and when

they traveled they saw African people who had more than they had in Birmingham, and the students around here tried to depict and get some pictures that would show this dichotomy. The one group wanted to show, like, right on one street, one block, one area close by that you could see both of those things—poverty and, then, quite a bit different, well off, doing better or whatever. And I thought—that's an example I would use because without that equipment I don't know how well they would have been able to tell us about it, to tell us what they wanted—how they feel about that.

Considering the wealth-poverty theme in the novel and their opportunity to represent it using DV led students to link their reading of the book to images of disparities in their own community. Their teacher, Tammy, suggests that students may have been unable to express their thoughts and feelings about this topic in relation to their own community without DV as a tool. Such learning opportunities can also spur ongoing inquiries about big issues that emerge when bringing literature and life together, as Tammy explains:

One particular student in that group was really passionate about that and she still continues trying to understand poverty. As we read novels, we read different poems that sort of related, and thinking about her group discussing Nikki Giovanni's poem, about her childhood, and all the time people thought this one child had a horrible existence when she was very happy. She had her family. She had love. So I think the student in this group was trying to show that, in some shape, coping about poverty and wealth. It's not just what you *see*, it's what's *behind* all that. That was a learning moment, and I think they're still trying to work those things through. But I think without the equipment, she would've been able to tell us about it, but it really helped us to see what she was saying, where her concerns are.

This student visualized a novel's theme in her own neighborhood, a "learning moment" of envisioning the connection between life and literature, which prompted a deeper concern, a big question that she took to her further reading and her group discussion. This kind of dialogic problem-posing is the source and guiding motivation of reflective and critical thinking (Dewey, 1933; Freire, 1970)—central goals of literacy learning. Raising such big questions is the real stuff of literature which, Greene (1995) argues, education must teach us to pursue "by sensitive inquiry, by dialogue, by connectedness" (p. 102). In this instance, DV production and the literature spurred discussions in the group, another powerful mediator of student thinking (Miller, 2003).

A few days after September 11, 2001, a group of distraught students at McKinley High School came to their City Voices, City Visions teachers with a question—what can we do? At first they planned to raise money, but in the ensuing discussion realized that, while a noble venture, "It wasn't going to allow them to express themselves, something that they needed emotionally," Keith remembers. Out of this talk, the student-produced video *Wings of Hope* was born. Students wanted to make a video expressing how deeply grateful they felt to the workers at Ground Zero in New York City. Amidst such terrible loss, they felt respect and pride. Set to haunting music from "The Wonder Years," the film opens with what they felt to be the most compelling images of rescue and caring—created as a collage on the outside of the computer box. Speeded up images of students between classes in the school hallway suddenly stop to focus on one student coming up the stairs, walking into frame, looking into the camera, saying, "Thank you for being an American hero." In their six-minute video made for those workers, that is their refrain.

There are close-ups of a firefighter carrying a woman through the silver smoke, of a weary firefighter getting oxygen from a paramedic, of a police officer guiding a group away from the fray. Then the fast-paced hallways with a pair of students stopping to look at these workers (it seems) and saying, "Thank you for being an American hero." Some students say more—with an earnestness and emotion that is unmistakable. (See the video at http://www.gse.buffalo.edu/org/cityvoices/). At the end of the video, each student speaks, the array of faces of many colors and voices of many accents coming together around this common feeling of sorrow and of pride. The very last scene was shot from a very tall ladder and includes the whole school standing in the auditorium joining in a vibrant chorus, "Thank You!"

It is a remarkable performance, initiated and produced by students, with the support of their teacher, Keith and also Shiarra. Aesthetically, it was beautiful and moving (there are few dry eyes when the film finishes). Literarily, it was tightly focused, but never boring; symbolic, but with direct impact. Cinematically, it just worked—the writing, the music, the movement, the structure, the pace, the shots, the transitions—everything worked together to communicate a strong theme that was not sentimental, just heartfelt. In the video, these students used the powers of DV as a source of "healing," as one student interviewed by the local television station put it, and as a means of creating roles for themselves as part of the post 9/11 civic conversation. And—this seems very clear—they were exceeding learning standards in social studies and English by quite a bit. The postscript which follows seems anticlimactic in light of what students had achieved in the film itself: all of Keith's students successfully passed the social studies graduation test in a school district where that is not a common occurrence.

CONCLUSION

Grounded in theory, City Voices, City Visions began with considerable confidence that DV integration into curriculum as a learning tool would activate and engage students. Still, we were amazed by the richness of that learning. At first, the notion of DV as a mediational tool was a compelling explanation of the usefulness of the technology in classrooms. As we have observed and talked to teachers and students, though, we have come to reenvision DV as more—as a learning and literacy supertool that combines the power of visual, written, and musical mediation for meaning-making and understanding. Teachers able to move beyond traditional notions of literacy and learning took up this supertool and put it to work with their students. We have strong evidence that teacher-supported DV production provided new opportunities for learning and success for diverse students. Not only did they meet learning standards in the context of meaningful DV activity, but they learned social and literacy strategies useful for a lifetime.

These explanations of the influence of DV on learning do not, however, capture the depth of the engagement, the joy of the learning, the heartfelt expression in some of the DV activity and production. Although we began the project with a notion of integrating DV *technology*, we now understand that DV is also an *art* that demands and provides an integration of meaning that profoundly engages intellect, emotion, and identity. DV as art is particularly evident in the process and product of the *Wings of Hope* video. But it is also evident in many students' entrancement with DV—those who spent their homerooms, lunches, after school time, and sometimes Saturdays working on school projects that opened to their worlds and community.

The special education student sitting at the computer with a self-selected poem on one hand, his storyboard on the other, and the computer where he imported visuals in the middle, turned to explain the poem: "It is about this young black man who is poor, but on the inside he has nice values, good character." The images he selected included one of a young black man's bound hands and feet. This young black student was creating, it seemed clear, something personal in his eloquent and moving interpretation of the poem. As urban students have such opportunities to reconstruct *who* they are in school through activities that reconstrue *what* counts as learning, we believe remarkable things can happen. DV production provides an artful supertool to help students move out of passivity, alienation, and powerlessness.

In the third year of the project we are attending to the many other bridges CVCV is building. In addition to students from one class becoming resources in other classes and the school, CVCV students graduate from middle school and become DV resources in high school buildings. In the first year of CVCV, we carried a poetry video made in one class to another school, where students first discussed the poem, then, with more interest and insight, discussed the student video interpretation of the poem. Since the fall of 2002, selected student-made videos have been published on the CVCV website (http://www.gse.buffalo.edu/org/cityvoices/) with streaming video, enabling urban student voices and visions to be seen, heard, and discussed across town and all over the world. In addition, we are developing curriculum and urban images archives for use in professional development for urban teachers and in teacher education. Recent presentations of CVCV videos to pre-service and in-service teachers promoted the notions of active learning and the possibilities for urban students and education rather than what these teachers said they had always seen and heard—negative urban images in the media (e.g., on COPS, on the evening news, and in newspaper) of intractable urban problems and failing schools.

Integrating DV production into the curriculum is a powerful strategy for active student engagement in literacy and learning. We hope, along with Jeannie Oakes, that these new "images and ideas . . . may embolden people in other places to act on their best dreams for American schooling" (see Oakes, p. 109). Such dreams belong not just in the suburbs, where most students succeed, but where students most need learning tools to link themselves to their schooling—in city voices and city visions.

NOTES

1. A team of University at Buffalo faculty created and supported the CVCV project, including Hank Bromley, Mary Finn, Patrick Finn, Lauri Johnson, Suzanne Miller, and Bob Stevenson. We are also grateful to Paulette Freyer, Don Jacobs, Dave Lanz, and Vicki Zimmer for their substantial support that led to the UB-BPS partnership.

2. Suzanne Miller is the CVCV Project Coordinator and Suzanne Borowicz is the CVCV Research Assistant who conducted the teacher interviews.

3. Teachers were promised anonymity and interview segments quoted use pseudonyms. All visual tapes and audiotapes were transcribed and coded. Videotapes were watched repeatedly and notes were recorded and coded for visual distinctions. Comparisons of teachers' perceptions and processes were made and taxonomies were created (Spradley, 1980) for the purpose of discovering domains. The domains were coded and then examined using the constant comparative method (Glaser and Strauss, 1999).

REFERENCES

Anyon, J. (1997). *Ghetto schooling: The political economy of urban educational reform*. New York: Teachers College Press.

Bakhtin, M. M. (1981). *The dialogic imagination: Four essays*. Austin: University of Texas Press.

Clark, C. M., & Peterson, P. L. (1986). Teachers' thought processes. In M. Wittrock (Ed.), *Handbook of research on teaching* (3rd ed., pp. 266–298). New York: Macmillan.

Dewey, J. (1933). *How we think: A restatement of the relation of reflective thinking to educative process*. Boston: D. C. Heath.

Eisner, W. E. (1998). *The kind of schools we need: Personal essays*. Portsmouth, NH: Heinemann.

Finn, P. (1999). *Literacy with an attitude: Educating working-class children in their own self-interest*. Albany: State University of New York Press.

Freire, P. (1970). *Pedagogy of the oppressed*. New York: New Seabury Press.

Glaser, B. G., & Strauss, A. L. (1999). *The discovery of grounded theory: Strategies for qualitative research.* Hawthorne: Gruyter.

Greene, M. (1995). *Releasing the imagination: Essays on education, the arts, and social change.* San Francisco: Jossey-Bass.

Gutierrez, K. D., & Stone, L. (2000). Synchronic and diachronic dimensions of social practice. In C. D. Lee & P. Smagorinsky (Eds.), *Vygotskian perspectives on literacy research* (pp. 150–164). Cambridge, MA: Cambridge University Press.

Heath, S. B. (1983). *Ways with words: Language, life, and work in communities and classrooms.* Cambridge, UK: Cambridge University Press.

Hobbs, R. (1997). Literacy for the information age. In J. Flood, S. B. Heath, and D. Lapp (Eds.), *Handbook of research on teaching literature through the communicative and visual arts* (pp. 7–14). New York: Simon and Schuster Macmillan.

Lave, J. W., & Wenger, E. (1991). *Situated learning: Legitimate peripheral participation.* New York: Cambridge University Press.

Leontiev, A. N. (1981). *Problems of the development of mind.* Moscow: Progress Publishers.

Miller, S. M. (2003). How literature discussion shapes thinking: Teaching/learning habits of the heart and mind. In A. Kozulin, V. Ageyev, S. Miller, & B. Gindis (Eds.), *Vygotsky's educational theory in cultural context* (pp. 289–316). Cambridge, UK: Cambridge University Press.

Rohde, G. L., Shapiro, R. J. et al. (October, 2000). *Falling through the net: Toward digital inclusion* [On-line]. A report on Americans' access to technology tools by the U.S. Department of Commerce, Economics, and Statistics Administration, & National Telecommunications and Information Administration. Available: http://www.ntia.doc.gov/ntiahome/fttn00/contents00.html

Spradley, J. P. (1980). *Participant observation.* Fort Worth: Harcourt College Publishers.

Vygotsky, L. S. (1978). *Mind in society: The development of higher psychological processes* (M. Cole, V. John-Steiner, S. Scribner, & E. Souberman, Eds.). Cambridge, MA: Harvard University Press.

Wells, G. (2000). Dialogic inquiry in education: Building on the legacy of Vygotsky. In C. D. Lee & P. Smagorinsky (Eds.), *Vygotskian perspectives on literacy research: Constructing meaning through collaborative inquiry* (pp. 51–85). Cambridge, UK: Cambridge University Press.

Wertsch, J. V. (1991). *Voices of the mind: A sociocultural approach to mediated action.* Cambridge, MA: Harvard University Press.

Wigginton, E. (1991). Culture begins at home. *Educational Leadership, 49*(4), 60–64.

Reforming Teacher Education to Improve Urban Education

9 Teaching to Change the World

Jeannie Oakes

Jeannie Oakes is Presidential Professor in Educational Equity and Director of UCLA's Institute for Democracy, Education, and Access (IDEA) and the University of California's All Campus Consortium on Research and Diversity (ACCORD). Oakes was the founding Director of UCLA's Center X, which is based on a commitment to social justice, to the interaction of theory and practice, and to partnerships with urban schools.[1] Center X integrates pre-service teacher education, a program for emergency credentials, and a doctoral program in urban education. In this chapter, Oakes describes how the teacher education program at UCLA's Center X, which prepares teachers to promote social justice and provide high-level academic instruction in low-income urban schools, is grounded in a conception of learning as "changed participation over time" and becoming a member of "a community of practice."

I AM NOT A TEACHER EDUCATOR BY TRAINING, although I was a teacher before I became an education researcher. I became a researcher because I was concerned about issues of educational equity. My early work was to document patterns of inequality and the ways that conventional school practices work against the education and life chances of low-income children of color. When I had an opportunity at UCLA to take leadership of the teacher education program, I thought it would be an opportunity to test some ideas about how good teaching and the pursuit of educational equity could actually be parts of the same project. But before I continue with how these parts fit together at UCLA's teacher education program, I want to mention two caveats. First, although we are extraordinarily proud of what we have been able to accomplish, we don't believe we have created a model for others to follow. At best, we hope we have created some images and ideas that may embolden others to act on their best dreams for American schooling. Second, while I may get carried away and speak as if we have a tight theory that points unambiguously to a program design (maybe on the order of a coherent "strategic plan"), most of what I am going to talk to you about is our challenging, difficult, and rewarding struggle. I will do this in three ways: I will tell you about what we are attempting to do; I will share some of the voices of our students and

Center X graduates Ciceley Bingenar (right) and Charlene Asis (left) in a Los Angeles classroom

graduates; and I will show some images of the children and teachers about whom I am talking. We should always remind ourselves that at the heart of our talk and theory are real teachers and learners.

We begin with the voice of Mary Ann Pacheco who was in the first cohort of teachers entering the redesigned teacher education program. Mary Ann is a Chicana who taught a bilingual class comprised largely of Latino immigrants. This is her reflection on her experience as a first-year teacher of first and second graders; her voice begins to capture some of the essence of what we are trying to do at UCLA:

> The class meeting was the first step in a long process that allowed the students to voice their concerns. . . . Before we began I disclosed my personal reasons for having chosen such an activity. . . . I shared that I wanted them to understand that we have the power to change things. It was a powerful experience to stand in front of a classroom of young children and tell them that I wanted to change the world.

It is important to know that in California we are experiencing a full-blown teacher crisis: not only will we need an extra 300,000 teachers over the next three or four years due to the rapidly growing population and the graying of the teacher workforce, but efforts to reduce class size have exacerbated the shortage of teachers. As of last year, over 10 percent of teachers statewide and up to 50 percent of teachers in many urban centers are on an emergency permit. Forty-six percent of the math teachers are unqualified, having neither a major nor a minor in secondary mathematics. Sixty percent of the teachers are over forty years old, 32 percent are over fifty. Moreover, new teachers aren't staying in the profession: there are rates of 30 to 50 percent attrition each year, with 50 percent of all teachers in the state leaving within the first five years. In many urban centers 50 percent of the new teachers leave within three years. As in many other states, California has a policy recipe consisting of incentives to attract people to the profession, expanding teacher education programs, increasing the quality of teaching by means of standards and testing, developing district-based programs for emergency teachers, support for first-year teachers, and increased professional development, peer assistance, and review, as well as the ability to release teachers who shouldn't be in the classroom.

These policies may help and, to the extent that we address working conditions and compensation, may encourage people to stay in teaching. Our concern at UCLA is that conventionally good teachers and the impact of these kinds of policies on teaching will not be enough. The stakes and standards are far higher and riskier than ever before in terms of life chances for students. California has seen radical changes in the composition of the student population. We now have much greater ethnic, cultural, and linguistic diversity in our students, but most of the mostly white teachers are not well prepared—and do not have the appropriate attitude—to foster a rich learning environment in this context. There also have been staggering increases in child poverty, which we all know is associated with various hazardous conditions, including violence, lack of health services, and limited pre- and after-school care. California public school students in the sixth grade face a school system in which more than half of them will be gone before they graduate from high school; for every five hundred entering ninth graders, only twelve will qualify for four-year colleges and universities when they graduate. So the challenge is not simply to "produce" qualified teachers, but to expand the understanding of "qualified" to include teacher characteristics such as a knowledge of diverse communities and languages along with a passion and commitment for teaching and remaining in schools in those communities.

At UCLA we are concerned that the policies of the state and traditional methods of teacher education do not encourage people to choose to teach low-income children of color in poor urban neighborhoods, to respect the diversity and the resources and assets that diverse communities bring, to commit for the long haul, and to work for social change or see that as their primary mission. We are worried that the policy environment is not sufficient to create social justice teaching. The teachers who go through our program see themselves as social justice educators, and while there are disagreements among all of us about what social justice really means and how one is a social justice educator, we all agree on the following:

- That social justice teaching considers the values and the politics that pervade education as well as having a healthy respect for technical matters of teaching and learning.

- That social justice teaching always asks critical questions about how conventional school practices came to be and who benefits from them.

- That social justice teaching pays attention to inequalities and, as it attends to them, seeks to alter them.

- That social justice teaching treats the diversity that we find in cities like Los Angeles not as a problem to be overcome, not as a difficulty to be accommodated, but as an asset to be valued.

The premise of our teacher education program is that a hopeful democratic future depends on all young people experiencing and succeeding in socially just and academically rigorous education. It is not always easy—it's never easy—to figure out what that means for us as teacher educators and for them as teachers, but we try to base everything we do on achieving this goal. Our aim is for our teachers to see themselves as public intellectuals, social justice advocates, and change agents, as part of a difficult and worthwhile struggle. This work is something more than doing good. Some people want to be missionaries, but that is not enough. The choice to do this work entails choosing a kind of life for yourself because it is the kind of life you want to lead, not simply because you want to do good for others.

Lisa, a science teacher, wrote the following reflection:

Schools can be socializing agencies or they can be sites of social struggle and transformation. As a teacher I have a certain responsibility to do all I can to reform the practices of education to address the needs of all children, black, white, female or male. If I am truly to be an agent of change, I must be self-critical, and question whether I am empowering my students or trying to force them into a mold that will only serve to confine and oppress. Am I feeding them information I think they should know or am I challenging them to think critically about life and their positions in society? Do I value the diversity and difference in my students or do I view it as an impediment to learning?

This kind of thinking led her both to deal specifically with issues of gender equity in science and also to think about opening up advanced science for kids who typically aren't thought of as being ready or eligible for such classes.

Mary Ann again:

Educators must understand that they are agents for social change—that what they say, think, and do in the classroom is both political and politically informed. . . . I intend to break the cycle of an education system that treats my current and future students as children who need to be controlled and 'schooled.'

Another of our goals is to educate teachers who are guided by research and theory, who see themselves as researchers and theoreticians as well as practitioners, who are able to use their classroom experiences as a vehicle for their own learning. We want our students to see teaching as a process of learning about children's cognition, as well as shaping the social context of the classroom and building the content of the curriculum. We want them to embody an interdependent mix of social justice values and rigorous academic content and to create a caring and democratic learning environment. One of the struggles we've had—especially as our program becomes more diverse—is that a caring democratic learning community can appear in different guises, depending on who the teacher is, who the students are, and what kinds of relationships they develop. There is no clear recipe. What a progressive white teacher may create as a caring classroom may be quite different than a caring classroom that a very traditional African American teacher might create. "Social justice" is not a matter of "anything goes," and critique is constantly needed; on the other hand, there is no litmus test for social justice practice and pedagogy. As long as there is a feeling of care and a willingness to examine one's own practice, the bumpy road to social justice teaching extends onward.

Cecily is a young African American woman who is in her fifth year of teaching in the Englewood school where she did her student teaching. In the fifties, the neighborhood was all white, but Englewood has been predominantly African American for a number of years. Over time, there has been a process of cultural transformation in order to build a school system that is healthy, vigorous, and positive for African American kids. Most of the school administration and city officials now are African American, but the student body is becoming predominantly Latino. This means that the school district faces the challenge of transforming itself again, as educators must deal with English language learners. There also are volatile tensions between the black and brown communities over what little opportunities there are for political influence and control in government and the school district.

Cecily begins her class each year with a unit on American history and democracy. Many people are surprised that she begins the year with a history unit for kindergarten students, but she says the following:

America is for everybody and our mission is to make it clear to our students that they and their families are no exception. So this year the kinders used the presidential campaign as the basis for a math project to accompany a unit on graphing. The kinders conducted a poll of first-, second-, and third-grade students to study and compare voter trends across grade levels. It was an exciting event and it continues to be in the forefront of their class discussion due to the controversy over the presidency. It is still surprising and pretty gratifying for us seeing five-year-olds taking such an independent interest in national politics.

As her students learn about the American political system and what democracy means, she is helping her Latino students, many of whose families are illegal immigrants, understand that they and their families are Americans too.

Jessica, also a fifth-year teacher, teaches high school English in a racially mixed school where most of the Latino students are in the lower-track classes. When she taught classes for ninth graders, she decided to include a unit on magical realism:

> In the unit on magical realism I wanted the students to experience the pure enjoyment of the story. I also want them to understand what magical realism is: imaginary becomes real and why it originated in Latin America. According to Gabriel Garcia Marquez, events in Latin America have become so extraordinary that realism is not adequate to describe people and events. The culminating project for the unit was a research project on an author or event or an historical figure. They needed to find a connection between their topic and the events or circumstance in Latin America that led to the development of magical realism. The strength of this unit is the material. The students really liked the stories because they were unusual and challenging. In addition my Latino students in particular enjoyed the opportunity to explore aspects of their character. They wanted to know more about the slaughter of Mayans and Aztecs—both were popular topics for the research project. I also think that this approach is powerful because it combines students' home culture and high status knowledge in an English curriculum. In an urban school we need to acknowledge our students' home communities but not at the expense of access to a rigorous academic curriculum.

Like Mary Ann and Cecily, Jessica provides a mix of a social justice values and rigorous academic curriculum.

The teacher education program at UCLA is nested in a unit called Center X. The name, Center X, was created as a temporary placeholder, since no one could agree on what the name should be. Seven years later, we are still Center X, officially defined as "the intersection of research and practice for urban school professionals." Center X integrates three kinds of activities: pre-service teacher education, a program for emergency credentials, and work with UCLA's doctoral program in urban education. Our pre-service teacher education program is a two-year master's program with an emphasis on bilingual, cross-cultural teaching. The first year is fairly traditional, including a combination of course work, fieldwork, and other activities. At the end of the first year, students sign a contract in which they agree to teach in Los Angeles city schools during what we call a year of residency. These novice teachers participate alongside experienced teachers who are engaged in their own professional development, which is also focused on urban schools and social justice. Teacher leaders from the professional development programs teach the subject matter and methods classes for new teachers. The program is very much guided by theories of "communities of practice" in which novices work and learn along with and from more experienced members of the community. I will say more about this shortly.

The second element is a program for emergency credentials, called "Teach LA," which tries to create a very rigorous social justice program for people who are on emergency credentials. The third component involves cooperation with UCLA's Ph.D. program in urban education, involving doctoral students who are studying and have acquired expertise on school policy, school leadership, curriculum theory, and bilingual education. Many of the doctoral students have been teachers, and as they gain experience in becoming teacher educators, they also support the novice teachers in teacher education. The doctoral students' research contributes to the field of teacher education generally as it more immediately informs various elements of Center X's program design.

Recognizing that most social justice programs are designed to help white teachers learn about teaching students from diverse backgrounds, one graduate student studied five African American teachers for two years after they entered our program in order to understand their experiences. We learned a great deal from that study and have changed our program as a result. Our goal is to integrate all these activities so that it is impossible to tell, at first glance, who is research faculty, who is clinical faculty, who is a Ph.D. student, or who is a master's student. That is not to say we have figured out how to do it smoothly, with no bumps, but that is our intention.

The theory of teacher learning pervading all these activities derives from sociocultural theory, particularly that which conceives learning as changed participation over time, as the teacher becomes a member of a community of practice. Under this model, the focus is on apprenticeship, on moving from peripheral to core participation as a member of the community of practice of social justice teaching in urban Los Angeles. As a result, relationships become extraordinarily important. We think of social justice teaching as a process of becoming a member of an oppositional community of practice that is in tension with state policy and many of the regularities in urban public schools in which we work. This forces all of us to have multiple identities, to be border crossers, to be both colleagues and critics within the system. What that requires, we believe, is a practice grounded in critical inquiry. Consequently, everything we do is held up to questions of whose interests are being served and what other possibilities might exist.

Finally, our theory of teacher learning is grounded in action. Our students teach in urban Los Angeles schools that are partners with UCLA. These are not ideal or exemplary schools; they have many teachers with emergency credentials. These schools have agreed to hire our second-year students as full-time, full-pay teachers, at least two at a time (so no one is alone in a school as a novice teacher). While we offer traditional university courses in which faculty stand up in front, our students also meet in cohorts of between fifteen and twenty-five students. These groups meet one another on their first day of their program and stay together for the entire two years, meeting at least once a week for three hours. Over the course of the program they become a community of support, and most of the students who are four and five years out are still very close to the members of their cohort.

Our students also spend a great deal of time in the school communities outside of school hours: for example, some are working with Latino immigrant mothers to help them understand what they should look for and what they should know about schools, including how to approach the school with their concerns about their children's school experiences. In response to an observation by Gloria Ladson-Billings that poor minority kids look much smarter outside of school than they do in schools, we design opportunities for student teachers to see their students and their families outside of school, undertake community studies that map resources in the community, and do a case study on a child from a background or culture that is not the teacher's own. Especially interesting and informative for some white faculty and students have been reports from minority student teachers who engage in a cultural study of students who come from affluent white families.

Overall, the community studies challenge preconceptions. For example, Jackie, a seventh-grade social studies teacher reported:

> I had heard horror stories about inner cities where the adults were the real culprits. Many days after school my teaching partner and I would walk over to the local community where most of my students live and made home calls to students we were concerned about. This, in itself, opened up a whole new perspective. It was one thing having a David Ferguson in my class, but meeting his parents, seeing the driveway where he hung out, and sitting on his living room couch while his mother admits that she also has trouble reading, forces you to change your priorities.

This is not somebody who is saying, " Oh, my, this poor family has no resources." This is someone who respectfully engaged with the mother about her own life and her own circumstances.

By the end of their first year, our students have satisfied the state's certification requirements as well as our requirements for what we call CLAD or BCLAD (cross-cultural language and academic development or bilingual cross-cultural language and academic development). Even though bilingual education is outlawed in California, we strongly believe that we need bilingual teachers—that teachers need to be able to speak the languages of their children whenever possible. Without this language facility, teachers' community of practice risks insularity—never opening to the outside of the school to allow community and family expertise to inform developing teacher identities.

This is what Mary Ann said, in the words of our theory, about moving from the periphery toward the core of her professional practice:

> I began the year afraid and gradually developed a more solid sense of who I was, what my profession meant to me, what I wanted for my students, whose lives I would touch forever. Perhaps my views and practices will change in the future, perhaps they will not. What's important is that I developed a new identity through teaching and this will sustain me through many more years. I expect that from a career in which I deal with real and diverse lives every day.

In the second year of the program, when students are working as full-time, fully paid teachers, we continue to support them with on-site mentoring and they continue to meet with their cohorts and attend seminars. Their master's work is conceived of as professional development, and their central task is to develop a portfolio. This entails revisiting all their theory-based papers and assignments they did as first year students and analyzing them in light of their subsequent practice. They analyze artifacts from their own teaching in terms of the theory they are now revisiting. At the end of the year, students defend their portfolios to a panel that includes research faculty, clinical faculty, a member of their cohort, and someone from their school. In effect, our master's degrees are granted in part based on the authority of the practitioners with whom students work. Over 95 percent of the teachers who enter our program finish with a master's degree and a successful first year of teaching.

The following reflection is a representative first-year story; it gives a sense of how important it is to have connections to theory and social justice values in the first year of teaching:

> Maintaining consistency between theory and practice is the trick to good teaching. It's often difficult to consider Vygotsky's theory of the zone of proximal development when you're planning a geography lesson, your principal's coming to observe you on Thursday, and the power goes out for two hours on Friday. It's easy to get caught up in the hectic pace of most teachers without stopping to consider the real goals that motivate us. Through personal reflection, reaction from my students, and comments from observers, I seem to keep my classroom practices grounded in both philosophy and the realities of teaching.

Another teacher sounds a cautionary note:

> Challenges come from other teachers who view my methods as
> inexperienced, naïve and unconventional. . . . Nothing excites me more
> than learning about teaching. However, at times I fear my aspirations
> are those of an idealistic student whose enthusiasm will be weathered
> by the frustration and stagnation that experience brings. I question
> whether or not I will fall into the rut of habit and mediocrity, and
> forgetting the real reason I turned to teaching in the first place.

Perhaps because they sense this risk of flagging enthusiasm and they recognize it in their more experienced colleagues, our students sought ways to stay
connected with UCLA and each other. In response, we developed the Early
Career Network, and now many of our graduates are actively involved in inquiry sessions. They gather a couple of times a month and explore their struggles
to maintain an oppositional community in a conventional urban school:

> I needed people with whom to discuss my struggle, and I found
> them. . . . Without these support options, I may have reanalyzed my
> teaching philosophy and gone back to a more traditional teaching
> style. . . . I am able to regain perspective from these interactions. They
> give me a place to express frustration and discouragement, but I am
> not left there. I have the opportunity to be a resource to others as
> well. I have forums in which to access the latest theory and pedagogy
> and reflect upon my teaching practice with other professionals.

We also have created an interactive online journal for our teachers and
their students, called *Teaching to Change LA*. For the first issue, which was
organized around the theme of democracy, Cecily and her kinders (who were
doing their democracy unit) posted some of their work on the journal Web
site. The journal also includes maps that show where in the city the student
work comes from, lesson plans, poetry, artwork, as well as discussions by teachers and parents about their struggles. The next issue focuses on the digital
divide. We realized that while we have video and film clips on the Web site,
some of the people in some of our schools don't have the technology to see
them. Consequently, we have instituted surveys of the digital divide in the city
and teachers all over the city are now engaging their students in questions
about the issue.

In the summers we work directly with kids and teachers to develop new
curricula. One group used a global positioning system to map resources in Los
Angeles and created a database of resources to empower their local communities. In summer 2000, our students studied various forms of access at and
around the Democratic National Convention. We also foster connections with
educational activists, engaging in such events as a peace march in a community

where there had been black/brown gang violence and a boycott of the SAT 9 test.

What have we learned about our students? We have learned that students value theory. They may complain about our emphasis on theory in the first year, but by the end of the second year they realize that theory can be quite practical as a powerful learning tool for themselves and their students. Our students also continue to seek the power of dialogue in professional communities. Finally, we have learned that while they may abandon bad schools, they do not abandon their students:

> It's been a difficult but transformative year. When I started teaching I was angry at the program for not giving me discrete examples and solutions that work in the classroom. Implementing a socially just agenda was difficult when I had discipline cases, district and school guidelines, deadlines, bureaucratic paperwork on top of tackling issues of literacy, cooperative learning, limited English proficiency, and lesson planning. . . . After reflecting on my practice I realize that all the theory I received has given me a self-conscious knowledge that I value and always use. Issues of cultural capital, biculturalism, transformative pedagogy, and the "unschooling" of the mind remain vital concepts needed to build a democratic community of critical learners. Even if the program had handed me lessons, I would chose which ones to adopt and how to alter them based on my philosophy—that is where theory plays the most important role.

As of last year 86 percent of our students are still teaching; 72 percent are in urban schools. Only 7 percent have left teaching altogether, the rest remain in education in some way. We are in the process now of collecting data on graduates and have had approximately a 95 percent response rate. We are hopeful that these numbers will rise and that this program and this approach will become more successful in keeping people in teaching.

What have we learned about teacher education? First, if you build it they will come. People thought we were crazy when we changed the UCLA program from being a one-year master's program for affluent white students who wanted to teach at affluent schools. We now admit twice our previous number of students each year, and we have about two applicants for every slot. We have learned that diversity makes for powerful learning, as students learn from each other, and we are working to increase the diversity of the cohorts. Again, Mary Ann:

> My teaching has taught me that it is essential to be critical about my practical approaches, my relationship with my students, the role of power in my classroom, and the theoretical perspectives informing my practice. These determine how successful I am. . . . Professional

challenges and personal dilemmas influence the way I think about culture, schooling, community, and teaching. I discover only through these dilemmas what issues are most important to me as a teacher, a Chicana, an agent of social and educational change, and an individual.

In conclusion, I'd like to leave you with three of our favorite quotes, by Vaclav Havel, Eleanor Roosevelt, and Walter Mosely, respectively:

[N]one of us—as an individual—can save the world as a whole, but . . . each of us must behave as though it were in our power to do so.

You must do the thing you think you cannot do.

You got to dream it. You got to make it up. And when you get it right then it'll be there.[2]

NOTES

1. Oakes left Center X in 2001 to develop the Institute for Democracy, Education, and Access (IDEA) in order to address the problems of schools and teacher education in the context of the larger political economy of California, focusing on access to college as part of an adequate education.

2. This paper originated as the Gail Paradise Kelly Memorial Lecture, given during Urban Educastion Month, organized by the Urban Education Institute at the University at Buffalo Graduate School of Education in March 2001.

OTHER RESOURCES

Internet:
Center X (includes education advocacy links): www.centerx.gseis.ucla.edu
IDEA: www.idea.gseis.ucla.edu
Teaching to Change LA: www.TeachingtoChangeLA.org

SELECTED READINGS BY JEANNIE OAKES

Oakes, J., Quartz, K. H., Ryan, S., & Lipton, M. (2000). *Becoming good American schools: The struggle for civic virtue in education reform.* New York: Jossey-Bass.

Oakes, J., & Lipton, M. (2002). *Teaching to change the world* (2nd ed.). New York: McGraw-Hill.

Oakes, J., & Quartz, K. H. (Eds.) (1995). *Creating new educational communities: Ninety-fourth yearbook of the National Society for the Study of Education. Part I.* Chicago: University of Chicago Press.

Oakes, J. and Lipton, M. (1990). *Making the best of schools: A handbook for parents, teachers, and policymakers.* New Haven: Yale University Press.

Oakes, J. (1985). *Keeping track: How schools structure inequality.* New Haven: Yale University Press.

10 Community Walk-About: Finding the Hope in Hopelessness

Ann Marie Lauricella

Ann Marie Lauricella, a doctoral student in the Department of Learning and Instruction at the State University of New York at Buffalo, describes an "urban experience" designed to expose predominantly suburban pre-service teachers to aspects of city life rarely represented in mainstream media through a "Community Walk-About" in which neighborhood activists served as guides for the students. Student journal responses indicated the "insider's view" provided by the Walk-About helped students better understand and appreciate the communities and the cultures in which their practice teaching experiences would take place.

> The stranger that sojourneth with you shall be unto you as the homeborn among you, and thou shalt love them as thyself; for you were strangers in the land of Egypt.

> —Leviticus 19:34

TEACHER EDUCATION IS DICTATED, in large part, by state departments of education. Courses in content-specific methods, field experience, instructional strategies, and the sociological and psychological foundations of education are the staples of most teacher education programs. The hurried pace of intensive one-year teacher preparation programs leaves little time for meaningful reflection. For that matter, providing the experience to reflect—what Schon (1983) so aptly argues is central to learning—is difficult to manage in a meaningful way given the time constraints. When the New York State Department of Education implemented a policy to place student teachers in "high needs districts" (read: urban areas), teacher preparation programs, including the Graduate School of Education (GSE) at the University at Buffalo (UB), considered how to best prepare student teachers to enter these school communities with more than a cursory preparation in cultural sensitivity. This chapter describes the evolution of an activity meant to provide experience, discourse, and reflection in preparation for a nine-week urban student teaching placement in Western New York, home to the second largest urban area in the state.

Rosa Gibson, President (at left), and volunteers Kathy Spencer (in the middle) and Ruth Coleman (at right) from the Community Action Information Center in Buffalo, New York, in the playground they built for neighborhood children. The Center has also established a food bank, neighborhood "crime watch" patrols, and several community gardens. Their mission is to "act as the eyes and ears of the community, to address community needs, and to promote unity, awareness, and appreciation of our culture."

Providing students with an opportunity to *experience* the commonalities, needs, and diversity that impact children (in essence, the issues of community and culture) remained at the core of the planning for what was eventually named the "Community Walk-About." Designed to offer pre-service teachers (PSTs) the experience of moving through the neighborhoods of the children they would soon be teaching in their high-needs urban placements, the event was informed by Schon's notion of learning as resulting not from experience, but from *reflecting* on experience.

So, with this in mind, we who were responsible for teaching and mentoring the PSTs set about planning an urban experience that would provide our mostly white, suburban, female, middle-class students an opportunity to develop new perspectives on urban life. We hoped the tour would offer an alternative to their views of city dwelling, which were formed in part by negative media images exploiting anecdotal tales of despair and hopelessness. We sought to challenge students' preconceptions by speaking frankly about the realities and by offering an opportunity for a deeper understanding of the children in urban schools. We thought that if an experience could be offered that exposed a sense of hope, it might encourage the resolve of new teachers and help them begin their journey into the profession with better understanding of urban children and their communities.

THE NEED FOR CULTURALLY RESPONSIVE PRE-SERVICE TEACHERS

The educational literature is replete with calls for educators to become more culturally sensitive and aware (Delpit, 1996; Groulx, 2001; Ladson-Billings, 1995; Sleeter, 2001). Yet many believe this call has not resulted in teacher preparation programs that effectively prepare teachers for success in diverse urban settings (Darling-Hammond, 1994: Murrell, 1997; Zeichner, 1996). Demographics indicate that the need to address this situation will grow. In 1993 Tamayo-Lott (1993) noted that 90 percent of the teaching population was white, with no significant change projected, at least for the next twenty-five years. By 2035, it is projected that approximately 50 percent of the children under eighteen years of age will be children of color. We are on the cusp of tipping the minority to majority within our nation's school population, with the results that the divide between children of color and the mostly white teaching population will continue to grow.

Given the research that supports the claim that current teacher preparation programs fail to meet the needs of urban children (Delpit, 1996; Irvine & Fraser, 1998; Sleeter, 1995; Sykes, 1997; Weiner, 1999), how can these programs best prepare pre-service student teachers to work with students different than themselves? PSTs tend to rate themselves as "committed individuals, having good parents, good values, a good education, and a good sense of what is expected of them as teachers" (McIntyre, 1997). Too often, however, these predominately white, middle-class teachers feel that the urban children they teach lack these things. Life in the suburbs can shelter or even skew a person's ideas of what city life is like. Recent studies have shown that pre-service teachers often bring little cultural sensitivity and understanding to the classroom and they often have rigid stereotypes about city people (Sleeter, 2001). Attitudes such as these cannot help but be conveyed while working with students. Teachers—consciously or unconsciously—try to impose their values and belief systems onto children in their classrooms. Sometimes this can benefit the student, when the teacher is seen as a positive role model. At other times, however, a teacher's assumptions can conflict with the cultural norms and values of the student, which can cause great distress for a student and result in lower grades, negative peer interactions, and resistant behavior.

Furthermore, teachers often hold lower expectations for working-class children and students of color (Anyon, 1981; Groulx, 2001) and students often conform to teachers' expectations, thereby creating a self-fulfilling prophecy (Rist, 1970). It has become common knowledge that urban school districts, where minority student numbers are highest, typically have a lower academic achievement level, a higher rate of expulsion and detention, a higher drop-out rate, and a lower (and oftentimes declining) proportion of high school graduates attending college. It is also the case that a "disproportionately high number of minority students are placed in low-ability groups or in special education" (Artiles, 1996, in Groulx, 2001). Often, it is the decision of the classroom teacher to recommend that a student be placed in a special education or low-ability setting. While many new teachers have been exposed to the concept of cultural bias in their course work in education, they may still fall short in implementing a culturally aware pedagogy in their own classrooms. It is not easy to do, and it takes practice.

Our nation's urban schools face a myriad of problems, ranging from a lack of adequate funding and scarcity of professional resources to ineffective governance and public apathy. It is a sad fact that "children and youth of color, especially African American and Hispanic learners . . . continue to bear the brunt of public school dysfunction" (Murrell, 2001). Teacher preparation programs, while aware that these issues plague urban schools, also face the challenge of working with pre-service teachers who are often resistant to grappling with the cultural differences of communities with whom they have had little or no experience. It is not uncommon to hear PSTs express faintly disguised discomfort with urban lifestyles and interactions. Student teachers sometimes feel that their lives are in danger or that students in poor school districts are "hopeless" due to their poverty and lack of familial education. While many PSTs are open to the notion that they will be working with students of other cultures, they often assume that this will happen in a suburban school setting. Work in an urban setting is rarely a new teacher's first choice; the urban placement is seen as a requirement that must be endured for the sake of obtaining professional licensure.

King's (1991) concept of "dysconscious racism"—the unexamined practices, beliefs, and attitudes of teachers who maintain, without question, the status quo—is an impediment to needed change in teacher education programs. The movement towards systematic change will come from those willing to connect with communities of people who have different social, racial, or cultural backgrounds. And who, once the connection is made, continue the dialogue in an open and reflective manner. Being culturally sensitive and aware is more than just a prudent idea in today's classrooms; it a way of proceeding that links the children, the community, and the schools. With this in mind, the teacher preparation program in the UB Graduate School of Education sought to provide an experience for pre-service teachers that enhanced understanding through community involvement.

COMMUNITY WALK-ABOUT: THE HISTORY

Beginning in the fall of 1997, the Teacher Education Institute (TEI) at the UB Graduate School of Education required that every pre-service teacher engage in an "immersion experience" that provided an opportunity to explore urban neighborhoods. The first immersion experience, the Community Plunge, was informed by a program at the University of Texas and was meant to promote an awareness and understanding of what urban students face on a daily basis. Billed as a strategy "to introduce PSTs to their students' cultural backgrounds," the Plunge focused more on neighborhoods than the cultural backgrounds of students. The rationale for the immersion experience was described in a September 1999 faculty handout:

> The majority of the students in the BRIET [former name of TEI] teacher education program are of European descent and come from suburban middle-class backgrounds with very little knowledge and/ or interaction with the city of Buffalo. Typically only a few pre-service teachers have any prior knowledge of the immediate area served by the schools in which they will student teach. Therefore, an initial hurdle to overcome has been the trepidation that student teachers bring to their urban placements. Based on media images of the city and its schools, many students believe the city to be a dangerous place, and the schools to be out of control.

The handout continued with descriptions of how the city schools are perceived by education students; how they fear, for example, gang activity, guns and knives, and fights in the halls. While some attempt was made to provide instructors with information about the diversity of the city schools in terms of size and numbers, the connection between walking through neighborhoods and addressing the fears and the preconceived notions about urban life remained sketchy at best, unexamined at worst. No guidance on this topic was offered to the instructors of the Field Experience class, in which the Community Plunge was a required activity.

In preparation for the Community Plunge, PSTs were assigned to small groups and required to select roles, including the following: tour guide, travel agent, recorder, and reporter. Each role was defined and students were encouraged to "undertake this plunge with sensitivity, creativity, and join together information and insights about your new community" (faculty handout, September 1999). Group members also were commissioned to take field notes and write a reflection about the experience, which we hoped would offer a starting point for the in-class debriefing to be held the following week.

The discussion that developed as part of the debriefing was surprising to many of the instructors of the Field Experience class. While the discussion was tentative at the start (the Plunge took place around the third week of the course, so many students did not really know each other), it gathered strength as students began voicing the criticism that the experience was a "forced diversity concentration." Below is a sampling of remarks gathered from the reflections offered in the student journals, which provide a milder version of the classroom dialogue once discussion got going. These comments are fairly representative of about one-third of a class of twenty-four:

> The experience was both contrived and superficial. I felt embarrassed to be roaming around people's neighborhoods with a clipboard taking down notes. We didn't belong there and nobody would talk to us. . . . I don't blame them, I wouldn't talk to us either. (PST—High School Chemistry)

> I grew up in the city. . . . I know what the city is like. So . . . when will we be doing a plunge in the suburbs where I want to teach! (PST—Elementary Education)

> We witnessed a drug deal. We saw money change hands, we saw a bag being passed, we were scared and after that, decided to leave immediately. What was I supposed to learn here? That the city was a dangerous place. . . . I already knew that. (PST—High School Social Studies)

> What was I supposed to learn? What was I supposed to take from this experience? That the neighborhoods are not as pleasant as the suburbs? Was I supposed to believe that the neighborhoods we visited were an accurate representation of all city neighborhoods? . . . suppose they were . . . what does this tell me about the students? (PST—High School Social Studies)

As one of the instructors, I listened to the concerns of the students and became increasingly aware of the negative aspects of the experience. I chided myself for my inability to foster a dialogue that would encourage thinking beyond a negative view of some of Buffalo's toughest neighborhoods. Instead of encouraging reflection on the possibilities, it seemed as though the whole experience made the PSTs even more wary of venturing into their urban placements. The students, armed with what seemed to be "actual evidence," perceived the city schools as more alarming than those in the suburbs.

As the time neared for their urban placements, students grew increasingly tense. As the semester moved on, the more I attempted to "sell" Buffalo to the cohort of PSTs I had been assigned to mentor, the more resistance I felt. Moreover, the reputation of the teacher education program, which did not lack for caring and committed people, suffered from a seeming mistrust from some students who were becoming suspicious of the emphasis the program placed on diversity. In sum, the defensiveness exhibited by some students toward the Community Plunge set a tone of defensiveness toward all matters of diversity that we were working to infuse throughout the program.

AN IDEA WAS BORN!

The claim that the Community Plunge seemed contrived struck me the hardest. How might the experience be enhanced to show the multiple realities of urban life? What was missing from the experience that might prove more meaningful to the students? Initially, four different walking routes were set up. Students were required to use public transportation (either bus or subway) to get to their starting point. No other direction was offered; the students were left to negotiate their own way. The routes were randomly assigned to groups of four to six students who were encouraged to walk around neighborhoods and observe, talk with people, and/or visit shops or restaurants.

Among the questions included on a sheet guiding the debriefing to be conducted by instructors were: What types of beauty or taste did you experience? What evidence of social conflict did you see? What types of businesses seemed predominant in the area? While there were fifteen questions in all, there was no resource available to the instructors suggesting how to probe students' responses. In other words, once the student observation was made, no suggestions were offered about where to take the discussion. How could the graffiti and the abandoned buildings be connected to and explained by such abstract concepts as "social conflict?" Was there a specific meaning behind the images that appeared both as graffiti and as a testimonial? Was all that appeared all that there was? We did not have any insider information—someone to explain the nuances of the neighborhood. Similarly, we (the instructors and mentors) were not prepared to discuss the student observations that exhibited an understanding of the urban landscape that was positive.

Coincidentally, in the fall of 1999, another type of "plunge" was taking place as part of a GSE research project. Members of the GSE faculty and student body joined several community groups in a door-to-door survey that involved visiting various Buffalo neighborhoods to gather information from parents of children in the Buffalo public schools (see Johnson, p. 157). As a result of participating in this experience, I attended a Coalition for Urban Education (CUE) meeting, one of the survey organizing groups. The more meetings I attended, the more I was invited into conversations with community members who were working hard to improve neighborhoods and schools. As a result, I began to conceive of community walks that *included the community!*

The survey project had asked parents to tell us about their children's schools, so why not ask members of the community to take PSTs around the urban neighborhoods and tell them about community issues? This idea came like an epiphany and seemed a nice balance between exposing students to the reality of city dwelling and exposing them to the possibilities cities offer. For help in organizing a new immersion experience for the PSTs, I turned to Dr.

Mary Finn, Director of the GSE Urban Education Institute. With the help of three community activists, we designed guided tours of various Buffalo neighborhoods for the fall of 2000. The Community Plunge, renamed the Community Walk-About, offered students a more in-depth look at the neighborhoods they toured because their tour guides were community activists.

THE ACTIVISTS

One activist, a Catholic priest, not only guided the students on a walk through the neighborhood, but also "behind the scenes" to look at what went into making improvements on a church property located in Buffalo. Students were given insight into the financial difficulties, political maneuverings, and community support that eventually led to a new roof being installed on the property. The priest also explained how he, along with the congregation, got the City of Buffalo to keep a promise to tear down twelve buildings that were "eye sores" and/or crack houses. Along the tour, he showed the corners where houses had been demolished and others where houses were slated for demolition. Students felt a sense of hope, which they remarked on in their journals as well as during the in-class debriefing:

> From this walk I learned a few interesting things. . . . I learned that even if the neighborhood appears run down, a closer look offers many homes that are well cared for. . . . It seems as though the area was what you made of it because both pastors and the woman that walked with us loved where they lived and wouldn't trade it for the world. They said that the only problems they had were people being inconsiderate and loud, not once did they mention violence. (PST—High School Chemistry)

> I was given a sense of both hopelessness and hope. In many ways the neighborhood has been going downhill for some time. Many people have moved out making way for poorer renters whose properties remain neglected by landlords. Drugs are more common along with widespread garbage and noise. Nonetheless, not all is bad. The priest said that he doesn't feel unsafe in the neighborhood and runs at night. The neighborhood is now ethnically diverse and for some immigrants, life is better than in their native countries . . . the neighborhood isn't all that run-down for a "bad" neighborhood, in fact, a number of homes were quite aesthetically pleasing. (PST—High School English)

Another team of activists offered a guided tour around the Quaker Meeting House in the Humbolt Parkway area. The third team was a mother and daughter who began their tour at the New Covenant United Church of Christ Church on Clinton Street downtown. The following reflections illustrate the ideas expressed during the classroom debriefing and summarize the prevailing views:

> As for the delve into the community... I was very touched by the commitment that Betty had for VOICE Buffalo, as well as the pride that she, along with her daughter, showed in their community... if we all had respect for our community the way Betty does, Western New York would be a beautiful place. (PST—Elementary Education)

> I enjoyed listening to Rosa Gibson, an African American activist living near Best Street. The history behind her organization [the Community Action Information Center] really brings to life issues discussed in books like Kozol's "Savage Inequalities." The Quaker church including the beliefs behind it was of interest. One, stereotypically of course, would picture a Quaker church to be full of purely white, educated, non-materialistic people. Therefore, it was a surprise to see this structure (house) standing in downtown Buffalo. I guess I am a walking stereotype. . . . (PST—High School Math)

In addition to the tours by community activists, the revised immersion experience included the use of a modified KWL organizer (Ogle, 1986) with an added "H" twist! That is, the students were required to consider their experience in light of the following four categories: the "K" represents what students already *Know* about the city and the schools in Buffalo; the "W" represents *What* was learned as a result of the Community Walk-About, being careful to consider what previous knowledge was confirmed, contradicted, or complicated; the "L" represents what the students might like to *Learn* more about. The added "H" represents *How* students might work towards gathering information to enhance their learning, such as where they should go to find out more. Each student completed this organizer and submitted it with their reflective narrative.

In the twenty-seven journal responses shared with me, none of the fall 2000 PSTs talked about being afraid of the neighborhoods, perhaps due in part to the explanations they heard about various homes and ongoing community projects. Also, the activists had a way of expressing the possibilities while acknowledging the work that still needs to be done. "This is where we live and play... there are good people here, people who need help, and people we would rather move someplace else . . . still, this is home to many of us and we will continue to work at making improvements." (Author's field notes, September 28, 2000).

FOCUS ON BUFFALO'S HISTORY

A guided walking tour of downtown Buffalo was another new component added to the Community Walk-About. In fact, it is how we started the day.

Approximately sixty students met downtown, broke into groups of about ten to fifteen people, and proceeded on a tour conducted by docents affiliated with the School of Architecture at the University at Buffalo. The goal of this part of the urban experience was to connect the city's rich historical past with the present, fostering an idea of a continuum that remains fluid and constantly evolves. This was viewed as key because we believed that if PSTs could envision a space where they could enter the changing face of the community—via the schools—their resolve might be encouraged by learning, and in some cases reviewing, Buffalo's powerful history. The historical narrative presented by the docents afforded an opportunity to critically analyze what had become of the city that Frederick Law Olmstead once described as "the most beautiful city in America" and to understand the hope very much alive within the community as seen by the activists.

The total urban experience lasted about five hours and, in contrast to the earlier Plunge immersion experience, the Walk-About elicited expressions of excitement and empathy from the PSTs as they anticipated their urban student teaching placements. Students seemed to enjoy the Walk-About and offered comments that invited dialogue rather than taking polarized positions of resistance. Some students even expressed a feeling of connectedness to the nation as a whole through the particulars of Buffalo's history. In a journal entry that typifies this understanding, one PST described history as "a people's legacy":

> I did enjoy several of the architectural sites downtown, the Calumet's terracotta tile exterior, City Hall and its Seneca decorations, . . . the Guaranty and Ellicott Square Building. Joseph Ellicott's innovative street-spoke design was new to me and so was the fact that Yamanski, architect of the World Trade Towers, designed a Buffalo building. As I looked up, I noticed the resemblance. I caught bits and pieces of the tour guide's explanations of the Pan-American Exhibition and the assassination of President McKinley. I listened as he explained that McKinley lay in state at County Hall as thousands of mourners waited in line to pass by. Today that building has been secured in the wake of terrorists' attacks and when he noted the building where Lincoln stayed, I couldn't help feeling amazed at the past and living history of the moment. As sirens signaled the end of the downtown tour, we all hoped it was a false alarm and I came away from this area with a sense that all of this should be protected and preserved. . . . I connected this 'bunch of old buildings' downtown with the progress and political struggle of our nation. In light of our present 'state of war' everything I saw this day seemed more emotional and more meaningful. History is really a people's legacy and even in the pouring rain, I could imagine the excitement and tragedy of world events happening right here in the city of Buffalo. (Karen Mahoney—PST, High School English)[1]

At the debriefing after the Walk-About, we considered the notion of history being a "people's legacy." What was there to learn about our role in the construction of Buffalo's ongoing history? As teachers entering classrooms, how might we envision the people's legacy in Buffalo? Many comments expressed a sense of connection with the past and hope for the future:

> staying here [in Buffalo] to teach is something I am definitely looking forward to doing. In a way, I (we) will be contributing to that which defines Buffalo, just like its architecture, theater district, etc. Hopefully, our prospective students will sustain the city. . . our work with them will set a solid foundation, similar to that which supports the strong old buildings downtown. The city, even in its beauty, still has a lot of unused potential. (Karen Mahoney—High School English, PST)

The phrase "unused potential" suggests enthusiasm for what is possible, an attitude that should be encouraged throughout urban teacher education programs. Most students from suburban backgrounds who want to become teachers express the desire to make a difference in the lives of children, but their ideas and preconceived notions about urban life—that little can be done in areas barraged with crime, "broken" families, and poverty—often lead to feelings of hopelessness. The rhetoric of despair needs to be challenged with all available senses. The education of new teachers who are willing to add to the legacy of hope should include the sights, sounds, and experiences of the city, supported by the optimistic intensity of community activists and their visions of what is possible and by a historical understanding of the shared roots and common desires, in order to help student teachers find connections between their lives and the lives of urban students. In the experience of one PST:

> It was the intensity of Cara's [a docent and parent of three children attending Buffalo's public schools] probing that really got me. She did what I would have done, that is, take advantage of the situation at hand. Here she was among a group of graduate students studying to be teachers and she polled every one of us for our thoughts on the schooling of her twin boys. One was identified as "gifted and talented" and the other needed extra help to keep up. When the district suggested that the more advanced son be moved to a different school, Cara wasn't sure that this would be good for the other twin that relied on his brother for remediation . . . there were so many issues. . . . Although we really didn't know what would be best for the boys, I was struck by the involvement, angst and lengths that this parent was going through to make a decision she would be comfortable with for her boys. Although not surprised by her involvement, it gave me my first taste of what parents go through

when dealing with the education of their children. . . . I could re-late to that! I hope I can see her again to find out what she decided but I mostly want to meet the boys (I had a "smart" twin too!). (PST—Elementary Education)

CONCLUSION

Students who participated in the Community Walk-About offered a number of suggestions for improving the program, including: (a) schedule time to meet and debrief directly after the tours instead of waiting a week; (b) go to lunch at the downtown restaurant where Buffalo high school students, learning to be chefs, complete an internship; (c) interact with "actual students" (the PSTs were adamant that sharing the tour with students would provide additional insights about the neighborhoods as well as the opportunity to meet and talk to their future students outside the classroom context); (d) use digital technology to capture the tour in order to review, inform, and assess changes throughout the years; and (e) make subject area connections to neighborhoods. For many of us who had been involved in the early urban immersion experiences (the Community Plunge), these student-generated suggestions indicated the success of the Community Walk-About in 2000. We saw hope and possibility in students' reflections on the experience of learning about the communities in which urban schools are located and in their willingness to discuss and consider improvements. The experience of the walk-about not only challenged students' unexamined assumptions about the hopelessness of urban life, but also seemed to strengthen their resolve to work in urban communities to make a difference in children's lives.

NOTE

1. All journal entries by pre-service teachers are anonymous, except for Karen Mahoney who wished to be identified in the text. The author gratefully acknowledges the contribution of Dr. Sandra Cimbricz for her "H" contribution to the KWL organizer and Dr. Mary Rose McCarthy and Dr. Kim Truesdell for their encouragement and helpful insights while planning this event.

REFERENCES

Anyon, J. (1981). Social class and school knowledge. *Curriculum Inquiry, 11*(1), 3–42.

Darling-Hammond, L. (Ed.). (1994) *Professional development schools: Schools for developing a profession.* New York: Teachers College Press.

Delpit, L. (1996). Skills and other dilemmas of a progressive Black educator. *American Educator, 20*(3), 9–11.

Groulx, J. G. (2001). Changing preservice teacher perceptions of minority schools. *Urban Education, 36*(1), 60–92.

Irvine, J. J., & Fraser, J. (1998). Warm demanders: Do certification standards leave room for the culturally responsive pedagogy of African American teachers? *Education Week, 17*(3), 42, 56.

King, J. (1991). Dysconscious racism: Ideology, identity, and the miseducation of teachers. *Journal of Negro Education, 60*(2), 133–146.

Ladson-Billings, G. (1995). Toward a theory of culturally relevant pedagogy. *American Educational Research Journal, 32*(3), 465–491.

McIntyre, A. (1997). *Making meaning of whiteness: Exploring racial identity with white teachers.* New York: State University of New York Press.

Murrell, P. C., Jr. (1997). Digging again the family wells: A Freirean literacy framework as emancipatory pedagogy for African American children. In P. Freire, J. Fraser, D. Macedo, T. McKinnon, & W. Stokes (Eds.), *Mentoring the mentor: A critical dialog with Paulo Freire* (pp. 19–58). Albany: State University of New York Press.

Murrell, P. C., Jr. (2001). *The community teacher: A new framework for effective urban teaching.* New York: Teachers College Press.

Ogle, D. M. (1986). K-W-L: A teaching model that develops active reading of expository text. *Reading Teacher, 39*(6), 564–570.

Rist, R. (1970). Student social class and teacher expectations: The self-fulfilling prophecy in ghetto education. *Harvard Educational Review, 40*(3), 411–451.

Schon, D. A. (1983). *The reflective practitioner: How professionals think in action.* New York: Basic Books.

Sleeter, C. E. (1995). Teaching whites about racism. In J. M. Larkin & C. E. Sleeter (Eds.), *Developing multicultural teacher education curricula* (pp. 117–130). Albany: State University of New York Press.

Sleeter, C. E. (2001). Preparing teachers for culturally diverse schools: Research and the overwhelming presence of whiteness. *Journal of Teacher Education, 53*(2), 94–106.

Sykes, G. (1997). Worthy of the name: Standards for the professional development school. In M. Levine & R. Trachtman (Eds.), *Building professional development schools: Politics, practice and policy* (pp. 159–193). New York: Teacher College Press.

Tamayo-Lott, J. (1993). Do United States racial/ethnic categories still fit? *Population Today, 21*(1), 6–7.

Weiner, L. (1999). *Urban teaching: The essentials.* New York: Teachers College Press.

Zeichner, K. M. (1996). Educating teachers to close the achievement gap: Issues of pedagogy, knowledge, and teacher preparation. In B. Williams (Ed.), *Closing the achievement gap: A vision for changing beliefs and practices* (pp. 56–76). Alexandria, VA: Association for Supervision and Curriculum Development.

11 Transforming Urban Education through the Massachusetts Coalition for Teacher Quality and Student Achievement

Dennis Shirley

Dennis Shirley is Professor and Chair of the Department of Teacher Education, Special Education, and Curriculum and Instruction at the Lynch School of Education at Boston College in Chestnut Hill, Massachusetts. A former VISTA volunteer and high school history teacher, his research has focused on community organizing and urban school reform, particularly the capacities of poor and working-class urban communities to develop effective strategies to improve public schools and urban neighborhoods simultaneously. In this chapter he uses Saul Alinsky's principles of community organizing as a conceptual lens to analyze school-university partnerships.

THE SIGNIFICANT CHALLENGES confronting urban school systems in the United States are rooted in a complicated confluence of political, economic, and educational factors (Anyon, 1997; Bowles and Gintis, 1976). Urban schools form part of the dual economy of metropolitan regions, which combine the class hegemony of an affluent, nomadic elite of symbolic analysts (Reich, 1992) with the poverty and disenfranchisement of the working poor and the working class (Goode and Maskovsky, 2001). In urban centers, the latter are increasingly, although not exclusively, communities of color, with a large influx of immigrants from all corners of the globe (Massey and Denton, 1993; Wilson, 1987). The complexity of new urban social formations, with truly transnational communication circuits superimposed upon older national identities and structures, require a variety of conceptual lenses to understand the contradictions and problems of contemporary metropolitan educational systems (Hargreaves, 1994; Best and Kellner, 1991).

These multiple lenses are helpful when attempting to understand the situation of teacher education programs preparing teachers to work in urban schools. Such programs are rife with contradictions. For example, elite universities with budget-busting tuitions proclaim themselves to be dedicated to social justice, but

The teaching team for the Fall 2003 "Social Contexts of Education" course includes (from left to right): Patrick Tutwiler, a history teacher at Brighton High School; Maria Teresa Sanchez, a doctoral student at Boston College; Professor Dennis Shirley, Chair of the Department of Teacher Education, Special Education, and Curriculum and Instruction at the Lynch School of Education at Boston College; Elizabeth MacDonald, a fourth grade teacher at the Garfield Elementary School; and Afra Ahmed Hersi, a doctoral student at Boston College.

their tuitions virtually guarantee that their student bodies will be predominantly white and privileged, thereby reproducing the racial division of labor in schools and society. Or teacher education faculty imagine themselves to be second-class citizens in the cultural universe of the college or university, but such faculty command salaries that place them in the top 20 percent of Americans. Or a third contradiction, admittedly subjective and from my own point of view, but observed too frequently to be anomalous: the more ostensibly "radical" faculty are those who are most disengaged from the work of urban schools, whereas apolitical or even conservative faculty often carry out impressive work directly with urban youth, their communities, and their teachers.

If teacher education is in and of itself in many ways a contradictory and tenuous profession, it is nonetheless remarkably resistant to change, an intransigence that in many ways reflects the fundamentally conservative nature of colleges and universities in the United States. Faculty guidelines for promotion and tenure, for example, are by and large indistinguishable from those in other professions, in spite of the need for teacher educators to be linked to the often turbulent and unpredictable challenges of urban schools. In this context one of the most noteworthy educational improvement efforts in the United States in the last fifteen years is the effort to create school, college, and university partnerships. Originally part of an attempt to reinvigorate the linkages between schools of education and public schools, these partnerships have evolved to include virtually all aspects of educational reform, from computer-assisted instruction in language arts classrooms to full-service schools with expansive pre- and after-school programs that serve a wide range of community residents. Evidence indicates that these partnerships have stimulated exciting exchanges between teachers, principals, and higher education faculty (Teitel, 2003); nonetheless, research thus far shows little evidence of learning gains by students in schools, the ostensible beneficiaries of partnerships (Valli, Cooper, and Frankes, 1997).

In this chapter, I offer some reflections on the current state of partnership work from the vantage point of a highly interested practitioner. I am the principal investigator and director of a United States Department of Education Title II Teacher Quality Enhancement Grant entitled the "Massachusetts Coalition for Teacher Quality and Student Achievement," which encompasses seven higher education institutions (Boston College, Clark University, Lesley University, the University of Massachusetts at Amherst, the University of Massachusetts at Boston, Northeastern University, and Wheelock College) and eighteen urban schools in Massachusetts' three largest cities (Boston, Springfield, and Worcester). In June 2003 the Coalition is in the fourth year of a five-year grant funding cycle; the size of the grant is $7 million.

I have come to the leadership of the Massachusetts Coalition from a somewhat unorthodox background as a teacher educator. Since 1992, I have been working collaboratively with the Industrial Areas Foundation (IAF), a community-based organization started by Saul Alinsky in Chicago in 1940. This background with the IAF has provided me with a unique frame of reference for conceptualizing urban school politics and the role of school and university partnerships within them. Consequently, the first purpose of the chapter is to characterize my prior work with the IAF. Alinsky organizing, I argue, provides a number of powerful conceptual tools for analyzing school and university partnerships. Second, I describe the theory of action and some of the dilemmas encountered by the Coalition in its first four years, attending in particular to the tensions, ambiguities, contradictions, and benefits that emerge in collaborations between schools, communities, and college and university faculty who engage in statewide partnership networks. Third, I describe a case study of one Massachusetts Coalition activity in the community organizing tradition of the IAF, in the hope that a balanced portrayal of the challenges and positive outcomes of Coalition-driven undertakings may support continued efforts in urban school reform.

PRIOR WORK WITH THE INDUSTRIAL AREAS
FOUNDATION (IAF) IN TEXAS

Saul Alinsky first gained national prominence in the 1940s with the publication of his book *Reveille for Radicals* (1946), in which he describes establishing and leading the Back of the Yards Neighborhood Council in Chicago, which organized low-income immigrant workers to contest established power structures and promote participatory democracy. "Alinsky organizing" entered the public lexicon in the 1960s when Alinsky's work with a wide variety of radical community-based organizations gained national recognition (or notoriety, depending on one's point of view). *Rules for Radicals: A Pragmatic Primer for Realistic Radicals* (1971) established Alinsky as the founder of an inventive, confrontational, and successful style of grassroots organizing highly attractive to a generation of newly radicalized youth.

Alinsky died in 1972, but his successor in the IAF, Ed Chambers, made the group more broad-based than it ever had been in Alinsky's lifetime. Where Alinsky was brash, confrontational, and theatrical, Chambers emphasized working-class respectability, patient negotiation, and the anchoring of the IAF in neighborhood institutions. Chambers was especially successful in anchoring the IAF in institutional membership in religious institutions, which paid dues to support organizers and staff.

I first connected with the IAF in Texas in 1992, while working on a project to start a new professional development school with Rice University (where I worked as a professor of education) and the Houston Independent School District. In planning the new school, it quickly became evident that neither HISD nor Rice knew successful strategies for bringing large numbers of low-income parents of color into the planning process. When I learned about a local IAF group, The Metropolitan Organization (TMO), and its organizing efforts in Houston's far-flung wards and barrios, its lead organizer Robert Rivera and I began monthly breakfast meetings to discuss the politics of education in Houston, the nation's fourth largest city. These initial primary contacts lasted for a year; once we established trust, Robert asked me to begin conducting research on the IAF school collaboratives.

The Texas IAF was then working in twenty-five schools scattered throughout the state, all of which were in intensely segregated communities of color characterized by high rates of poverty. The IAF had organized the schools into a loose network known as "Alliance Schools," which convened their own assemblies, shared samples of best practices, and debated strategies for enhancing parent engagement. Although well documented, this project is insufficiently known by teacher educators and school reformers (Murnane and Levy, 1997; Osterman, 2002; Sarason, 2002; Shirley, 1997, 2002; Sirianni and Friedland, 2001). Organizers work with community leaders using strategies that start with "one-on-one" conversations, evolve into "house meetings," develop capacity through "home visits" and "research actions," and culminate in large public "accountability sessions," in which elected officials, civil servants (such as police, health, or school officials), and business leaders commit themselves to the given community organization's agenda. These strategies have been honed over decades and have proven effective in developing civic capacity between faith-based institutions, schools, and community-based organizations. In the following, I briefly describe three facets of this organizing approach.

The first is the legendary "iron rule" of this variant of community organizing: "never do anything for others that they can do for themselves" (Shirley, 2002, p. 11). The iron rule often is difficult for teacher educators and school reformers, who can be caught up in "the culturally mainstream perspectives of faculty and students and their tendencies toward 'helperism' in relationships with school and community partners" (Murrell, 2001, p. 35). This "helperism" is endemic in the literature of professional development schools and urban schools; it often is used to acquire external grants for colleges and universities and transforms higher education institutions into perpetual grant-seeking machines as well as auxiliary social service agencies. The well-intentioned argument that urban schools are under-resourced and that urban populations are disenfranchised can lead to an assertion of professional expertise that reduces citizens to clients and transforms political problems into issues of technical inefficiency. Unless checked, the tendency of such professionals as professors, teachers, social workers, and school counselors can be to reinforce a sense of dependency upon external actors, not only for urban parents but also for teachers in urban public schools.

The iron rule is the philosophical corrective for this tendency to helperism, but it is not intended to convey indifference to social injustices or to legitimize the withdrawal of civic engagement from the body politic. Community organizers in the Alinsky tradition recognize that the working poor in many American cities attended schools that practiced de facto racial and class-based segregation and emphasized order and discipline over content knowledge and participatory democracy (Texas Interfaith Education Fund, 1990). Learning to translate vague grievances into political problems, developing social capital through networks of broad-based civic engagement, and acquiring the public speaking and organizing skills to confront and persuade power holders requires careful mentoring and support for adult learners.

A second aspect of Alinsky organizing is a focus on "winnable issues," based on the belief that community organizations in poor and working class neighborhoods can afford only a small number of defeats and must carefully select their battles. Alinsky organizations are sometimes faulted for focusing on topics that seem relatively trivial, such as installing a traffic light at a dangerous intersection, shutting down a single crack house, or improving neighborhood drainage systems. The important point, from the IAF's perspective, is not the particular change, but the development of a measure of confidence on the part of the community that change can be brought about at all. Organizers need to identify and work with indigenous community leaders to develop the confidence that political engagement can produce visible results.

The third strategy used by IAF organizers is that of actively listening to community concerns and using those concerns—and not the organizers' assumptions of what the community might most need—as the point of departure for organizing. House meetings, in which community residents and stakeholders meet to identify core grievances and develop political strategies, are the primary vehicles for developing civic capacity; they can be held in a church, school, health clinic, apartment building, or neighborhood center. The purpose of a house meeting is for stakeholders to address problems in their communities, brainstorm possible solutions, and generate both the leadership and strategies for attacking those problems.

These principles of community organizing—the iron rule, the selection of winnable issues, and the importance of active listening—shaped my own education as a teacher educator and school reformer. By studying the development of the Alliance Schools in Texas, I saw that community stakeholders in poor and working-class neighborhoods could use the principles to develop the civic clout to improve their schools and communities simultaneously. The principles also have shaped my engagement in the founding and maintenance of the Massachusetts Coalition for Teacher Quality and Student Achievement from 1999 to the present.

ORIGINS OF THE MASSACHUSETTS COALITION

The Massachusetts Coalition was formed in response to a unique funding opportunity provided by the Office of Postsecondary Education of the U.S. Department of Education in 1999. The original purpose of Title II was to promote the training, recruitment, and retention of high quality teachers for urban schools. Drawing on the extensive body of research documenting the dramatic inequities that exist between urban schools and those in suburban or rural settings (Anyon, 1997; Kozol, 1991; Stone et al., 2001), Title II intended to augment resources that would address those inequalities by assuring urban students access to highly qualified teachers. After a round of preliminary applications, a few organizations, including the Massachusetts Coalition, were invited to submit a full fifty-page application. The Coalition, which included higher education faculty, teachers, urban school administrators, and affiliated community leaders, formed an ad hoc writers' group to compose the application.

From the outset, the task entailed contradictions and ambiguities. For example, the Request for Proposals (RFP) emphasized both engaging arts and sciences faculty in teacher preparatory work and involving a wide range of community stakeholders in planning the grant. The Coalition made both a priority in its application, but in convening large groups of stakeholders from schools, community-based organizations, and businesses in two needs-assessment forums, we heard little (actually nothing) about the need to engage arts and sciences faculty in teacher education. For most teachers and parents, academic subject mastery was a low priority compared to the relentless daily pressures in schools. The funding guidelines also called for business involvement in school reform, but as with the involvement of arts and sciences faculty, there is little evidence to support the assertion that business involvement per se has any predictive value in terms of raising student achievement or improving teacher education.

The needs assessment found that the teachers' first priority was classroom management, broadly construed. Urban schools are perceived by teachers to be turbulent and unsafe places, both for their students and themselves, and teachers wanted assistance with managing and instructing large numbers of city youth. Second, teachers and parents wanted help learning how to teach diverse learners. Students in urban schools come from all over the world; some know no English; some come from conditions of extreme poverty and are unfamiliar with the cultures of schools; some come from thriving, entrepreneurial, and ambitious families and enter schools well-prepared to excel academically. This tremendous range of learners in urban schools presents teachers with daunting instructional situations. Third, teachers and parents were concerned about the disconnection between teachers and parents and sought ways to develop stronger ties between teachers and parents, so that areas of mutual concern could be addressed and children's learning advanced.

According to political scientists Michael Cohen, James March, and Johan Olsen (1988), policy formulation in the United States is best described with a "garbage can" metaphor. That is, decision makers throw ideas into policy proposals—in this case, the Massachusetts Coalition grant proposal—just as a variety of disposables get tossed into waste receptacles. The U.S. Department of Education wanted arts and sciences and business involvement in the preparation of urban teachers, so those goals had to be "thrown" into the proposal by the writers' group. Teachers and principals wanted help with classroom management, diverse learners, and working with parents, so those themes were added. At the request of Thomas Payzant, the Boston Superintendent of Schools, a focus on improving students' literacy was included as well.

At the same time, urban education is part of what Clarence Stone and his colleagues (2001) have described as a "high-reverberation" system. Such systems, they contend, "are characterized by frequent reshuffling of mobilized stakeholders, multiple and strongly felt competing value and belief systems, deeply held stakes by both educators (the professional providers of education) and parents (the consumers), and ambiguous boundaries, making the prospects for establishing a new equilibrium more problematic than is formally the case" (Stone et al., 2001, p. 50). In situations of such dynamic complexity, leadership has to both flexible and stable.

Although the "garbage can" theory is apt, it obscures a key component of Alexis de Tocqueville's (1969) classical analysis of American democracy. Tocqueville's *Democracy in America* illuminated the educative role of civic associations in the

United States, which enabled individuals to transcend their narrow areas of interest or specialization and brought them into contact with others from entirely different backgrounds and vocations. Through such connections, voluntary associations work against the "atomization of society"—that is, the tendency of individuals, especially prominent in market economies—to pursue their narrow self-interest at the expense of the public good. The value of coalitions is, from this point of view, profoundly educational. In the words of Carmen Sirianni and Lewis Friedland (2001), innovative coalitions should support "an extended process of social learning" and challenge "value fundamentalism" that can undermine the compromises and negotiations needed to build broad networks of civic engagement.

For networks in civil society to promote social learning, individuals need public spaces in which they can articulate their beliefs, hear other points of view, and negotiate their differences—exchanges that can be quite profound. All the stakeholders in the Massachusetts Coalition agreed on the need for highly qualified teachers in city schools, for example, but in fact had very different opinions about what actually constitutes teacher quality. Nor did we agree on how student learning should be assessed. Were we willing to focus on raising student test scores in our partnering schools? While some of us accepted standardized test scores as valid and reliable ways of measuring student learning gains, others were cautious, if not cynical, about the value of such tests.

In addition to questions of definition, we all had to negotiate a host of issues raised by the grant. Would the grant pull some of the best faculty out of our higher education institutions and make them less accessible to our own students who were paying expensive tuitions in our colleges and universities? Would the grant, by pulling talented teachers out of urban classrooms and "promoting" them into administrative roles in the Coalition, unintentionally cull some of the best urban teachers out of high-need schools, at least in terms of the daily contact between pupils and teachers? By emphasizing school partnerships, would the grant inadvertently undermine the research mission of the university and thereby reinforce the already poor image that many arts and sciences faculty have of their peers in schools of education? We had aspirations that the Coalition be as democratic as possible, but the Principal Investigator was ultimately accountable for how money was spent. How could we adjudicate conflicts when they arose, especially when no consensus could be found among decision makers?

These problems were addressed but not resolved in the grant-writing phase in the summer of 1999. The writers' group did assemble and submit a fifty-page proposal to the Department of Education. The proposal emphasized six separate goals: 1) increase the participation of arts and sciences faculty in teacher education to ensure strong content knowledge for beginning teachers; 2) expand the school and community-based nature of teacher education to provide greater practical, field-based experiences as part of teacher preparation; 3) organize broad-based "communities of inquiry and practice" among school, university, business, and community stakeholders to inform teacher education; 4) improve instruction in literacy across the content areas both in teacher education and in our partnering public schools; 5) recruit, train, and retain cohorts of ethnically diverse beginning teachers; and 6) promote the Coalition's capacity to conduct research and inform public policy on issues of teacher quality. The proposal explicitly emphasized the role of arts and sciences faculty in teacher education and advocated a stronger community-based role for teacher education.

The Coalition's proposal was approved in September 1999; however, the initial request for a budget of $15 million was cut to $7 million. Given the funding reduction, we considered whether to cut back on some of our objectives—reducing the total of six to four, for example. While there was a general sense that reducing the ambitiousness of the Coalition would make sense in light of the funding realities, we were unable to settle on one or two objectives to be cut. In spite of the many problems identified above, we remained hopeful that we would be able to play a role in improving teacher education and placing highly qualified teachers in Boston, Springfield, and Worcester.

THE CHALLENGES

Political scientists, economists, and sociologists have explored the arena of collaborations between different institutional stakeholders, variously called "interorganization domains," "resource exchange networks," "social partnerships," or "interorganizational fields." These studies map out the origins, development, regularities, and kinds of assessments that are appropriate when organizations with very different cultures attempt to collaborate (Sarason and Lorentz, 1979; Waddock, 1989; Warren, 1967), information that is helpful in identifying and articulating the host of problems created when institutions as disparate as urban public schools and higher education institutions—or as fluid and politically disenfranchised as urban "communities"—attempt to form coalitions or networks. This section describes some of the challenges of the Massachusetts Coalition, drawing upon interorganizational research to illuminate the deeper nature of these dilemmas.

Once the funding arrived, the Coalition had to establish a stable organizational structure that could serve for the five years of the grant. We settled on seven different partnerships; each would match a higher education institution with at least one and perhaps as many as five urban schools. Tom Payzant, the Boston Superintendent of Schools, asked the Boston-based higher education institutions to limit their collaborating schools to one or two at most, hoping that a concentration of resources in single buildings would yield better results than a more scattershot approach. Each of the seven partnerships would receive one-eighth of the Coalition budget each year, with another eighth set aside for Coalition-wide activities, such as conferences and the salary of a full-time Coalition manager. In addition to the Principal Investigator, the leader of each partnership was designated a "co-PI," with fiscal responsibility for his or her partnership.

The writers' group evolved into a Steering Committee, with representation from each of the seven partnerships. Although each partnership ideally would have sent a delegation of higher education faculty, teachers, and community members, in reality Steering Committee meetings were primarily comprised of education faculty from the writers' group. In large part, this was due to differences in teachers' and professors' work schedules; it also evidenced the problems inherent in organizing a statewide coalition. Few teachers were willing to attend Steering Committee meetings after work, especially if it required travel, and a shortage of substitute teachers, as well as other institutional constraints, made it difficult for teachers to attend meetings during the day. On the other hand, arts and sciences faculty from higher education institutions were disinclined to join the Steering Committee, viewing the work of the Coalition as unrelated to their teaching interests and research specializations.

When higher education institutions receive a grant, funders typically designate the grant by the lead institution's name, such as "the Boston College grant" in this case. Such nomenclature makes it sound as if the higher education institution has endorsed the purposes of the grant. On one hand, the endorsement is genuine, especially as research universities are increasingly manifesting "academic capitalism" and a keen sense for the financial benefits to be accrued through successful grants (Slaughter and Leslie, 1997). On the other hand, the endorsement is superficial, and the deeper transformations called for by a grant can meet with tenacious resistance, especially when they challenge deeply held institutional prejudices. At the same time, some faculty use a grant to pursue their prior initiatives and interests, exploiting benefits, such as course releases, stipends, or summer salary, but make no real contribution to the grant's purpose.

In the Massachusetts Coalition, these paradoxes and contradictions were acted out many times with infinite variations. A faculty member who was a principal investigator or co-PI and who had some expertise in issues of teaching and learning had perforce to evolve into a fiscal manager, institutional arbiter, and political street fighter. Although grants nominally are intended to reinforce and help focus faculty activities, the on-the-ground reality is far more complex. Economists refer to these complications as "transaction costs" that can undermine the efficacy of an organization and, if not dealt with, can ultimately destroy it. How should money be divided up? What projects within a partnership should be funded and which should be turned aside? In schools, how does one explain why one teacher is chosen to become an on-site coordinator, while others are not? In higher education institutions, how does one explain to a colleague why his or her proposal cannot be funded by the grant, but one initiated by a school or community-based organization can be? Some partnerships hired full-time parent liaisons to work in schools, who asked questions and agitated institutional cultures in ways that were not always welcomed by teachers or principals. These issues go to the core of an institution's culture and of individuals' sense of control of their workplace. If not handled well, coalitions can undermine collegiality and inadvertently subvert the idea of collaborations between schools, universities, and communities.

None of these dilemmas were addressed in the grant proposal, but the grant brought all of them with it in its wake. Out of these ambiguities, a host of further problems emerged. Peter Marris and Martin Rein (1982) have observed that the dynamics of collective action require all groups to balance concerns of *participation, action,* and *research.* Although the Coalition never formulated its activities in such terms, they are useful for examining our evolution. The Steering Committee, for example, was concerned from the beginning that we did not have sufficient participation from teachers or community members. Given the research (Cuban and Usdan, 2003; Shirley, 1997; Stone et al., 2001) that indicates that broad-based networks of civic engagement are indispensable to successful urban school reform, this preoccupation with the logic of participation was well placed. Further, Marris and Rein emphasize that coalitions cannot simply convene; rather, they must *act* if they are to garner credibility and be effective. As will be shown below, the Coalition undertook a wide range of interventions that meet the criterion of action in school and university settings. The Coalition was successful in researching its work, both internally and through an external agency (Abt Associates of Cambridge, Massachusetts).

Participation in the Coalition was stressful. Many Coalition leaders received no release time from other aspects of their work from their schools or higher education institutions; rather, Coalition activities constituted high-stakes and uncompensated supplementary work. As Andy Hargreaves (1994) has shown, this sort of intensification in the area of school improvement is often self-generated by educators, who possess ambiguous professional identities, are values-driven, and given to self-abnegation. At the same time, one must note that intensification has its rewards in terms of the logic of action. At numerous conferences, summer institutes, workshops, and Steering Committee meetings, for example, Coalition members often—not always, but often—experienced a sense of fulfillment based on the conviction that their engagement was truly making a difference in preparing high quality teachers to serve in urban school contexts.

The challenges identified above are typical of the dilemmas faced when individuals attempt to create new settings along complex interorganizational lines. Ideally, each group of stakeholders brings their unique strengths to the new setting—in this case, the Coalition. Ideally, colleges and universities bring tremendous reservoirs of intellectual talent; public schools bring personnel who are drawn to teaching out of idealism and who serve working-class and immigrant children of color in the face of widespread social skepticism; and diverse urban communities that are protean and bring enormous reserves of untapped leadership potential. However, as Howell Baum (2000) has noted, this ideal vision can be counterproductive if it is not balanced with a realistic appreciation of the tremendous obstacles to coalition building. For example, school-university partnerships can include higher education institutions with dubious track records regarding support for school reform, urban school systems that have generally failed to educate the youths in their charge to the minimal levels of competence required to earn a living wage in a globalizing economy, and urban communities that are impoverished and unsure of how to access and influence power in the schools their children attend. Tremendous political skills are required to hold coalitions together given the many human frailties that mitigate against collaboration.

As if the problems of coalition building and interorganizational development were not daunting enough, the larger context of urban school politics is strewn with legacies of failed programs and shattered dreams. For whatever reasons—failure of public will, breakdowns at the level of implementation, factionalism, bureaucratic resistance, racism, or sustained assaults by advocates of privatization—urban schools as currently constituted find few champions and consistently generate low student-learning outcomes. Nor are reform efforts immune from criticism: teachers resent "reform du jour" impositions by outcomes-driven administrators; parents feel disconnected and alienated from efforts that ignore community desires for participation in school improvement; and the urban communities of color who should be served by the schools find that allegedly race-neutral measures such as teacher tests have a devastating effect on the recruitment of teachers of color into the profession (Hargreaves, 1994; Oakes et al., 2000; National Research Council, 2001; Stone et al., 2001). Seymour Sarason (1995) has warned that most school reformers who seek to build coalitions have "a catastrophically oversimplified notion of what they are up against" (p. 59). Given this context, simply the act of building a broad-based coalition that perdures over many years, brings together disparate stakeholders, and keeps public attention focused on the garnering of small victories over time should be interpreted as a major achievement. The art of coalition building would appear to lie in identifying assets possessed by the full range of coalition stakeholders and bringing these into new ensembles of productive learning, while mindfully recognizing and working through the multiple barriers to change.

Despite the complexity of the dilemmas that faced the Coalition, the number of self-interested actors opposed to change, and the uncertain nature of outcomes from our activities, I nonetheless submit that the Coalition has been highly productive in its first four years and has subtly begun reshaping the culture of urban education and higher education in Massachusetts. As an example of a way in which community organizing traditions can benefit school and university partnership work, consider the following case study of parent organizing in an urban high school.

PARENT ENGAGEMENT AT LEWES HIGH

Boston College has for many years collaborated with schools in what is now called "Cluster V" of the Boston Public Schools. These schools are concentrated in the northwest segment of the city known as Allston-Brighton, one of the nine largest neighborhoods in Boston and home to roughly 30,000 people. One urban high school, Lewes High (a pseudonym), serves roughly 1,200 students. Of these, approximately 27 percent come from Allston-Brighton; the other 73 percent are bused in from the other neighborhoods and many of the pupils travel for more than an hour each way on public transportation. Sixty-five percent of the students qualify for free or reduced-price lunches; because of the high poverty level, the entire school receives Title I funding.

As part of my work with the Massachusetts Coalition, in the fall of 2001 I began teaching my classes on-site at Lewes High, which served as a site for masters-degree level teacher candidates and doctoral students to study instruction, curriculum, and assessment issues. In addition, leaders from community-based organizations such as the Dudley Street Neighborhood Initiative, the Boston Parents Organizing Network, and the Greater Boston Interfaith Organization (the local Alinsky organization) spoke to my classes about their efforts to strengthen school and community relationships. The initial period of relationship building entailed learning about the culture of the school and its many strengths and challenges; in terms of community organizing it corresponded to the initial phase of "one-on-one" meetings and "research actions" deployed by Alinsky organizers.

Roughly two-thirds of the way through this school and university "courtship," in April 2002, the headmaster and faculty at Lewes High asked if Boston College would participate in a day of professional development activities planned for the school. The district's "whole-school improvement plan" was to include a strategy for working with parents and community members, but the school was at a loss as to how to build these relationships. Although Lewes High previously had a parent liaison, the funding had expired and the position had been terminated. The location of the school, far from where the majority of students lived, was another obstacle to close school and community ties. Parent participation in Parents' Night activities was low—generally below 150 each fall—and teachers sensed that they had failed to build appropriate bridges to communicate with parents.

Over thirty Boston College faculty and administrators agreed to work with the school on the professional development initiative; they listened to teachers' frustration and anger about low levels of parent engagement in the school. Teachers were especially irate that although over 40 percent of their students had a grade point average below 1.65 and thus were disqualified from sports, clubs, and holding class offices, few parents asked about the academic status of their children. As I listened to the teachers, I wondered if this discontent could be shifted away from attacking the parents and toward developing civic capacity between teachers and parents.

Over the summer I worked with the headmaster, teachers, parents, and community-based organizations at the school to develop an action plan for increasing parent engagement. I teach a graduate class on the "Social Contexts of Education" each fall on-site at the school and, in collaboration with the Lewes High faculty, agreed to explore the possibility of linking that class with some yet-to-be developed parent engagement strategies. Together, we decided to see if the class could play a role in promoting greater parent engagement at the November Parents' Night.

In September, the Social Context class convened weekly in the Career Services Library of Lewes High and interviewed teachers, students, and parents to learn about multiple facets of the Lewes High pupils' lives relevant to education. The teacher candidates also studied research on community organizing, parent involvement, urban education, and multicultural education, and brought questions generated by the readings to the class' engagement with the organizing process. Grant funds from the Massachusetts Coalition provided tuition for four teachers from the school to take the class, and those teachers educated the entire Social Context class, including the professor, on the real challenges (as well as the significant victories) they experienced on a day-to-day basis in school.

At the same time, a Boston College-based team began meeting with teachers, parents, and representatives of community-based organizations to plan the Parents' Night activities in November. Targeting the Parents' Night as a priority months in advance was a first for the school, which had previously waited until November to set the date for Parents' Night. Throughout the fall, a broad base of teachers and community activists were brought in to coordinate strategies for the Parents' Night and to lay the groundwork for a long-term parent engagement component for the school's "whole-school improvement plan."

Much of this work was tenuous and difficult. Although many of the day-to-day routines of teaching and learning at Lewes High operate smoothly, sporadic incidents related to violence, drug-dealing, or truancy will intermittently deflect the school from its academic focus. Michelle Fine (1994, p. 30) has commented on the high level of "communitarian damage" experienced by urban high schools due to years of disappointing student achievement outcomes on one hand and bureaucratic intractability from central administrations on the other (p. 23).

Throughout the fall, a small cadre of teachers from Lewes High, led by those taking the class, nurtured relationships with parents, primarily through extensive telephone calls, as well as mailings and notifications sent home with pupils. Those notifications were primarily in English, but Spanish and Portuguese translations were also prepared. A parent liaison working with GEAR

UP, a federally funded college preparatory program, made phone calls to the Spanish-speaking parents to keep them abreast of developments.

We also planned to use Parents' Night to survey parent opinions about Lewes High and to solicit their ideas about ways to improve school and community ties. I chair the Community Engagement Task Force of UNITE (Urban Networks to Improve Teacher Education), a national network of higher education faculty, teachers, administrators, parents, and community activists, which had developed a survey that would measure not simply *parent involvement* (in which parents help reach goals already established by the school) but a more robust sense of *parent engagement* (in which parents develop civic leadership and fuse the school's academic goals with broader community concerns) (see Shirley, 1997, p. 73). The students in the Social Context class agreed to approach parents at the fall Parents' Night and ask them to complete the survey, either while they were waiting to meet with a teacher or between activities. Spanish-speaking students in the class would translate the survey for parents so that their perspectives could be solicited.

Given the themes of parent engagement and civic capacity that emerged during the planning process, the planning group worked to include a broad array of community-based organizations in the Parents' Night activities; a wide variety of organizations were contacted and became part of the planning team. The plan for Parents' Night evolved into a "Community Fair," where organizations could inform parents about their activities and solicit participation in work related to youth development, health services, and community organization. Part of the school's cafeteria, where parents would be receiving their children's fall semester report cards, would be turned over to the community groups, whose services would be offered alongside the food and drinks set out for the parents.

When Parents' Night finally arrived, attendance rose from 145 in 2001 to 231 in 2002—an increase of 59 percent. Although the increase might seem small, given the effort that went into recruitment and student enrollment, the faculty, parents, and teacher candidates were delighted. Teachers who had worked in the school for years reported that the turnout was the highest they had ever seen; some had lines of parents waiting outside their classrooms, a sight that none of the teachers had previously experienced in the school.

Where did the "iron rule" fit into this organizing effort? The significance of the work at Lewes High School is not that parent participation in Parents' Night rose, although that was an important first step. More important is that school faculty, parents, and Boston College teacher candidates learned that they could change the culture of a school and collaborate to raise parent participation. The critical contribution of the iron rule was the development of local leadership capacity. My role, and that of the Boston College teacher candidates, was supportive: we convened meetings, researched the topic, met with parents and students to gain their perspectives, and kept the parent engagement theme on the school's agenda, but the critical work of directly contacting the parents and developing their capacity was done by the Lewes High School community of teachers, staff, and parents.

The selection of the fall Parent Night as a target for raising parent participation also proved to be a "winnable issue" in the sense used by the IAF, referring not to a spectacular triumph but to a cultural shift. After the fall Parents' Night, the collective sensibility that low parent participation was a "naturalized" part of the school culture was disrupted. Teachers saw that parents could and would come to the Parents' Night, given sufficient prior notification, phone calls at home, and hand-outs to students. The theory behind Alinsky organizing is that the sense that things *can* be different is tremendously important to leadership development—and that this understanding is far more important than mere parent turn-out, programmatic changes, or other objective outcomes.

The parent engagement work at Lewes High is only beginning. In January 2003, teachers, parents, and activists in community-based organizations formed a Parent Engagement Task Force to develop long-term strategies for enhancing parents' roles in the high school. The independent convening of this group indicates that Lewes High did indeed "own" the issue and is now driving it forward on its own accord—exactly the outcome that one should want as the result of an organizing effort. It is at this juncture that external partners—whether community organizers (as in the case of Alinsky organizers) or university faculty (as in the case at hand) should either recede or should shift their attention to other facets of community organizing.

At the microlevel, the experimental design of the class in the Social Contexts of Education—organized around a Lewes High faculty-identified priority—appeared successful. Student evaluations were overwhelmingly positive, although some students clearly found the unpredictability entailed in working with a large urban school around community engagement daunting. Many had specific ideas for improving the Parents' Night—providing a map of the building, having individuals on hand to help parents understand report cards, or separating more distinctly the distribution of report cards from the more festive information booths about community-based groups—that have been submitted to the Parent Engagement Task Force and may prompt modifications in the future. In a final survey of the students, all twenty-nine agreed that the class should continue to be taught on-site at Lewes High, and twenty-eight agreed that the class should "continue to link Lewes High School goals with Social Contexts curricula."

CONCLUSION

Partnership work in the arena of school reform is demanding. Nonetheless, despite the many problems generated by interorganization collaboration and large-scale coalition building, much good can be accomplished, as the above case study illustrates. Even with the irrationalities evidenced in the garbage-can model of policy formation and working under conditions of high-reverberation policy subsystems and interorganizational turbulence, coalitions can create positive outcomes. The community organizing tradition of the IAF, with its emphasis upon the iron rule, winnable issues, and active listening, provides one useful strand of a broad-based and efficacious political strategy for school reform that can be appropriated by teacher educators, teachers, and community activists to improve urban education. Flexible leadership, respect for interorganizational ecologies, an inventive use of financial resources, clarity of vision, and leading by one's example are also critical components of civic capacity. Hence, partnership work, as it has evolved in the last fifteen years, does have a role to play in improving both urban education and teacher education.

The origins and trajectory of the Massachusetts Coalition do not offer any panaceas for school reformers, teacher educators, or community stakeholders. Urban school reform work is demanding and turbulent, and changes can never be easily transplanted from one context to another. On the other hand, by demonstrating the feasibility of a broad-based school, university, and community partnership in uncertain times, the Massachusetts Coalition has become a powerful force for change in the politics of educational reform in the Commonwealth.

REFERENCES

Alinsky, S. D. (1946). *Reville for radicals.* New York: Vintage.

Alinsky, S. D. (1971). *Rules for radicals: A pragmatic primer for realistic radicals.* New York: Vintage.

Anyon, J. (1997). *Ghetto schooling: A political economy of urban educational reform.* New York: Teachers College Press.

Baum, H. S. (2000). Realities and fantasies of university-community partnerships. *Journal of Planning Education and Research, 20,* 234–246.

Best, S., & Kellner, D. (1991). *Postmodern theory: Critical interrogations.* New York: Guilford.

Bowles, S., and Gintis, H. (1976). *Schooling in capitalist America: Educational reform and the contradictions of economic life.* New York: Basic Books.

Cohen, M. D., March, J. G., & Olsen, J. P. (1988). A garbage can model of organizational choice. In J. G. March (Ed.), *Decisions and organizations* (pp. 294–334). New York: Basil Blackwell.

Cuban, L., & Usdan, M. (2003). *Powerful reforms with shallow roots: Improving America's urban schools.* New York: Teachers College Press.

de Tocqueville, A. (1969). *Democracy in America.* Garden City, NY: Anchor Books.

Fine, M. (1994). *Chartering urban school reform: Reflections on public schools in the midst of change.* New York: Teachers College Press.

Goode, J., & Maskovsky, J. (2001). *The new poverty studies: The ethnography of power, politics, and impoverished people in the United States.* New York: New York University Press.

Hargeaves, A. (1994). *Changing teachers, changing times: Teachers' work and culture in the postmodern age.* New York: Teachers College Press.

Kozol, J. (1991). *Savage inequalities: Children in America's schools.* New York: Crown Press.

Marris, P., & Rein, M. (1982). *Dilemmas of social reform: Poverty and community action in the United States* (2nd Ed.). Chicago: University of Chicago Press.

Massey, D. S., & Denton, N. A. (1993). *American apartheid: Segregation and the making of the underclass.* Cambridge: Harvard University Press.

Murnane, R. J., & Levy, F. (1997). *Teaching the new basic skills: Principles for educating children to thrive in a changing economy.* New York: Free Press.

Murrell, P. C., Jr. (2001). *The community teacher: A new framework for effective urban teaching.* New York: Teachers College Press.

National Research Council. (2001). *Testing teacher candidates: The role of licensure tests in improving teacher quality.* Washington, D.C.: National Academy Press.

Oakes, J., Quartz, K. H., Ryan, S., & Lipton, M. (2000). *Becoming good American schools: The struggle for civic virtue in education reform.* San Francisco: Jossey-Bass.

Osterman, P. (2002). *Gathering power: The future of progressive politics in America.* Boston: Beacon Press.

Reich, R. (1992). *The work of nations.* New York: Vintage.

Sarason, S. B. (1995). *School change: The personal development of a point of view.* New York: Teachers College Press.

Sarason, S. B. (2002). *Educational reform: A self-scrutinizing memoir.* New York: Teachers College Press.

Sarason, S. B., & Lorentz, E. (1979). *The challenge of the Resource Exchange Network.* San Francisco: Jossey-Bass.

Shirley, D. (1997). *Community organizing for urban school reform.* Austin: University of Texas Press.

Shirley, D. (2002). *Valley interfaith and school reform: Organizing for power in south Texas.* Austin: University of Texas Press.

Sirianni, C., & Friedland, L. (2001). *Civic innovation in America: Community empowerment, public policy, and the movement for civic renewal.* Berkeley: University of California Press.

Slaughter, S., and Leslie, L. L. (1997). *Academic capitalism: Politics, policies, and the entrepeneurial university.* Baltimore: Johns Hopkins University Press.

Stone, C. N., Henig, J. R., Jones, B. D., & Pierannunzi, C. (2001). *Building civic capacity: The politics of reforming urban schools.* Lawrence: University Press of Kansas.

Teitel, L. (2003). *The professional development schools handbook: Starting, sustaining, and assessing partnerships that improve student learning.* Thousand Oaks, CA: Corwin.

Texas Interfaith Education Fund. (1990). *The Texas IAF vision for public schools: Communities of learners.* Austin: unpublished ms.

Valli, L., Cooper, D., & Frankels, L. (1997) Professional development schools and equity: A critical analysis of rhetoric and research. In M. W. Apple (Ed.), *Review of research in education: Vol. 22* (pp. 251–304). Washington, DC: American Educational Research Association.

Waddock, S. A. (1989). Understanding social partnerships: An evolutionary model of partnership organizations. *Administration and Society, 21*(1), 78–100.

Warren, R. L. (1967). The interorganizational field as a focus for investigation. *Administrative Science Quarterly, 12,* 396–419.

Wilson, W. J. (1987) *The truly disadvantaged: The inner city, the underclass, and public policy.* Chicago: University of Chicago Press.

University Partnerships for Parent Empowerment

12 Giving Voice to Urban Parents: Using a Community-Based Survey to Leverage School Reform

Lauri Johnson

Lauri Johnson, Assistant Professor in Educational Leadership and Policy at the State University of New York at Buffalo, describes how a partnership of parents, community activists, and university faculty created a community survey to assess parent perceptions of their children's schools and their views on parent involvement and good schooling in a high poverty, urban school district, and how the survey sparked other projects that involved parents in school district reform.

PARENT INVOLVEMENT HAS BEEN identified as a critical element in the improvement of urban schools by teachers, administrators, policy makers, and researchers (Comer, Ben-Avie, Haynes, & Joyner, 1999; Sanders, 1999). Educators who aim to increase parent involvement often uncritically adopt well-known national models (Epstein, 1995) or design local outreach programs for parents. This top-down approach to involving parents in the life of the school assumes that as educators we understand parents' perspectives on schooling and their views on parent involvement. As Fine (1993) notes, however, this top-down approach to decision making can result in (ap)parent involvement, where programs designed by others fail to authentically involve parents or to challenge existing power relations at the individual school site and the district level.

Studies about parent involvement have often focused on either descriptions or evaluations of actual parent involvement programs and the processes through which these programs were developed and/or implemented (e.g., Cochran & Henderson, 1986). Similarly, efforts to assess parents' views about urban school reform have also been limited, often focusing on parent support for specific reform proposals. For instance, surveys have been conducted to assess urban parents' views concerning magnet schools (Smrekar & Goldring, 1999), school choice (Wells & Crain, 1992), charter schools (Becker, Nakagawa, & Corwin, 1997), vouchers (Morken & Formicola, 1999), desegregation efforts (Wells & Crain, 1997), and the racial achievement gap (Public Education Network, 2001).

This mother on the lower west side has four children in the Buffalo Public Schools, one in a bilingual early childhood center, two in a bilingual elementary school, and one at a "academically selective" high school. Her vision of good schooling includes a school with adequate and current books, "art and music for every grade and every child," smaller classes, and good communication between parents and teachers. She would like the school district to provide additional programs that would benefit single and working parents, such as a program for latchkey children and a mentoring program for single mothers. Her view of good schooling approaches the notion of a "full service" school, one that provides after-school tutoring programs and summer enrichment. She is also concerned about the unequal distribution of resources between schools and feels that children of color are under-represented in the academically selective magnet schools.

—Parent Survey Responses from
The Parent Partnership Report:
Parent Perceptions of the
Schools We Have, the Schools We Need

There have been few open-ended attempts to examine how urban parents view parent involvement and to give voice to their concerns about their children's schooling as part of a conscious strategy for urban school reform. The importance of listening and documenting urban parents' views is under-scored by long-term ethnographic studies that have demonstrated that parents who are poor or working class or from diverse racial and cultural backgrounds may have different notions about parent involvement than white, middle-class educators (see e.g., Lareau, 2000; Macias & Garcia Ramos, 1995;Valdes, 1996).

Listening to urban parents' concerns and documenting their visions of good schooling also provides an avenue for the involvement of parents in the "public engagement" aspect of school reform. Public engagement holds out the promise that school reforms are more likely to succeed if the public's concerns are heard and addressed (Farkas, Foley, & Duffet, 2001). The hope is that by inviting diverse stakeholders (e.g., parents, teachers, administrators, community members) to have more say in what schools should look like, support and commitment for urban public schools will increase.

This chapter examines the question: How might an open-ended parent survey designed by a coalition of parent advocacy groups give voice to diverse parents' concerns and create public spaces for dialogue and deliberation by parents, teachers, administrators, and community members about the schools we have and the schools we need (Katz, Fine, & Simon, 1997)? I begin by describing how a partnership of parents, community activists, and university faculty implemented a democratic, grassroots survey in a high poverty, urban school district to assess parent perceptions of their children's schools and their views on parent involvement and good schooling. The results of the parent survey are summarized, as well as the responses of the participants about the development and implementation of the survey. Finally I discuss how the process of collaborating on the parent survey jumpstarted several other parent involvement projects and public engagement efforts to dialogue about urban school reform.

THE CONTEXT—SCHOOL REFORM IN BUFFALO

Buffalo is a mid-sized urban school district in New York State comprised of approximately 43,000 students. The racial composition of the student population is 57.8 percent African American, 27.7 percent white, 11.8 percent Hispanic/Latino, and 2.7 percent other (including Native American, Asian, and Arab students.) The poverty rate district-wide is high—over 74 percent of the students qualify for free or reduced school lunches (New York State District Report Card, 2003). The last district-wide school reform efforts took place in the late 1970s, when several magnet schools and early childhood centers were created as part of a court-ordered desegregation plan. In 1999 the district was declared unitary and the school district removed race and gender as selection criteria for placement in the magnet school programs. In practice, some of the magnet schools are perceived by parents as more prestigious and desirable than others, particularly two high schools and three elementary schools that require entrance tests and accept primarily "academically successful" students. As an African American father remarked at a recent public meeting when a district-wide choice plan was unveiled in Buffalo, "It sounds like the haves and the have-nots."

Interviews with parent activists date recent parent organizing in the Buffalo Public Schools to the "parent walkout" that occurred a few years ago. In an effort to meet the statewide mandate for district site-based decision making, in the spring of 1996 Buffalo's new Superintendent formed a District Stakeholders' Committee. This committee contained several parents who had been active in local parent-teacher groups as well as principals, teachers, and union officials. Audra Wood (pseudonym), an African American parent on the Committee, reported that parents quickly became frustrated because district officials, building-level administrators, and union representatives held a different perception of what constituted "authentic" parent involvement. As she described it,

> They wanted to define parental involvement for us. For instance, although it is the superintendent's (decision) to put whomever he likes on the negotiating committee of the unions, the unions kept telling us it was against the contract, which we knew it was not. They didn't want us involved in those big decisions. . . . Hiring, budgets, all those decisions that made an impact, parents were not to be involved in.

After a year and a half of meetings, in the winter of 1998 fourteen of the sixteen parents on the District Stakeholders' Committee met and decided to resign en masse to protest the district's failure to include parents in a meaningful way in district decision making. The walkout made the front page of the local newspaper. Shortly afterwards some of these parents formed an independent organization called Parents for Public Schools (see description below) to advocate for increased parent involvement in the Buffalo schools.

HISTORY OF THE PARENT PARTNERSHIP

Two key events in the spring of 1999 coalesced attention on parent concerns in Buffalo and brought together a consortium of four organizations that would become known as the Parent Partnership. First, the Education Fund for Greater Buffalo (a local education fund described below) received a substantial grant from the Mayor's office to fund projects that would link individual schools and their nonprofit partners to increase parent involvement in the schools. Julie Murphy (pseudonym) described the response of the community:

> When everybody found out that we had this money to devote to parents there was an immediate rush by a number of organizations . . . telling us about the kinds of parent work they could do. Few (of the organizations) were grass roots . . . it made us realize that a lot of these folks didn't really know much about parents, and that we didn't either.

Secondly, as part of a new urban education emphasis in the Graduate School of Education at the University at Buffalo, a citywide Urban Education Dialogue was held that involved fifty-five stakeholders (i.e., parents, community members, teachers, administrators, and university faculty) to identify current issues in the Buffalo schools. At this dialogue, attended by several parent activists, a key concern arose—the need to assess the views of Buffalo parents about their experiences with their children's schools and their views about the type of parent involvement they wanted and needed. Because of the success of this dialogue, the faculty who organized it decided to form an ongoing coalition, which became known as the Coalition for Urban Education (see description below).

In May 1999 the Education Fund for Greater Buffalo brought together several organizations interested in parent involvement to discuss coordination of their efforts and strategies to determine parents' needs. Out of this meeting a consortium known as the Parent Partnership was formed that agreed to jointly conduct a parent needs assessment. A brief description of the four participating organizations in the Parent Partnership follows.

EDUCATION FUND FOR GREATER BUFFALO

A local education fund created in 1998 to raise private sector support for the Buffalo schools, the Ed Fund provides seed money for collaborative projects between individual schools and their community partners that are designed to improve teaching and learning in schools of the greatest need. The Ed Fund has made grants to several Buffalo schools in the areas of family support, parent involvement and student literacy, special education, and workforce preparation, and has staged community focus groups about education and race, parent involvement, and academic standards.

PARENTS FOR PUBLIC SCHOOLS

A local chapter of a national parent organization, PPS is dedicated to supporting and strengthening the public schools through parent involvement. The core group of parents in this organization remain active in their local school parent-teacher organizations but seek a wider decision-making role at the district level. Their organization's informal motto is "No More Bake Sales." They developed a far-ranging parent involvement policy based on Epstein's (1995) model which was formally adopted by the Buffalo School Board in December 1999.

VOICE BUFFALO

A faith-based community organization that seeks to strengthen its member congregations, increase civic participation, and affect fundamental change at the root cause through community organizing, VOICE Buffalo incorporates many of Saul Alinsky's (see Shirley, p. 138) strategies developed to organize and empower low income neighborhoods in Chicago in the 1960s and 1970s. Recent organizing successes in Buffalo have included pressuring city officials to tear down several abandoned crack houses and to provide free garbage cans to all housing units in central city neighborhoods in an effort to control the rodent problem.

COALITION FOR URBAN EDUCATION

Formed by university faculty in the spring of 1999 as part of the university's new urban education focus, the Coalition for Urban Education (CUE) sponsored a series of community-wide dialogues to discuss issues of concern in the Buffalo schools. CUE worked to facilitate communication and cooperation between all urban education stakeholders (i.e., parents, students, teachers, administrators, community and university members) in an effort to improve the Buffalo schools.

SURVEY DEVELOPMENT

The parent survey was developed collaboratively by a committee that included representatives of the four partnership organizations in a series of meetings between June and September 1999. The survey was conceived as a vehicle that would go beyond the district's agenda and provide "a platform for parents to talk about their issues." Questions were drawn from existing parent surveys and the committee members' perceptions of important issues regarding parent participation in the schools. The Education Fund wanted survey questions about parents' awareness of the new statewide standards. Parents for Public Schools lobbied for questions about parent decision making in schools. The Coalition for Urban Education requested that questions about cultural diversity and literacy education be included.

As Julie Murphy from the Ed Fund described it, constructing the survey became a constant "process of negotiation." One prominent debate in the group was whether or not information would be collected about the race and ethnicity of the parents interviewed. Some members of the committee felt it would be insulting to ask parents to identify their race or ethnicity. In Julie's words,

> It was an issue among the partners. You had grassroots organizations, you had foundation-like organizations, you had higher ed institutions—they are just not the same. You negotiate things. In the process of that, afterwards you (say) why did we do that? I remember I really wanted that information (about parents' race). I think it might have been (VOICE Buffalo) that didn't want that. So the data never got collected. You just run into different philosophies.[1]

By the time that everyone's questions were included, the survey had become overly long, and some questions had to be eliminated. The final survey began with four open-ended questions that asked parents what they liked best about their child's school, what concerns they had, their visions of good schooling, and their parental role in their children's education. The survey also included checklists that asked parents to rate their satisfaction or awareness of a variety of issues, including school cleanliness, discipline, respect for cultural diversity, their knowledge of state standards, and their desired involvement in school decisions.

THE COMMUNITY WALK

The plan for administering the survey was unique in the district. VOICE Buffalo had conducted several "community walks" where volunteers survey residents door-to-door in a particular neighborhood about community problems and needs. The Parent Partnership committee decided that the community walk idea could be expanded to survey parents throughout Buffalo, with four headquarters in local churches located in the North, South, East, and West sections of the city that would be led by members of each of the four organizations.

The Parent Partnership hoped that a door-to-door survey would reach parents who wouldn't necessarily come to school or answer a written survey. As Julie Murphy described it,

> When we realized that nobody really knew as much as we'd hoped (about parent involvement), that's when we said we've got to get out there and find out what parents are really thinking. And try to have some contact with parents, just regular folks. And we thought if we went out to their neighborhoods . . . we would get a really broad cross section that way.

Not all of the partners were equally enthusiastic about the parent survey, but they agreed to support the community walk. Audra Wood from Parents for Public Schools expressed her skepticism:

> I'll be quite honest with you. I wasn't that crazy about doing another survey. We've been surveyed to death. Parents are surveyed to death. We've already got information. What are we doing with the information we already have? But I liked (the) concept of going into the neighborhoods and the one-on-one, door-to-door survey. And maybe going into neighborhoods that normally don't get a voice.

INTERVIEWS

Interviewers were recruited by each of the partner organizations and included parent activists, church pastors and priests, graduate students in teacher education, university faculty, and board members from the participating organizations. Some of the volunteers (e.g., several university faculty and some of the graduate students) were experienced interviewers. Others had participated in earlier community walks organized by VOICE Buffalo. The multiracial group of seventy-five interviewers included several who were fluent in Spanish. Interviewers met in the church headquarters on the day of the community walk where they participated in an orientation session conducted by VOICE Buffalo and the Coalition for Urban Education. They reviewed questions on the survey and practiced interviewing each other.

The community walks were conducted on two Saturdays in October 1999. Interviewers traveled door-to-door in teams of two, with one conducting the interview and the other recording parent comments in as much detail as possible. The average interview lasted about twenty minutes, although some interviewers reported that a few interviews lasted over thirty minutes when the parent had lots of "war stories" to tell. Neighborhoods canvassed included several predominately African American areas, a predominately Latino neighborhood, a multiracial working class neighborhood in South Buffalo, and a predominately white middle class neighborhood on the west side of the city.

Because the Buffalo school district had declined to supply lists of parents, interviewers used address lists of households with children generated by a local market research firm. The address lists that were provided often proved inaccurate, however, and interviewers reported relying on a variety of means to determine which households to interview, including noticing "Halloween decorations in the window" and toys in the yard. In the public housing project canvassed, community center workers from the neighborhood accompanied each group of interviewers and introduced them to local households they knew with children. About thirty of the families contacted in various neighborhoods had children in private schools and those surveys were eliminated.

In the final tally, 250 parents of children in the Buffalo Public Schools were interviewed representing 410 school children who attended sixty-two different Buffalo schools. Ten interviews that were conducted in Spanish and several others that included both Spanish and English comments were later translated by a fluent bilingual translator on faculty at the university.

SURVEY RESULTS

Survey results were analyzed both qualitatively and quantitatively by a team of four university researchers, two of whom were associated with the Coalition for Urban Education.[2] Open-ended responses were transcribed and analyzed recursively to identify common themes. Checklists of overall satisfaction, specific areas of concern, and specific areas for increased services and parent involvement were tabulated and statistically analyzed by individual schools and areas of the city.

In an analysis of parents' open-ended comments, patterns of parent satisfaction and dissatisfaction seemed to vary based on the kind of school their children attended. To examine those patterns more closely, the research team conducted another analysis sorting parent responses by the following three groupings: 1) those whose children attended "academically selective" magnet programs; 2) those whose children attended all other elementary/middle schools; and 3) those whose children attended all other high schools. The definitions used for each of these groups follows.

ACADEMICALLY SELECTIVE MAGNET SCHOOLS

This category included two high schools and three elementary school programs in Buffalo that require special testing and teacher recommendations for entry and are commonly characterized by the school district and parents as programs for academically capable students. These schools are among those with the lowest poverty rates of all Buffalo schools. At one of the high schools, only 11 percent of the students qualify for free or reduced school lunches, while at the other high school the rate is 29 percent. In the three elementary programs the number of students who qualify for free or reduced school lunches ranges from 19 percent to 37 percent across the three campuses.

ELEMENTARY/MIDDLE SCHOOLS

The next grouping of parent surveys included all other elementary schools. The poverty index in this grouping was considerably higher than the academically selective magnet schools. The percentage of students who qualified for free and reduced lunches in this grouping generally ranged from 57 percent to 100 percent.

HIGH SCHOOLS

The last grouping included all other high school campuses (other than the two defined here as academically selective) and included both neighborhood and magnet schools. The free and reduced lunch rate in those schools ranged from 46 percent to 62 percent.

Chi-square tests were used to determine if there were significant differences between school types and satisfaction/dissatisfaction rates on overall satisfaction and specific school factors such as information about report cards and test results, teacher responsiveness, and helpfulness of the office staff.

PARENT SATISFACTION (OR LACK OF IT) WITH THE SCHOOLS

About half of the Buffalo parents surveyed (52 percent) reported they were very satisfied with the schools, while 28 percent were somewhat satisfied and 21 percent were somewhat or very dissatisfied. Although the parent partnership survey didn't sample parents randomly, this dissatisfaction rate was similar to Buffalo's ranking on a nationwide Educational Testing Service (ETS) telephone survey on school satisfaction levels across fifty-five metropolitan areas in the U.S. In that random telephone survey of Buffalo residents with at least one child,

Buffalo ranked sixteenth out of the fifty-five cities with a dissatisfaction level of 19 percent. The average rate of dissatisfaction in the ETS survey was about 10 percent (Carnevale & Desrochers, 1999).

Patterns of parent satisfaction varied, however, depending on the type of school their children attended. Parents with children in the academically selective magnet schools were significantly more satisfied with their children's school than other parents, with 95 percent saying they were satisfied or very satisfied. Their satisfaction held across many indicators, including significantly more satisfaction than other parents with teaching and learning (79 percent), teacher responsiveness (62 percent), and student safety (65 percent). These parents reported that their children were academically challenged and encouraged to accept leadership roles.

Parents of high school students, on the other hand, were significantly less satisfied with their children's schools (37 percent were somewhat or very dissatisfied) as compared to other parents. They were significantly more dissatisfied than other parents with information about performance and graduation requirements (36 percent), school safety (30 percent), teaching and learning (28 percent), and teacher responsiveness (24 percent).

SPECIFIC ISSUES AND CONCERNS

On the checklists, parents rated the availability of books and computers as their number one concern (31 percent), followed by the helpfulness and responsiveness of office staff (26 percent), information about performance and graduation requirements (22 percent), student safety (22 percent), and the quality of teaching (19 percent).

In the analysis of the open-ended questions, several themes emerged that pointed to the importance of relationships and communication between teachers and parents and parents' desire for an expanded role for the school in the community.

CONNECTING AND COMMUNICATING WITH TEACHERS/SCHOOLS

In the open-ended responses, parents related the quality of their child's school experience to the quality of their communication and relationships with teachers. The need for schools to be "caring" environments emerged as a major theme. Satisfied parents responded that good communication and caring and concerned teachers were their major sources of satisfaction. The lack of caring relationships with teachers and the lack of responsiveness of the staff and administrators were concerns for some parents, particularly those of high school students, many of whom reported that they were only invited to come to the school when there was a discipline problem with their son or daughter. Dissatisfied parents wanted to be able to "walk into their child's classroom" and desired increased communication between the home and the school.

VIEWS OF PARENT INVOLVEMENT

As Scribner et al. (1999) found in their study of high performing Hispanic schools, many parents in the Buffalo survey cited informal activities at home as the most important contributions they could make as a parent to their children's success in school. In their responses Buffalo parents conceptualized parent involvement as home based and described ways they attempt to support the total well-being of their children. However, many were also interested in being involved in important school decisions such as the selection and evaluation of administrators and teachers (65 percent), what is being taught and how (65 percent), and school budgets (58 percent).

FULL SERVICE SCHOOLS

Some parents also envisioned the need for "full service/community schools" that would be open extended hours and provide services that would benefit the entire family, including social work, counseling, preparation for college, GED classes, parenting classes, English as a second language, and programs to help parents help their children to achieve the new state academic standards.

PARENT PORTRAITS

In an effort to personalize the anonymous survey results and give voice to individual parents, the research team created parent portraits that included selected data and quotes from individual surveys. These portraits, placed throughout the final research report, were used to illustrate particular findings and demonstrate the range of parent responses. A sampling of the parent portraits follows.

PARENT PORTRAIT #1

This parent of a sixth grader who attends a neighborhood elementary school in the east section of Buffalo is generally satisfied with her child's school, commenting that "the teachers and staff act professionally, the school seems well run, and the building is clean and well cared for." Still she wonders if her son's education is "adequate to ground (him) with what he needs—not just to be successful in the job market but as a citizen." She wants her child "to care about his country and to know how it works." In her vision of good schooling she would like to see a more personal relationship between teachers and students, citing that the "teachers seem a bit rushed and focused on performance" and that "kids can get lost in classroom demands."

PARENT PORTRAIT #2

A parent from the south section of the city who has four children in four different schools contrasted her high satisfaction with two of the schools and high dissatisfaction with the other two. She emphasized that children need to feel respected, valued (a respect for cultural differences), and safe (one of her child's school supplies were stolen), and they need a sense of physical well-being (warm food in the school cafeteria, not cold lunches and inflexible menus).

PARENT PORTRAIT #3

This mother on the lower west side has four children in the Buffalo schools, one in a bilingual early childhood center, two in a bilingual elementary school, and one at a academically selective high school. Her vision of good schooling includes a school with adequate and current books, "art and music for every grade and every child," smaller classes, and good communication between parents and teachers. She would like the school district to provide additional programs that would benefit single and working parents, such as a program for latchkey children and a mentoring program for single mothers. Her view of good schooling approaches the notion of a "full service" school, one which provides after-school tutoring programs and summer enrichment. She is also concerned about the unequal distribution of resources between schools and feels that children of color are underrepresented in the academically selective magnet schools.

PARENT PORTRAIT #4

A parent living in the north section of Buffalo has two children in a neighborhood school and one child in an academically selective elementary/middle school. She is very satisfied with both schools her children attend but believes that her child in the academically selective school is "made to think independently," is challenged with projects, and that the school "pushes kids into leadership."

USING SURVEY DATA TO LEVERAGE SCHOOL REFORM

A report of the survey findings was distributed to every school in Buffalo and presented at a citywide Principals Meeting and a Buffalo School Board meeting in June 2000 (Miller, Johnson, & Truesdale, 2000). Even the presentation of the report was collaborative. Members of the four organizations took responsibility for presenting different sections of the report, and several parents stood up in the audience and read parent portraits as part of the presentation.

Shortly after the report was presented a new superintendent was appointed when the former superintendent's contract was not renewed following a public controversy concerning mismanagement of funds by his business officials. In part to restore public confidence, the new superintendent (and the

Board of Education president) initiated an independent study of the Buffalo school system by the Council for Great City Schools. Their report, which recommended sweeping changes in the governance and decision-making structure of the Buffalo district, referenced the Parent Partnership survey in their recommendations for greater parent participation in the district.

Although the Parent Partnership unofficially disbanded after the survey, the four participating organizations continued to work together on specific parent involvement projects. Their collaboration on the parent survey helped to jumpstart several initiatives in parent involvement and public engagement in Buffalo.

The Coalition for Urban Education sponsored four additional Urban Education dialogues. The findings of the Parent Partnership Survey were presented at a community-wide dialogue in the spring of 2000 and teachers, parents, community members, and university faculty generated action plans to increase parent involvement in the schools. In the fall of 2000, a community dialogue on reforming teacher education to respond to the needs of urban schools was attended by the deans and faculty members of several local colleges and universities. In March 2001, parents, teachers, school officials, and community members met to discuss the recommendations of the Council for Great City Schools' recommendations for the Buffalo schools. In the spring of 2002, the Coalition for Urban Education joined with Parents for Public Schools to stage a day-long dialogue on the creation of democratically organized "small schools" in Buffalo.

Some of the graduate students who participated in the community walk became active members of the Coalition for Urban Education (see Lauricella, p. 121) and helped plan and facilitate the Urban Dialogues. Having developed a reputation as a "hot ticket" in Buffalo, the community dialogues were attended by school district leaders, several school board members, and city officials as well as parents, community members, teachers, and university faculty.

Parent activists from Parents for Public Schools enlisted the assistance of the other partnership organizations to press the district for implementation of the new Parent Involvement Policy. They received a national grant to provide leadership training for parents to become active members of the school site-based management teams.

The Education Fund for Greater Buffalo applied for and received a grant to hire parent liaisons and create parent centers in several local schools. When questioned about the impact of the Community Walk, Julie Murphy acknowledged that the survey findings informed their thinking about the parent liaison program. She describes the parent survey as part of a "blossoming" of change in the school district:

> I think this is an organic process . . . we fall into this business management thinking . . . (that) it's all linear and this leads into this. But there's a point where (one) thing happens and that thing happens, and (something) over here. And (there is) a blossoming of something new (in parent involvement). I think the community walk was a part of that.

Members of VOICE Buffalo worked with the Coalition for Urban Education on a literacy and parent empowerment project (funded through the Education Fund) at a local school to develop "powerful literacy" to empower parents and their children to "read the word and the world" (see Finn, Johnson, Finn, p. 193). They used the results of the parent survey and excerpts from parent interviews in their workshops to help parents think critically about parent involvement and the issues in their own school that they would like to change.

CONCLUSION

Calls for greater partnerships between schools and communities, particularly in urban areas, target parent involvement in schools as a critical component for student success. Yet many top-down approaches to parent involvement fail to create either involvement or ownership by parents. This bottom-up, democratic approach to the development and implementation of a parent survey enlisted parents and community members as collaborative partners in the needs assessment process, facilitated community dialogue about school reform, and served as a catalyst for school change projects in a bureaucratic urban school system. Buffalo's Parent Partnership models a collaborative process by which parents, community members, and university faculty can join together to create authentic parent participation and give voice to parent needs and concerns. The Parent Partnership may have ended, but the dialogue about how to improve Buffalo's schools continues through the collaborative networks and relationships that were established in the process.

NOTES

1. I have contacted several interviewers to question them verbally about the race of the parents they interviewed to get a general sense of the racial and ethnic composition of the survey respondents. Based on the responses of the interviewers and the survey organizers, I would estimate the racial composition of the families interviewed is fairly representative of the Buffalo Public School student population as a whole.

2. My sincere thanks and acknowledgement to all the volunteers who participated in the community walk and to the other members of the research team (Suzanne M. Miller, Kim Truesdale, and Sue Gerber) who worked collaboratively to analyze the survey results and write the research report that summarized the survey findings.

REFERENCES

Anderson, G. (1998). Toward authentic participation: Deconstructing the discourse of participatory reforms in education. *American Educational Research Journal, 35,* 571–603.

Becker, H., Nakagawa, K., & Corwin, R. (1997). Parental involvement in contracts in California charter schools: Strategy for educational improvement or method of exclusion? *Teachers College Record, 98,* 511–536.

Carnevale, A. P., & Desrochers, D. M. (1999). *School satisfaction: A statistical profile of cities and suburbs.* Princeton, NJ: Educational Testing Service.

Cochran, M., & Henderson, C. (1986). *Family matters: Evaluation of the parental empowerment program.* Ithaca, NY: Cornell University Press.

Comer, J. P., Ben-Avie, M., Haynes, N. M., & Joyner, E. T. (1999). *Child by child: The Comer process for change in education.* New York: Teachers College Press.

Epstein, J. L. (1995). School/family/community partnerships: Caring for the children we share. *Phi Delta Kappan, 76*(9), 701–712.

Farkas, S. , Foley, P., & Duffett, A. (2001). *Just waiting to be asked? A fresh look at attitudes on public engagement.* New York: Public Agenda, http://www.publicagenda.org.

Fine, M. (1993). (Ap)parent involvement: Reflections on parents, power, and urban public schools. *Teachers College Press, 94,* 682–710.

Katz, M. B., Fine, M., & Simon, E. (1997). Poking around: Outsiders view Chicago school reform. *Teachers College Press, 99,* 117–157.

Lareau, A. (2000). *Home advantage: Social class and parental intervention in elementary education.* Lanham, MD: Rowman & Littlefield.

Macias, R. F., & Garcia Ramos, R. G. (Eds.). (1995). *Changing schools for changing students: An anthology of research on language minorities, schools, and society.* Santa Barbara: University of California Minority Research Institute.

Miller, S., Johnson, L., & Truesdale, K. (2000). *The Parent Partnership Report: Parent perceptions of the schools we have, the schools we need.* Unpublished manuscript.

Morken, H., & Formicola, J. R. (1999). *The politics of school choice.* Lanham, MD: Rowman & Littlefield.

New York State District Report Card. (2003). District comprehensive information report: Buffalo City School District, 2001–2002. Retrieved on December 8, 2003.   xc

Public Education Network. (2001). *Quality now: Results of national conversations on education and race.* http://www.publiceducation.org

Sanders, E. (1999). *Urban school leadership: Issues and strategies.* Larchmont, NY: Eye on Education.

Scribner, J. D., Young, M. D., & Pedroza, A. (1999). Building collaborative relationships with parents. In P. Reyes, J. D. Scribner, & A. Paredes Scribner (Eds.), *Lessons from high-performing Hispanic schools: Creating learning communities* (pp. 36–60). New York: Teachers College Press.

Smrekar, C., & Goldring, E. (1999). *School choice in urban America: Magnet schools and the pursuit of equity.* New York: Teachers College Press.

Valdes, G. (1996). *Con respeto: Bridging the distance between culturally diverse families and schools: An ethnographic portrait.* New York: Teachers College Press.

Wells, A., & Crain, R. (1992). Do parents choose school quality or school status? A sociological theory of free market education. In P. Cookson (Ed.), *The choice controversy* (pp. 65–82). Newbury Park, CA: Corwin Press.

13 Structural Barriers and School Reform: The Perceptions of a Group of Working-Class Parents

Gillian S. Richardson

Gillian Richardson, Assistant Professor in the Education Department at Canisius College in Buffalo, New York, reports the results of her study of working-class parents' perspectives on the politics of literacy education. Richardson shared progressive education research with a focus group of seven working-class parents on such topics as the difference in teaching methods in working-class and affluent schools; the close fit between middle-class discourse and school discourse; the impact of working-class students' "resistance" to schooling; the benefits of critical pedagogy/literacy; and educational reformers who use public engagement methods to achieve a more just and equitable education for working-class students.

IN COMPARISON TO THEIR UPPER-CLASS COUNTERPARTS, working-class parents have historically been less involved with their children's education, a problem that often is attributed to lack of cultural capital (Lareau, 1987), and thus the interests of their children are commonly ignored.[1] Unless working-class parents bring pressure upon the educational system to better meet the needs of their children, we can expect that class disparities in educational outcomes will continue to persist. While the sociopolitical nature of literacy and education attainment is well known within sociology of education circles, it is basically unknown to those most affected, members of the working class themselves. This study sought to overcome the power differentials in access to information by bringing literature regarding the education of working-class children to the attention of a focus group of working-class parents.

By exposing working-class parents to the hidden curriculum in school that advantages certain social groups over others and by uncovering issues critical for engaging them in positive change in the education of their children, this study encouraged parents to critique the social, cultural, political, and economic structures that limit the literacy and academic achievement of their children and to develop greater insights into how such structures can be

---

Quotes from Parents

"I felt that participating would give teachers better insights and awaken them about the need to start stepping up more." [Ray, factory worker]

"I came in with the attitude 'you can't fight city hall.' And then after these discussions, I found that there are ways to change it, you just have to work at it." [Vicki, stay-at-home-mother]

"After talking and listening and reading, I feel there are many different forms of literacy. If you don't engage in all forms, you tend to stay in a life style that could be damaging to your knowledge. People will only see you for what you are and not what you can be." [Bill, road maintenance worker]

—Quotes from parent interviews in
Making Literacy Political: Incorporating a Critical Pedagogy in the Facilitation of a Focus Group of Working-Class Parents (Richardson, 2001)

---

altered. Specifically, this study sought to answer the following questions: 1) What values, attitudes, beliefs, and behaviors do working-class parents bring to the issue of literacy and education in general, including those related to power, conformity, and authority? 2) How does the exposure of the social, political, cultural, and economic contexts of literacy and education affect these values, attitudes, beliefs, and behaviors? 3) In light of such exposure, how do working-class parents feel that schools can better meet the needs of their children and how do they perceive their role in the process of change? 4) What effect did the focus group discussions have on parents' attitudes towards power, conformity, and authority?

METHODOLOGY

In a small urban school district in the northeast United States, which here will be called Montrose, the working classes are the predominant economic strata of the city, with a large factory as the main employer. There are eight elementary schools, two middle schools, and one high school in Montrose; the elementary schools and middle schools are divided along class lines.

A series of five focus group sessions was used to collect data for this study. Connaway (1996) describes this kind of group interview as

> an in-depth, face-to-face interview of a purposive sampling of a target population. It is similar to the case study and structured interview as a research technique. The discussion is carefully planned and focused on a particular topic to explore the perception of the interviewees in a non-threatening, permissive environment. (p. 231)

Each focus group session incorporated a sixty- to ninety-minute discussion period that was audiotaped and transcribed. Videotapes of these sessions were produced in order to capture nonverbal gestures and communications. Rough field notes were written and elaborated immediately following each focus group session.

Eight white, working-class parents participated in the five sessions, with one parent withdrawing from the study after two sessions. Given the complexity of class identity and the fact that participants are in the best position to determine with which social class they identify, self-identification was the basis of participant selection. However, parents were asked to list their parents' occupations and highest educational level, as well as their own, on the intake surveys. Of the eight participants, none held a postsecondary degree, seven were high school graduates, and one had earned a GED (General Equivalency Diploma). Occupations included: three stay-at-home mothers (Rachel, Vicki, and Lynn), three factory workers (Julie, John, and Ray), one welder (Jim), and one road maintenance worker (Bill).

Literacy with an Attitude: Educating Working-Class Children in Their Own Self-Interest (1999), by Patrick Finn, was the primary basis for discussion in the sessions. This book reviews many of the landmark studies in the sociology of education, presenting the arguments of critical theorists in plain language. Rather than requiring participants to read the book, Finn prepared thirty-minute videotaped summaries of key chapters, which were viewed at the beginning of each focus group session as a catalyst for group discussion.[2] Facilitated by the researcher, the discussion was organized by a set of questions that had been developed in an earlier study.

The main analytic strategies used in this study were thematic analysis (Aronson, 1994); an inductive approach, in which theoretical categories emerge from the data rather than from preestablished classes (Goetz & LeCompte 1984; Tesch, 1990); and sociocultural mediation analysis, which links systemic structures with social action (Morrow & Brown, 1994). A three-stage model of responding to oppressive conditions, developed by Alfred Alschuler (1980), was the instrument used to measure the effect of the discussions on the parents' attitudes and beliefs. Alschuler's model incorporates three stages of problem solving in response to oppressive conditions: magical-conforming, naïve-reforming, and critical-transforming. Within each of these stages are distinct ways of naming a problem, analyzing the cause of the problem, and taking action to confront the problem. According to Alschuler and other critical theorists, consciousness-raising involves the facilitation of movement from a magical-conforming or naïve-reforming stage, both of which are viewed as playing host to an unjust system, to a critical-transforming stage, in which the system itself is transformed. Figure 1 summarizes each of the three stages in Alschuler's problem-solving model.

RESULTS

FIRST SESSION

An Education Appropriate to Their Class—Finn Discussing the Research of Jean Anyon.

Summary: Jean Anyon (1980) completed an ethnographical study of five elementary schools in communities that differed according to social class. She observed differences in classroom work, as well as such things as background of the teachers, styles of teacher control, and dominant themes within the classroom. According to Anyon, the findings of her study suggest that the hidden curriculum of the school contributes to the reproduction of the social strata.

In their discussion of Anyon's study, which uncovered class-based differences in education, the group rejected the idea of schools operating as social equalizers, demonstrating an awareness of class bias in the educational system. This awareness was not particularly surprising given their lived experiences; what was surprising was the lack of outrage that one might have expected. No great overt emotional response to Anyon's findings was discernible. Instead, a general sense of subdued resignation permeated the group.

The group expressed their belief that schools tend to tailor instruction to the occupational expectancy of students based upon the prevailing occupations within the community. Participants frequently spoke about the fact that the schools in Montrose are divided along class lines, with the upper-class children attending schools with much higher achievement levels and the working-class children relegated to several "working-class schools" that are characterized by low student achievement and numerous discipline problems. Participants also noted that the "ghettoing" of working-class students in inferior schools is common knowledge within the city and is generally accepted by the community as "the way it is."

Several participants talked openly about having felt segregated within mixed socioeconomic classrooms when they were students because of their working-class status. Their perception was that class segregation in the class-

Developmental Responses to Oppression

	Playing Host to the System Passively (Magical-Conforming)	(Naïve-Reforming)	Changing the System Actively (Critical-Transforming)
NAMING THE PROBLEM	NO PROBLEM: Problem denied or avoided; Difficulty accepted as a fact of existence	PROBLEMS ARE IN INDIVIDUALS WHO DEVIATE FROM RULES AND ROLES OF THE SYSTEM: Self deviates; Peer deviates; Oppressor deviates	PROBLEMS ARE IN RULES AND ROLES OF THE SYSTEM: Exploitation, injustice; Blocked human development; Interpersonal conflict, lack of love
ANALYSIS OF CAUSES	MAGICAL CAUSES BEYOND LOGICAL EXPLANATION: Fatalism, uncontrollable external forces; Fears of change	NAÏVE BLAMING OF INDIVIDUALS: Accepts oppressor's explanations; Blames others: feelings of anger, resentment, hostility; Blames self: self-deprecation causes feelings of doubt, inferiority, guilt, pity, worthlessness	CRITICAL ANALYSIS OF SYSTEM CAUSES: Understands how system works; Understands all past actions that played host passively and actively
TYPES OF ACTION TAKEN	NO OR LITTLE ACTION TAKEN; CONFORMING: Pessimism, accommodation to the status, resignation; Waiting for change to come from external forces	REFORM INDIVIDUALS TO MAKE SYSTEM WORK: Personal reforms to model oppressor, or live up to standards of system; Scapegoating a peer; Avoid and/or oppose an individual oppressor; Gregariousness with peers, support without action.	TRANSFORMATION IN SYSTEM OR SELF: Change the rules and roles through dialogue, cooperation, democratic action; scientific approach; Self-actualization through personal and ethnic esteem, appropriate role models, faith in peers, boldness, risk taking, reliance on community resources, learning.

Figure 1. Alschuler's three-stage model of responses to oppressive conditions.
From *School Discipline: A Socially Literate Solution* (p. 88), by Alfred S. Alschuler, 1980, New York: McGraw-Hill Book Company.

room was often the result of ability grouping, with working-class children frequently classified as low-ability students and often ignored. As Lynn put it, "I felt I was denied an education." Participants also agreed that the institution-alization of domesticating policies in working-class schools contributed to the limited opportunities offered to working-class students; that is, mechanical schoolwork and authoritarian control disempower working-class children in school and ultimately in the larger society.

The type of work that participants most associate with working-class schools is mechanical in nature, involving such activities as copying notes from the board, isolated seatwork, completing ditto sheets, and answering textbook questions, with little or no discussion. Teachers in the participants' schools tended to expect transmitted knowledge to be accepted unconditionally by students, with no explanation of the reasoning behind the answers or any allowance for student questioning. Many participants spoke about how they were unable to learn using these methods, causing them to develop a negative attitude towards school and creating teacher-student conflict when they re-jected learning by methods they perceived to be ineffective and unmotivating.

In addition to rote learning, participants identified authoritarian control, both intellectual and physical, as characteristic of working-class schools. All the participants remember having had little power within the classroom as stu-dents, with little opportunity for voicing their opinions or having their ideas valued. Memories of punishment, not infrequently physical, were often shared in the group discussions. According to John, "That's what sticks out most in my mind—is the punishment."

While none of the participants said their children were being exposed to the type of physical discipline they had experienced as students, they did note that their children are exposed to other forms of control that equally disempower them. Just as in their school experiences, participants believe that the opinions and ideas of their children are disallowed by teachers or disregarded when they are expressed. According to Lynn, "The child's ability to have his own knowl-edge of things is not allowed." Participants also expressed the belief that their children are often disrespected and humiliated by teachers, with every partici-pant sharing at least one such incident.

SECOND SESSION

Unconsciously Playing Host to the System: The Role of Working-Class Parents and Students—Finn Discussing the Research of R. Timothy Sieber, Lois Weis, and Paul Willis.

Summary: Sieber (1981) studied the ways in which a group of upper middle-class families who moved into a working-class neighborhood were able to implement changes in the local school in such a way that they served the interests of their children. Weis (1990) studied a high school in an American working-class community in order to learn how the closing of the local steel mills had impacted the high school. Willis (1977) studied a group of working-class "lads" who perceived school knowledge as antithetical to their culture, theorizing that subtle societal mechanisms often produce a conflictive relationship in schools.

In response to the ideas of Sieber (1981), Weis (1990), and Willis (1977), the group discussed the covert nature of class-biased education and the need for working-class parents to confront it. Rather than acting in the interest of working-class children, the group agreed, inaction on the part of both parents and teachers contributes to the perpetuation of the situation in American schools. Unlike parents from the upper classes, working-class parents tend to accept the status quo in education rather than challenge perceived injustices within the system. The group identified several factors that contribute to this reaction: feelings of powerlessness, a lack of a sense of entitlement, lower expectations for their children, and contradictory attitudes towards education.

The overriding factor contributing to parental inaction, the group agreed, is a feeling of powerlessness that is commonly shared by those in the working class. The issue of class disparities in terms of social and economic power resonated deeply with the group. The participants spoke about feelings of powerlessness and hopelessness in regard to having any major impact on their children's education. They acknowledged begrudging conformity and sometimes total disengagement in the decision-making processes in schools.

The group also related parental acceptance of the status quo to two values common in the working class: an admiration for common sense and practical skills, and an aversion to a sense of entitlement. Everyone in the group expressed discomfort with the methods they view as commonly used by upper-class parents to ensure their children are provided an education in their best interest. For example, "brown-nosing" administrators and/or board members, pressuring the system through social and political networks, and becoming overly involved in the school were viewed negatively. They consider many of those in the upper classes who use such tactics to be "selfish," "pushy," "arrogant," and "snobbish," in contrast to members of the working class, who they characterize as "grassroots" people who use common sense and practical skills to deal with situations.

The group also believed that working-class acceptance of the education provided to their children is related to the fact that working-class parents generally have lower expectations for their children than do upper-class parents. They attributed the lower expectations of working-class parents to the conservative tendency of the working class to stay with what they know and are comfortable with. Lacking the cultural capital (i.e., knowledge base, finances, etc.) to encourage their children to pursue fields of study with which they have no familiarity, working class parents generally expect their children to follow in their own footsteps, namely into the working-class sector, in which high levels of education have historically not been necessary. As a consequence, working-class parents are generally content that their children are being provided an education sufficient for their future needs. The group contrasted this situation with that of middle- and upper-class parents, who know their children need a quality education to retain the social status of the family—and thus expect it and demand it.

Finally, the participants suggested that working-class parents rarely challenge the type of education provided to their children because they hold contradictory attitudes towards education as a consequence of the changing economy. On one hand, higher levels of education historically have not been necessary to acquire "good" jobs in the working-class sector, those jobs that provide a livable income and secure lifestyle. Consequently, high levels of education were generally deemed unnecessary by the working class. With industry down-sizing and increasing literacy demands in all sectors, the group believes, those in the working class have been forced to look towards education as their only viable option. Rather than viewing education as inherently valuable, however, they tend to perceive it as a forced commodity, necessary as a credential for continued survival in a changing economy. The group pointed out that as a consequence of the forced nature of this valuing, the stated emphasis on higher levels of education does not always translate into student and parent behaviors that would promote this outcome. Additionally, the group believed that as long as a number of industrial jobs are still available, many working-class parents will continue to be content with the education their children are receiving.

A secondary discussion, which related to Willis' (1977) study, revolved around the issue of working-class students rejecting high status knowledge when it is offered at school. Though none of the participants associated with the blatant oppositional behavior of "the lads," several acknowledged that they often had rejected school knowledge as irrelevant to their lives and perceived future work. According to Jim, "I do feel there's some stuff at school that they teach you that has no big bearing on your life." Jim explained that in high school he knew he wanted to be a welder just like his father. Jim stated that, as a result, he found English boring and meaningless but wanted to learn math because "it was part of my future."

Also emerging from this discussion was the notion that even when they saw the relevance of school knowledge, such as in Jim's case with math, the mechanical nature of the instruction that was typical of their experiences often led to student disengagement and student-teacher conflict. Participants remembered methods such as copying notes from the board, filling in ditto sheets, and answering textbook questions as ineffective and unmotivating. According to Bill, "I couldn't learn like that." Jim talked about conflict with his math teacher because he could not learn using these methods, and said that when he spoke up, he was disciplined for being disruptive. Despite entering high school motivated to learn math, Jim stated, "That experience sort of put a shell on me when it came to math. I had a problem with math from then on."

THIRD SESSION

The Disconnection Between School Literacy and Language and the Working-Class Experience—Finn Discussing the Research of Basil Bernstein and Shirley Brice Heath

Summary: Basil Bernstein is an English sociologist who wrote about the language habits of the English working and middle classes. Bernstein (1971) traced patterns of language use to cultural characteristics, such as attitudes towards conformity, styles of exercising authority, the amount of contact with "outsiders," and how people deal with government, institutions, and agencies. Shirley Brice Heath (1983) studied emergent literacy experiences in two working-class communities and one middle-class community, observing that early literacy experiences differed according to the predominant social class of the community.

In addition to types of classroom work and control that act as structural barriers to reducing social class differences in educational experiences and the factors that keep working-class parents from challenging these barriers, the participants also discussed how the literacy practices and language demands of school are different from those to which working-class children are exposed in their homes and communities. The form of literacy expected in school was not commonly found in their homes as children, much as Heath found in her study. Reading and writing were activities that were unrelated to their everyday lives as children; all reported a lack of emphasis on reading in the home. Few remembered being read to as a young child, seeing their parents engage in reading and writing activities, or being encouraged to read to any great extent once they were older students.

Additionally, reading was not viewed as a meaningful and enjoyable activity in which one engages for its intrinsic value, but instead one related only to school and often forced. When their parents had promoted reading, it was almost always directly tied to schoolwork. For instance, early parent-child interactions commonly involved formal and informal basic instruction aimed at preparation for school entry. Further, as older students, reading and library usage were promoted by parents only as a means to achieve good grades. The group also identified the fact that their parents had engaged them in only literal interpretations of texts as a factor in their difficulties with school literacy. Unaccustomed to "how," "why," and "what-if" questions (types of questions commonly asked in school), participants felt they were unprepared to handle abstract texts involving complex structures once they moved beyond the basic texts of their early school years.

All participants said they had read to their children when they were young, but approximately half of them indicated that their interactions surrounding books had followed the same patterns to which they had been exposed as children rather than the interactions recommended by research on children's language acquisition. For these participants, reading interactions took on an instructional tone, again reflecting Heath's findings. As in the Heath study, these participants spoke about reinforcing a literal interpretation of the text, providing few opportunities for their children to go beyond the text or to tie the text to their own experiences. In fact, several participants indicated their lack of awareness that these elements have a positive effect on the academic success of children and should be encouraged.

In addition to literacy assumptions and practices, participants identified language as an arena in which school expectations and working-class practices differ. The group agreed with Bernstein's (1971) contention that the working class relies on implicit, context-dependent language, a language of "intimates" where understanding relies on shared knowledge. (Bernstein contrasted this language pattern to the explicit, context-independent language emphasized in middle-class communities and in the schools.)

The group also explored the four characteristics that Bernstein (1971) relates to the language patterns of the working class, namely, attitude towards conformity, exercise of authority, attitude towards power in relation to society, and contact with strangers. With the exception of Rachel (who frequently expressed a conscious effort to "break away" from the assumptions of her background), all the parents agreed with Bernstein's (1971) view that the working class tends to be conformist and subsequently engages less frequently in communication where explicit, context-independent language is required.

Based upon their own experiences as children, the group instantly recognized the authoritarianism within the family to which Bernstein alluded. Participants agreed that they had few opportunities to practice social negotiation skills entailing explicit language use in their homes; decisions were not made collaboratively and thus there was little need for explicit explanations.

Bernstein (1971) also theorized that people who feel powerless avoid confronting societal institutions, which necessitates the use of explicit language. In terms of attitude towards power, the responses were mixed at first. Through continued discussion, the general consensus reached by the group was that Bernstein's (1971) characterization of the working class as feeling powerless had validity. There was some feeling, however, that the working class has a recognition of power that is available to them through group solidarity, which appeared to be tied to exposure to union tactics in the factory.

Finally, while the group alluded to the view that the working class tends to have less contact with strangers than the middle class and thus less practice in using explicit language, the main focus of discussion was on the caution with which the working class approaches outsiders in terms of communication, particularly those from the upper or better-educated classes. This suggests that participants are aware of language differences among the social classes, which can be a potential roadblock for teachers who want to open up dialogue with working-class parents.

Moving Towards a Liberating Education: Reforming the System—Finn discussing Paulo Freire's Literacy Campaigns and Freirean Educators.

Summary: Paulo Freire was a Brazilian educator who developed literacy campaigns to teach literacy to poor adults in his country. Freire believed that past literacy campaigns had failed because the poor tend to view literacy as being part of upper-class culture, a culture to which they do not belong. He also thought that those who are oppressed view their condition as natural and thus have little awareness of the possibility of change. As a consequence of these views, Freire (1970) developed a unique approach to teaching literacy, one that motivated and empowered students. Robert Peterson (1991) and William Bigelow (1992) are two American educators who have incorporated Freirean principles and methods in their classrooms in working-class schools.

Using a list of instructional elements adapted from Finn's book (1999, pp. 198–199), the participants identified nine specific areas most in need of reform in the Montrose "working-class" schools:

1) Instruction is typically copying notes and writing answers to factual questions.

2) Students are rarely given an opportunity to express their own ideas.

3) "Writing" consists of filling in blanks or lines on teacher-constructed handouts or workbook pages.

4) Students are rewarded for passivity and obedience, not for initiative and inquisitiveness.

5) Teachers focus on correctness before expression.

6) Knowledge gained from textbooks is valued more highly than knowledge gained from experience.

7) Knowing the answers and knowing where to find the answers are valued over creativity, expression, and analysis.

8) Knowledge taught is not related to the lives and experiences of the students.

9) Teachers make derogatory remarks to and about students.

As this list indicates, reforms in these problem areas should center on increasing student expression and initiative, developing critical analysis skills, relating knowledge to students' lives, and decreasing teacher disrespect of students. When asked which one reform was the most important to them, the group was evenly divided between two: 1) Students need to be given frequent opportunities to express their own ideas; and 2) Creativity, expression, and analysis need to be made essential, beyond knowing the answers or knowing where to find them. Interestingly, both of these identified reforms involve allowing and encouraging more student expression in the classroom. The lack of such opportunities for working-class children was a source of much discussion throughout the sessions.

The group's discussions of Paulo Freire's literacy campaigns and teachers in the United States who incorporate his ideas into their classroom instruction further verified the importance of increased student expression. Briefly, Freire's main teaching objective was consciousness-raising about the connections among literacy, culture, technology, and power. The primary method used to reach this goal was dialogue, which Freire (1970) defined as communication between equals, in which one person does not control the ideas of the other.

The group reacted positively to Freire's (1970) approach to teaching literacy, identifying the primary benefit of Freire's (1970) methods as the engagement of students as active learners, critical evaluators, and creators of knowledge rather than as passive learners who act as mere receptacles of others' knowledge. The participants believe that Freirean methods encourage working-class students to think for themselves and to challenge existing knowledge and systems, that incorporating such methods brings students' experiences and perspectives into the classroom, empowering them by placing value on their ideas and thus motivating them to learn. While the benefits of Freirean methods were unanimously lauded within the group, concern about the realities of implementing these methods in conservative school environments was expressed and explored. The consensus was that without parent-teacher collaboration and support, such change is not possible.

FIFTH SESSION

Factors in Organizing Working-Class Parents for School Reform—Finn discussing community-based education reform organizations

Summary: Examples of community-based organizations and other groups aimed at school reform were provided. Some of the organizations discussed were: The Annenberg Institute on Public Engagement for Public Education (1998), The Alliance Schools Project of the Interfaith Education Fund, Mothers on the Move (MOM), and the Cross City Campaign for Urban School Reform.

All the participants expressed a willingness to become involved in organizing efforts to better the educational situation of their children; however, all but one specified that they would be willing to act only in a "behind the scenes" type of role, such as attending meetings, making phone calls, and doing mailings. Only Ray, who was the most vocal member of the group, stated a willingness to take a leadership role.

Given the participants' perception of the roles they were willing or unwilling to assume in organizing efforts, it is not surprising that they focused on the need for leadership. The group felt that an outside organizer is needed to serve two essential functions: to help dissolve the working-class acceptance and passivity to which they have been encultured, by making them aware of the issues and revealing the mutability of conditions, and to provide training in organizing strategies. Change will also require a significant event about which they feel strongly and a response that would be viewed as operating for the common good. The group cautioned that what others might perceive as relatively trivial can in fact be an issue around which parents will organize, if the problem affects many children and is an issue about which parents feel strongly. As such, "significant" becomes a relative term, one in which parent group members themselves determine what is important and what is not.

The idea of collective action was expanded to include both parents and teachers cooperating in a unified effort for change. Participants believed that unless teachers are willing to incorporate changes at the classroom level, no amount of parent organizing will reform the schools to any great extent. On the other hand, the group agreed that teachers need the backing of parents to ensure that they can implement the desired changes without jeopardizing their careers. The group recognized that even the most well-intentioned teacher will be limited without such collective action.

The group also expressed awareness that for school reform to be successful, parents must support teachers' classroom efforts by playing a more active role in their child's learning. Rather than placing most of the responsibility for their child's learning on teachers, participants recognized that they need to play an equal role in that process. The group noted that many working-class parents erroneously believe that once their children enter school, parents no longer need to be as involved in their learning.

Participants believed strongly in the importance of incorporating democratic principles in reform initiatives: all agreed that they would be unwilling to participate in a group that advocates breaking laws or resorts to forms of violence as a means to an end. The group members were willing to participate in the struggle for improved schools, but both the cause and the methods must be just.

GROUP PROBLEM-SOLVING TRANSFORMATION:
FROM PASSIVITY TO POSSIBILITY

Using Alfred Alschuler's (1980) three-stage model of problem solving, changes in the group's problem-solving perspective across the sessions indicated group transformation in terms of critical consciousness and group empowerment. In the initial sessions, it was evident that the group approached problems in the education system mainly from a magical-conforming perspective, described above. The following statements were typical: "That's just how it is" [Lynn]; "You come back to—'You can't fight city hall' " [John]; "Your hands are tied" [Rachel]; "We're comfortable with basic knowledge" [Bill]; "You hear 'no' once—okay, fine. Who am I?" [Jim]; "They [teachers] know what they're doing and we'll just follow along" [Ray].

The analysis of the last session revealed a significant transformation in the group's problem-solving perspective, from the magical-conforming to the critical-transforming stage, also described above. In the last session, participants expressed their belief that the problems in education rest in the oppressive nature of the educational system itself, one that operates to limit working-class parents, working-class students, and teachers. As a consequence, the group began to question the rules and roles of the system, as well as to explore the ways in which they have unconsciously played host to this oppression and ways in which the oppression can be ameliorated.

The group's awareness and empathy with the conflicted position of teachers in a system that demands conformity clearly demonstrate that the group had indeed moved into the critical-transforming stage—one in which people are valued and systems are criticized. In addition to a transformation from perceiving problems in education as an immutable fact of existence to the view that the situation can be changed, the group also demonstrated a marked change in their analysis of the causes of the problems. In the initial sessions, the problems were seen as caused by historical inevitabilities (e.g., the state has always controlled the curriculum) or uncontrollable external forces (e.g., politics). In the last session, the group talked at length about how the working class has unconsciously played host to the educational system by accepting the type of education provided to their children.

Finally, the group's attitude towards taking action to confront problems in education was dramatically transformed as well. Foremost, the group now expressed the assumption that change is possible and actually inevitable, specifying that success lies in collaborative action that involves democratic principles. For instance, when the group was asked if parental organizing efforts would work in Montrose, Ray responded, "There's nothing that *cannot* be changed. I found through the group that it's possible."

DISCUSSION

Researchers have contended that working-class children are hindered by structural barriers that impede their academic success (see Bowles & Gintis, 1976; Haberman, 1991; Waxman & Pardon, 1995). This study supports Jean Anyon's (1980) research that suggests that working-class children are mainly exposed to easy work, few opportunities for creative expression or critical analysis, authoritarian control, and, not infrequently, disrespectful treatment. Participants immediately recognized this type of education as that to which they had been exposed as students and, with a few notable exceptions, as characteristic of the type of education that their children are being provided. This finding is noteworthy, given the fact that Anyon's study was completed over two decades ago. While some have argued that the status of working-class children in American schools has improved significantly in recent decades, this evidence indicates otherwise.

The goal of education should be to provide all students with a type of education and level of literacy that does not limit their options in life. Not all students want to pursue higher education or enter the professions, and indeed any work that contributes to society is honorable and valuable, but the choice should be the student's and should not be determined by an educational system that provides different types of education to children based upon their social class. Improving the academic outcomes of working-class children by creating schools that operate in the interests of all students will take a concerted effort on the part of both educators and parents. Placing blame on either side is counterproductive and only acts to perpetuate a system that is not meeting the needs of working-class children.

This study also supports and adds to the work of Lois Weis (1990), R. Timothy Sieber (1981), and Paul Willis (1977), identifying covert mechanisms that operate in schools to maintain the status quo. For instance, as in the Weis (1990) and Sieber (1981) studies, this study found parental acceptance of inferior schools was tied to cultural traits within the working class that hinder the active involvement of parents in school reform to better meet the needs of their children. Rather than blaming parents for what is often perceived as a disinterest in their children's education, educators must understand the role of social, cultural, and economic factors if they are to develop constructive ways of bringing parents into the process.

Additionally, participants in this study acknowledged that just as Willis (1977) noted in his study of "the lads," many working-class students reject school knowledge as antithetical to their culture. Often valuing practical skills over abstract knowledge, such students perceive school knowledge as meaningless and irrelevant to their lives. The tendency to disengage from the learning process often is exacerbated by the rote teaching methods that Anyon found in her observations of working-class classrooms. With such methods, even when the knowledge is perceived as useful, students are unmotivated to learn.

If working-class students are to be brought into the learning process, their ideas and experiences must be validated in the classroom. Higher-order skills must be tied to the lives of working-class students in their homes and communities in order to develop a connection between school and home. Additionally, democratic classrooms, in which authoritarianism is replaced with teacher-student collaboration, dialogue, and negotiation, would encourage student expression and active engagement in learning. Such classrooms empower and motivate students as well as provide frequent opportunities to develop critical analytical skills.

Working-class children not only are provided a different education, but also do not enter the educational system on an equal footing with middle-class children (see Anderson & Stokes, 1984; Teale, 1986). This study finds that working-class children bring ways of using language, of thinking, and of acting that often are different from those required for school success. As in the working-class communities in Heath's (1983) study, all the participants had had only limited exposure to literacy events in the home when they were children, and all but one had experienced reading difficulties in school. Although every participant stated that, unlike their parents, they routinely read to their children when they were young, six of the eight participants reported that their children were placed in remedial reading programs at an early age. This might be tied to the fact that despite reading to their children, these parents acknowledged, their parent-child book interactions tended to follow the patterns that Heath noted in the working-class community she observed. Namely, they tended to emphasize a literal interpretation of the text and rarely encouraged going beyond the text or tying the ideas to the everyday experiences of the child.

This finding suggests that many working-class parents have received the message about the importance of reading to their children at an early age, but that assisting parents in effective ways of interacting with their children while reading aloud may be equally as important. For instance, most of the participants were surprised by the suggestion that asking "what if" questions rather than sticking "to the facts" was a skill to be encouraged. Family literacy programs that provide parents with guidance in how to effectively interact with their children during reading aloud can help prepare children for the literacy demands of school.

In addition to entering school with different literacy experiences, working-class children also bring with them different language patterns. Confirming Bernstein's (1971) theory, the participants in this study identified working-class language patterns as emphasizing implicit language that is context dependent. In other words, it is a language "of intimates" in which commonly shared knowledge is assumed. This is in contrast to the explicit context-independent language that is more common in middle-class homes and is expected at school. Tied to cultural traits involving conformity, power, and contact with strangers, working-class children often enter school with much less exposure to the type of language required for school success.

Rather than assuming that all children enter school with middle-class assumptions about literacy and language, teachers need to understand that discourse differences—not deficits—place working-class children in a disadvantaged position upon entry to school (see Gee, 1991). By becoming aware of these differences, teachers can develop instructional programs that specifically teach the skills and patterns to which many working-class children have had limited exposure.

Throughout the discussions, the need to incorporate more creativity, student expression, and critical analysis emerged consistently. Given this fact, it is not surprising that the group reacted so positively to Freire's (1970) methods of instruction and the American educators who integrate his methods in their classrooms. The group was particularly attracted to Freire's (1970) notion of dialogue, a methodology that they perceived as giving voice and value to their children's ideas and perspectives and encouraging higher-level analytical skills. This suggests that working-class parents are open to progressive instructional methods when there is a perceived value for their children. Parents can be a potential source of support for educators who are committed to empowering forms of education.

Working-class parental activism to implement change in the system is crucial; without such pressure, a system that is structured to perpetuate inequality by acting in the interests of the more powerful middle- and upper-class groups will not spontaneously challenge these interests. Due to working-class parents' general lack of cultural capital and tendency not to challenge the authority of the more educated classes, outside assistance to provide information about how schools work and strategies for organizing reform initiatives might be necessary for the successful reform of schools. Any such assistance must be cautious about disempowering parents by taking over the cause rather than acting as guides and facilitators. If the initiative is not parent-led and something about which they feel strongly, it is most likely doomed to fail.

Parent activism needs to include the support of teachers who express a commitment to implementing progressive changes in their classrooms, particularly in situations where such changes are not supported by the school administration. The power held by a unified group of parents can bring about changes that an individual teacher might otherwise not be able to implement. In addition to supporting teachers' commitments to reform, parents need to reinforce the teachers' classroom efforts. Parents must understand their role in preparing their children to meet ever increasing academic standards by themselves. A partnership between home and school is critical if children are to meet these higher standards.

Successful change will come about only through increased dialogue between teachers and working-class parents. Many misconceptions and past negative experiences have created a situation where mistrust, tension, and outright animosity often permeate the relationship between these two groups. Breaking down these barriers will need to be the first step. As the discussions demonstrated, dialogue that analyzes the status of education from a critical perspective can move working-class parents beyond blaming individuals to looking at systemic problems and constructive solutions that victimize no one and empower all.

NOTES

1. According to Vacha and McLaughlin (1992), "Cultural capital refers to parents' skills in dealing with the schools, their strategies for helping their children, their understanding of how schools work, their beliefs about the role of the family in education, and their possession of prestigious knowledge such as familiarity with highbrow culture" (p. 12).

2. A copy of the book was provided to the parents at the first focus group session. Though not required to read the text, all the participants expressed reading the book in its entirety and frequently made reference to it.

REFERENCES

Annenberg Institute on Public Engagement for Public Education. (1998). *Reasons for hope, voices for change: A report of the Annenberg Institute on public engagement for public education.* Providence, RI: Annenberg Institute on Public Engagement for Public Education, Brown University. (http//:www.aisr.brown.edu)

Alschuler, A. S. (1980). *School discipline: A socially literate solution.* New York: McGraw-Hill.

Anderson, A. B., & Stokes, S. J. (1984). Social and institutional influences on the development and practice of literacy. In H. Goelman, A. A. Oberg, and F. Smith (Eds.), *Awakening to literacy* (pp. 24–37). London: Heinemann.

Anyon, J. (1980). Social class and the hidden curriculum of work. *Journal of Education, 162*(2), 67–92.

Aronson, J. (1994). A pragmatic view of thematic analysis. *The Qualitative Report, 2*(1) [Electronic Journal], pp. 1–2. http://www/nova.edu/ssss/QR/BackIssues/QR2-1/aronson.html

Bernstein, B. (1971). *Theoretical studies towards a sociology of education.* London: Routledge and Kegan Paul.

Bigelow, W. (1992). Inside the classroom: Social vision and critical pedagogy. In P. Shannon (Ed.), *Becoming political: Readings and writings in the politics of literacy education* (pp. 72–82). Portsmouth, NH: Heinemann.

Bowles, S., & Gintis, H. (1976). *Schooling in capitalist America: Educational reform and the contradiction of economic life.* New York: Basic Books.

Connaway, L. S. (1996). Focus group interviews: A data collection methodology. *Library Administration & Management, 10*(4), 231–239.

Finn, P. J. (1999). *Literacy with an attitude: Educating working-class children in their own self-interest.* Albany: State University of New York Press.

Freire, P. (1970). *Pedagogy of the oppressed.* New York: Seabury Press.

Gee, J. P. (1991). What is literacy? In C. Mitchell & K. Weiler (Eds.), *Rewriting literacy: Culture and the discourse of the other* (pp. 3–11). New York: Bergin & Garvey.

Goetz, J. P., & LeCompte, M. D. (1984). *Ethnography and qualitative design in educational research.* New York: Academic Press.

Haberman, M. (1991). Pedagogy of poverty versus good teaching. *Phi Delta Kappan, 73,* 290–294.

Heath, S. B. (1983). *Ways with words: Language, life, and work in communities and classrooms.* Cambridge: Cambridge University Press.

Lareau, A. (1987). Social class differences in family-school relationships: The importance of cultural capital. *Sociology of Education, 60*(2), 73–85.

Morrow, R. A., & Brown, D. D. (1994). *Critical theory and methodology.* Thousand Oaks, CA: Sage.

Peterson, R. E. (1991). Teaching how to read the world and change it: Critical pedagogy in the intermediate grades. In C. E. Walsh (Ed.), *Literacy as praxis: Culture, language, and pedagogy* (pp. 156–182). Norwood, NJ: Ablex.

Richardson, G. S. (2001). *Making literacy political: Incorporating a critical pedagogy in the facilitation of a focus group of working-class parents.* Unpublished doctoral dissertation, University at Buffalo, Buffalo.

Sieber, R. T. (1981). The politics of middle class success in an inner city public school. *Journal of Education, 164,* 30–47.

Teale, W. H. (1986). Home background and young children's literacy development. In W. H. Teale & E. Sulzby (Eds.), *Emergent literacy: Writing and reading* (pp. 173–206). Norwood, NJ: Ablex.

Tesch, R. (1990). *Qualitative research: Analysis types and software tools.* New York: Falmer Press.

Vacha, E. F., & McLaughlin, T. F. (1992). The social structural, family, school, and personal characteristics of at-risk students: Policy recommendations for school personnel. *Journal of Education, 174*(3), 9–25.

Waxman, H. C., & Padron, V. N. (1995). Improving the quality of classroom instruction for students at risk of failure in urban schools. *Peabody Journal of Education, 70*(2), 44–65.

Weis, L. (1990) *Working class without work: High school students in a de-industrializing economy.* New York: Routledge.

Willis, P. E. (1977). *Learning to labor: How working class kids get working class jobs.* Wesmead, England: Saxon House.

14 Workshops with an Attitude

Patrick J. Finn, Lauri Johnson, and Mary E. Finn

Patrick Finn, Associate Professor Emeritus in the Department of Learning and Instruction, Lauri Johnson, Assistant Professor in the Department of Educational Leadership and Policy, and Mary Finn, former Director of the Urban Education Institute of the Graduate School of Education, State University of New York at Buffalo, report on a two-year literacy project conducted in a Buffalo public school serving a poor and working-class neighborhood. Over the course of the workshops, parents came to see themselves as their children's first teacher; participating teachers and parents developed better communication and a sense of community; and parents organized to address problems in the school. The chapter describes how the theory and practice of "powerful literacy" interacted to produce these results.

> Just from growing up in the same area and stuff, you think nobody really has these concerns, and then you walk in here and its like, wow, there are other people out there. It might help if we get together and maybe make some changes for our children.

> —Jan, Lakeview School parent

THIS CHAPTER IS ABOUT A PROJECT—a series of workshops conducted by university faculty for parents and educators intended to develop "powerful literacy"—but it's also about the place of theory and practice in action for change. In the fall of 1999, the Mayor's office, through the Education Fund for Greater Buffalo, put out a call for proposals for increasing literacy in the Buffalo Public Schools. Three educators from the University at Buffalo, Patrick Finn and Lauri Johnson, faculty and co-chairs of the Urban Education Committee, and Mary Finn, Director of the Urban Education Institute, wrote a proposal and were funded to conduct workshops for parents and educators in one of Buffalo's low-performing schools that would a) familiarize parents with progressive, child-centered, collaborative methods of teaching reading and writing so they could provide effective support at home; b) encourage teachers to use more progressive, child-centered, collaborative methods in their classrooms; and c) empower parents for effective advocacy in their children's education and

Joseph Gilley's response to "My Dreams for My Grandson" written by his grandmother, Joan McComas.

participation in school governance.[1] Patrick and Mary Finn planned and facilitated the workshops; Lauri Johnson observed and evaluated the workshops using qualitative research methods.

THE COLLABORATORS

Lauri Johnson brought to this project a background in multicultural literacy, urban school reform, and parent activism. She has worked with urban schools in New York City, Seattle, and Buffalo for the past twenty-five years to make them more equitable places for students from diverse backgrounds and their families. Her main interest in participating in the workshops was to experience the process of parent empowerment in action. As the parent of two children in the Buffalo Public Schools, she attended the workshops in a dual role, as a parent and a participant observer. While this chapter reports and discusses the workshops from the facilitators' point of view, comments by parents and Lauri's observations appear throughout the chapter in sections titled "Observer's

Notebook." They are intended to provide a lens through which to view the workshop activities from the participants' perspectives.[2]

Patrick and Mary Finn brought to the project forty years of reading, teaching, debating, and writing based on the work of such people as John Dewey, Paulo Freire, Alfred Alschuler, Saul Alinsky, Jean Anyon, John Ogbu, Basil Bernstein, Shirley Brice Heath, John Wilinsky, Gordon Wells, Robert Peterson, and Linda Christiansen. They brought experience as facilitators in the Alternatives to Violence Project (AVP), as teachers of conflict resolution, cooperative learning, and other small group learning techniques, and as community organizers. They also brought certain assumptions, a theoretical framework.

THE FACILITATORS' ASSUMPTIONS

EFFECTIVE CHANGE CALLS FOR THEORY *AND* ACTION

When university faculty join forces with teachers, parents, and community activists to address school problems, a conflict usually arises. Teachers, parents, and community activists tend to view themselves as actors and to view university faculty as talkers. They tend to view professors as unnecessarily theoretical, complex, idealistic, and hesitant, while they tend to see themselves as plain speakers who are pragmatic, who identify themselves with right versus wrong, and who are out to win.

However, actors who disparage talk frequently do not examine the assumptions that underlie their actions. They identify a problem, attempt to nail it (or, more often, nail the perpetrators), and move on. Years of experience have taught us that viewing problems in isolation and nailing them or their perpetrators without trying to understand how the entire system works and how the present problem fits into that system doesn't get lasting results. And of course understanding how the entire system works and how the present problem fits into it is theory.

NOTHING FOLLOWS NATURALLY FROM LITERACY

In this chapter we will refer to three levels of literacy:[3]

- functional literacy—the ability to meet the reading and writing demands of an average day of an average person (e.g., read *Reader's Digest*, fill out a job application, understand directions for using a household gadget, and write a note to leave on the kitchen table). Functional literacy is associated with working-class work.

- informational literacy—the ability to read and absorb the kind of high-status knowledge that is associated with ideal schools and to write examinations and reports using this knowledge.[4] Informational literacy is associated with middle-class work.

- powerful literacy—the ability to use reading and writing to influence people and events in the public sphere and negotiate to advance one's self-interest. Powerful literacy is associated with the affluent professional and executive class.[5]

These three levels are somewhat hierarchical, but they also develop simultaneously and interactively. Unfortunately, too many people who advocate literacy as the cure to social ills believe that once you teach a child (or adult) to read, he or she will naturally proceed to acquire informative literacy and even powerful literacy. It simply is not so.

In a community where adults operate primarily at the functional level, children tend to acquire this level and proceed no farther. In communities where adults function primarily at the informational level, children tend to acquire functional literacy and aspects of informational literacy somewhat simultaneously. Five-year-olds in such communities tend to know classic fairy tales and understand allusions to some myths and Bible stories (high status knowledge compared to cartoon and comic book characters) as they learn to read and write at the functional level. In communities where adults operate frequently at the powerful level, children tend to acquire functional and certain aspects of informational and powerful literacy somewhat simultaneously as well. Five-year-olds in such communities are likely to ask kindergarten teachers why they are doing such-and-such and expect an explanation. They acquire powerful and informational literacy as they learn to read and write at the functional level.

Today in America, nearly all middle- and upper-grade students in regular classrooms can read and write at a functional level, even in "schools at risk." But most children in poor and working-class schools never become ready to read and absorb the kind of high-status knowledge that is associated with middle-class and more affluent schools or to write examinations and reports using this knowledge. They are less ready to use language to influence people and events in the public sphere and negotiate to advance their self-interest. It would seem that it is the responsibility of the schools to teach informational and powerful literacy to all children, but as long as it is generally assumed that such progress occurs naturally, even in working-class schools, this teaching does not happen. Instead the students are blamed for not doing what is "natural."

FACILITY WITH EXPLICIT LANGUAGE IS CRUCIAL

The language of both informational and powerful literacy tends to be explicit. The speaker/writer spells things out fully. He or she does not leave it to the listener/reader to "fill in" information based on knowledge or experience he or she presumably shares with the listener/writer. Basil Bernstein (1971, 1973a, 1973b) observed that working-class culture (compared to middle-class culture) tends to promote implicit language and provides fewer experiences that demand explicit language. This makes it more difficult for working-class people to acquire informational and powerful literacy.

Bernstein observed that compared to the middle class, working-class people tend to have fewer occasions where they need to deal with "outsiders." They move in what has been referred to as a "society of intimates" (Givon, 1979). They tend to rely on allusion to shared experience and knowledge for communication. This encourages them to use implicit language habitually. On the other hand, middle-class people's occupations and position in society lead them into far more frequent contact with people whom they do not know, who live far away, and who are from different ethnic, social, and economic backgrounds from their own. They move in what has been referred to as a "society of strangers." They cannot rely on shared experience because they cannot be sure of what the other person knows or thinks. This encourages them to use explicit language habitually.

WORKING-CLASS CULTURE DOES NOT ENCOURAGE EXPLICIT LANGUAGE

Bernstein observed that in working-class homes parental control tends to be more authoritarian than in middle-class homes where parental control is often negotiated to a greater degree. With authoritarian parental control, there is simply less language. For example:

Pop: Be home by 11.

Son: Why?

Pop: Because I said so.

On the other hand, when children expect to negotiate scenes like the following are more typical:

Pop: Be home by 11.

Son: Why can't I be out till 11:30?

Pop: Because the streets are dangerous after 11.

Son: But they're not any more dangerous at 11:30 than at 11:00. Can't I stay out until 11:30?

Pop: No. You need to get up for school in the morning. Make it 11.

Son: But a half hour isn't going to make a difference.

Pop: I said 11, and that's that!

The son questions the father's order with an explicit counterproposal; the father states a reason for his decision that gives the boy an opening to challenge the father's reason. The father gives further reasons that the boy challenges. Finally, the father resorts to his authority, but not before several explicit statements are exchanged.

Finally, Bernstein observed that working-class people feel powerless (You can't fight city hall!), and so there were fewer occasions to make plans, express them to others, defend them, and convince others to follow them. And so once again, there is very little necessity for using explicit language. On the other hand, middle-class people are more likely to believe that their opinions count, that they can fight city hall, and they have the political savvy to get what they want or at least put up one hell of a fight. They are more accustomed to joining together with comparative strangers (often absolute strangers) and stating their positions, finding common ground, and planning unified action. This demands explicit language and a lot of it.

Of course, middle-class people don't use explicit language constantly. Although they spend a lot of time in a society of strangers, they also have families and friends among whom they can be as implicit as the most working-classed of the working class. And working-class people are certainly capable of using explicit language when they understand that it is called for. Bernstein observed comparative, not absolute, differences.

THE WORKSHOPS

The Setting and the Parents

We conducted the workshops at Lakeview Elementary School, a small elementary school located in a poor and working class neighborhood.[6] The school is bounded by a large 1960s-era housing project on the north that is being phased out, where several buildings have been boarded up as families move out. A freeway exit ramp lies on the east side of the neighborhood, and rows of modest single-family frame houses on the south. Lakeview School stands in the shadow of abandoned grain elevators and warehouses, a constant reminder of Buffalo's faded industrial past. About twelve blocks from the center of downtown, many families in the neighborhood are without a car, and the infrequent bus service means that even a trip downtown for families with several small children is a major undertaking. The residents of the neighborhood remain physically cut off—from each other and from other parts of the city.

The families of Lakeview School also are socially isolated, with deep racial and ethnic divisions that historically have kept them apart. State Street, which runs in front of the school, acts as a symbolic racial divide. On the north side of the street, the Cooper Projects have been home to two generations of African American and Latino families. On the south side, third generation Irish Americans live in an area that we will refer to as the Old Town. The two areas maintain separate community centers, churches, and community organizations. Lakeview School, whose student population is approximately one third white, one third African American, and one third Latino remains one of the few community institutions with the potential to bring these groups together.

The staging of the Powerful Literacy parent workshops involved extensive support and resources. Child care was provided at every after school or Saturday session, with sometimes as many as twenty children being cared for in a separate room. Refreshments were provided at every workshop, and both teachers and parents were paid a stipend to attend.

Observer's Notebook: Payment for the workshops remained a tension throughout the two years of the program because the checks (which were processed by the university budget office) often took weeks to arrive. Parents eagerly looked forward to their workshop checks, expressed irritation when they were late, yet felt guilty about getting paid for something that they perceived as so useful. As one parent put it, "I can't believe how much this has done for me and I'm getting paid for it. I can talk to my kids" (quoted to Mary). Two of the most active parents freely admitted that it was the "paychecks that [initially] drew them in" but the workshop activities that kept them coming back.

THREE STRANDS

We planned and carried out the workshops believing that functional literacy is not enough and that poor and working-class people do not acquire informational and powerful literature "naturally." We believed we needed to work consciously on facility with explicit language and on participants' ability to negotiate in their own self-interest with those in authority. Based on Bernstein, we believed that facility with explicit language is impeded among poor and working-class people by their lack of experience in a community of strangers, by their style of exercising authority and responding to it, and by feelings of powerlessness.

There were three strands of workshop activities:

- building community (functioning in a society of strangers).

- parent involvement in their children's literacy learning.

- parent empowerment (acquiring and using language to influence people and events in the public sphere and negotiate to advance one's self-interest—or in this case one's children's self-interest).

Of course, the objectives of these strands overlapped.[7]

BUILDING COMMUNITY (FUNCTIONING IN A SOCIETY OF STRANGERS)

We addressed isolation by attempting to form a community in a society of strangers—parents from two separate and possibly antagonistic communities, teachers, school administrators, and university faculty. Following principles of the Alternatives to Violence Program (1986), our "Gatherings" and "Light and Livelies" were designed to help people who were accustomed to a society of intimates to feel comfortable operating in a society of strangers.

Gatherings. Each workshop began with a Gathering. Sitting in a circle each participant gave his/her name and addressed a topic briefly, such as "What I like about Lakeview Elementary School." As trust and community developed, we moved into more high-disclosure topics such as "My Dreams for My Child."

Journal Sharing. Participants were assigned to engage in the literacy activity they learned in the workshop with their child at home (or in their classrooms), and they were asked to write briefly in a journal on the experience. Journal entries were frequently shared in Gatherings and in small groups.

Light and Livelies. About half way through each workshop there was a Light and Lively (Alternatives to Violence Project, 1986). Big Wind Blows, for example, is a variation of Musical Chairs. A good Light and Lively gets everyone moving and laughing and usually involves physical contact. It's easier to address stressful topics with someone who would be considered an outsider in your community if you've just been laughing and engaging in a friendly scuffle over the last chair in a game like Big Wind Blows.

These activities are not designed to demonstrate that we are all the same after all; they are designed to assuage fear of strangers while accepting differences. Once some of the mistrust and fear of strangers is reduced, we can express opinions to people who we know hold different or opposing opinions. This of course requires more explicit language than referring to or expressing shared opinions with those in one's intimate circle (those from your side of State Street in this case.)

Observer's Notebook: Loretta, a young White mother of a kindergartner, describes how the powerful literacy workshops sometimes felt like a "big therapy group":

> some of the things that we discussed like our dreams for our children and a bad or good experience [in school] that happened to you, and being able to share it with other people . . . parents also realizing that they handled the situation, and you could get it out. It felt like a big therapy group to me. . . . I left here [the workshop] every Saturday with such a good feeling. It was such a good, positive environment. (Loretta, Lakeview parent)

Many of the workshop participants were single parents with several young children who talked about how they rarely got the opportunity to talk with other adults. Julie, a white woman with four young children she was raising alone, described her response to the workshops:

> I really enjoyed [the workshops] . . . because I'm a single parent and it's hard. . . . I was saying about my cousin, I talk to her on the phone, other than that [I don't talk to other adults]." (Julie, Lakeview parent)

Other parents in the Powerful Literacy workshops related how the workshops "brought them out of their shell." Mary, who became a workshop facilitator and later a leader in the parents' movement to protest the school's closing, began to bring her neighbor Marisol to the weekly workshops, a woman she described as "isolated." At first, Marisol said little in the workshops. By the second round of workshops, however, Marisol volunteered to help facilitate meetings for new parents. As Mary explained Marisol's situation:

> she's going through some changes, she's going through a divorce and stuff like that. She's coming out, she enjoyed [the workshops] so much because her mother always kept her like timid, and then her husband kept her timid. You know what I mean? And I don't think she ever had a chance, but she said . . . she really looks forward [to the workshops], she was turned on. She said she feels like it's preparing her to go out and get a job, where she's less shy and stuff. She's talking to people." (Mary, Lakeview parent)

The Lakeview parents appeared to use the Powerful Literacy workshops to overcome the isolation they felt from the school as parents. The workshops provided a place to learn new skills, socialize, to share their thoughts and feelings with other parents, and to create a "community of learners" within the group. This sense of community bridged the traditional distance between teachers and parents and, to some extent, crossed the boundaries of race and class differences as well.

In each workshop we taught parents a progressive, child-centered, collaborative method of teaching reading and writing so they could provide effective support for their children's literacy learning at home. Parents, who expected to learn yet more inventive ways to teach phonics, were surprised and delighted by what they learned. We hoped teachers who were not using such activities as a general rule in their classrooms would be encouraged to do so. Data collected from observations and interviews with participants indicate that because these literacy activities engaged adults and children in more collaborative (democratic and child-centered) ways of learning, subtle changes also occurred in the balance of power and ways of using authority, especially in child and parent relationships.

Observer's Notebook: Sarah, a young white woman who worked nights and attended the workshops the next morning without sleep, described how her interaction with her 5-year-old daughter had changed:

> Before this workshop it was, just do your home-work, I'm cooking dinner. Now it's "I'll help you with your homework . . . we'll share together. . . and I watch (her more) . . . she's a teacher too. I let her make more decisions than I would normally have. . . . (Before it was) this is the way it's going (to be). And (now) it is more teaching her to think. (Sarah, Lakeview parent)

Activities designed to involve parents in their children's literacy included teaching parents ways to read with their children and to talk about reading and books, about what can be learned from pictures and text, and about language. We included writing experiences as well. In an activity taken from James Vopat (1994) we talked about the challenges our children face in a typical day and asked how often we talk to them about their problems and express sympathy, empathy, and encouragement. Then we supplied paper, envelopes, and stamps and asked each participant to write an encouraging letter to her child. We mailed the letters and asked parents to a) write in their journal about what happened when their child received the letter, and b) ask their child to write a response or draw a picture in response to the letter. At the next session, we talked about the experience. There was usually not a dry eye in the house. Some experts call this kind of talk between parents and children around reading and writing a "literacy event." Research shows that the frequency of literacy events in a child's home is highly correlated to a child's success in school (Wells, 1991).

In a later session we started a writing project that resulted in a publication entitled "Our Dreams for Our Children." It included an essay by each of the participants as well as something their child wrote or drew in response to their essay (Vopat, 1994). Each parent wrote a paper entitled "My Dreams for My Child [Children]," which they revised and edited in "peer conferences," where participants could comment and ask questions about one another's papers. This, of course, called attention to the use of implicit language and encouraged the use of explicit language. Participants revised their papers at home and shared them with their children. We asked participants to use peer conference techniques in praising and asking questions about their children's writing and drawing, and to write in their journals about the experience.

Observer's Notebook: Typical educational approaches to parent involvement, and literacy workshops in particular, aim to "train" parents in particular methods or techniques. Lopez, Scribner, and Mahitivanichcha (2001) refer to this as the deficit approach to parent involvement, in which parents are viewed as in need of remediation. For example, parents are taught how to read aloud to their children, to help with their children's homework assignments, and to keep a journal of home literacy activities.

On the face of it, many of the activities in the Powerful Literacy workshops involved explicit aspects of this approach. Reading aloud strategies that involved predictions and writing activities that required parents to describe their "dreams for their children in the future" and write and mail letters to their children were designed to teach parents additional literacy strategies to work with their children. However, it was often the process of disclosure and emotional sharing that took place during these workshop activities that appeared to have the biggest impact on the participants. The "Dreams for Our Children" booklet, in particular, became a vehicle for parents to publicly affirm their hopes for their children amidst the sometimes difficult circumstances of their lives. As Julie described it in her journal:

> My dream is just that they live healthy, productive lives. In the world today it's an uphill battle, and my children are strong-willed, just like me. They come in to battle. And they flounder and falter, but if we stick together as a family, we can do it. (Julie, Lakeview parent)

PARENT EMPOWERMENT

We define parent empowerment as acquiring and using language to influence people and events in the public sphere and negotiate to advance one's self-interest—or in this case, one's children's interests. We addressed parent empowerment in two ways: 1) through activities that taught the use of explicit language and negotiating techniques, and 2) through experiences in negotiating with those in authority.

"Pass the Hat," designed to teach the language of negotiation, required participants to take turns expressing and supporting an opinion, and to accurately paraphrase the opinion of another participant. Next we role-played a parent and a school official, with the parent using paraphrasing to good effect:

School Official: Lakeview Elementary School is doing a really great job considering the caliber of the students and their families.

Parent: You don't believe that smaller classes, a bigger budget for materials, more teacher aides, more progressive methods, or greater parent involvement would do any good because the students in this school are incapable of performing any better than they do now because of some deficiency in them and their families.

We meant to demonstrate that you can nail an opponent without expressing outrage or calling them names, just by paraphrasing what they have just said. In the role-plays (and in life) the person who made the initial remark begins to back-peddle furiously, and the discussion continues. After outrage or name calling, however, the conversation usually ends.

In "Ask the Right Question"[8] we asked participants, "If your fifth grade child brought home this paper, what question would you want to ask the teacher?"

My dad and me went to the circus. We tigrs and lion. The Pink panter was chasing the clown. My Dad bout me tiger flash lite. We came home late.

Teacher's grade: C

Some typical responses were:

Did you notice the spelling (and other) errors? Why didn't you correct them?

How many Cs did you give on this assignment?

How did you arrive at this grade? What would my child have had to do to get a B?

As a final step in this exercise, participants role-played parent-teacher conferences.

We repeated this activity using a report card with all "A"s and a fourth grade arithmetic curriculum that was obviously too easy for fourth graders. Our objective was not only to give parents practice in negotiating, but also to teach parents that they have the right and duty to ask questions, and that asking honest and reasonable questions is a more effective way to approach those in authority than expressing hostility (the fight or flight approach typical of people who feel powerless).

Observer's Notebook: Parents mentioned "increased communication" as one of the main skills they gained from the Powerful Literacy project. In response to the "Ask the Right Question" activity, Denise, an African American mother of a first grader who rearranged her work schedule to attend the workshops, responded:

> This part of the course was great because I was hesitant on sending [my son] to Lakeview because of all the stories I heard. This part helped me to realize that if I know the right questions to ask I can send [my son] anywhere. (Denise, Lakeview parent)

Sonia, an African American parent with three children who was attempting to move off welfare, noted the listening skills she learned in the workshops helped her in a recent job interview:

> It was one of the questions on my job interview— "How can you be a good listener?" And the first thing I thought of was one of our workshops. So a lot of things have helped me that I actually learned

---

at the workshop. How to be a good listener, a good speaker, not to go too far into the question itself, just answer it and then go into experience." (Sonia, Lakeview parent)

Roxanne, a young white woman with three children who had recently moved to the area, felt the workshops helped her communicate better with her husband and her children, "to not just hear what they say but to actually listen to them." Shirley, an African American mother of two older children, described how the workshops helped her to learn how to get her ideas across to others:

I learned how to listen much better, even if I don't agree with whomever is speaking, to let them have their say, and not to verbally disagree, but suggest something that you think might be a little better than what the other person is talking about. (Shirley, Lakeview parent)

Parents also described how the discussions during the workshop sessions helped them learn how to communicate better with other parents. As Sonia described it:

I liked the way we got to discuss things that are going on with our children in school. Because by me having all of these kids . . . as far as getting together with other parents, I never did that before. And this is a great way to do that. (Sonia, Lakeview parent)

In order to address the problems of powerlessness and lack of experience with negotiated authority, we ran the workshops in as democratic and egalitarian manner as we knew how, following the format of Alternatives to Violence Workshops. In the first session we asked participants to develop their own ground rules (for example, don't interrupt; don't talk too long; and everyone has the right to pass). Everyone was addressed by the name they chose. In fact, everyone chose to be addressed by his/her first name, including administrators, teachers, parents, and facilitators. Off-duty facilitators engaged in the exercises as participants. We avoided contextual signs of superiority such as speaker/audience formats and tried to be seated whenever the participants were seated. We supplied a written agenda and reviewed it at the beginning of each workshop. This left participants a little less at our mercy. There was an evaluation at the end of each workshop led by a participant, and we made a point of responding to criticisms and suggestions in subsequent workshops.

In the first session we also brainstormed a list of the barriers to communication that exist between parents and school personnel and then generated suggestions for how these barriers, most of which could be paraphrased as "They out-gun us and we're afraid to speak," could be addressed, ranging from parents being able to call teachers on the phone to joining the PTA. We displayed this list of barriers at all future workshops and referred to them frequently while conducting exercises.

Observer's Notebook: During some workshop sessions, particularly the series that was held outside the school in the local Catholic community center on Saturday mornings, the Powerful Literacy workshops became a "safe space," a place where parents and teachers could meet together on an "equal playing field." For two hours once a week, the workshop facilitators and teachers shed their roles as academics and professionals and responded as parents. The parents, in turn, respected the fact that their children's teachers came "right down on our level." In the photographs of those sessions, you can't tell who are parents and who are teachers and workshop facilitators—everyone is wearing sweatshirts and jeans and sitting in a circle engaged in conversation. Mary, a white woman who had recently become guardian of two older children, describes how her view of the teachers who participated in the workshops had changed:

> I've seen the teachers come [to the workshops] so
> I know that they are really caring. And the views

that they gave and everything . . . that means a lot, because they were right down on our level. They didn't intimidate us or anything. A lot of parents are worried about that. . . . I see it becoming more of a friendship between the parents and the teachers. (Mary, Lakeview parent)

Several parents described previous negative experiences where they experienced resistance from Lakeview teachers whom they felt wouldn't listen to parents. As Mary described it, "Before it used to be like, I felt like, why bother, you know, they got their say, teachers are going to feel intimidated [if you question them]" (Mary, Lakeview parent).

One parent expressed her satisfaction with the communication in the workshop on an anonymous evaluation form: "I liked the interaction between parents and teachers. It was great to discuss some of my fears, triumphs, and hopes while also listening [to] others." Loretta confirmed the comfort level she felt talking to her daughter's teacher who was a regular participant in the workshops: "It made me more, actually, more able to ask her questions without, you know [feeling intimidated]. . . . we're on the same level" (Loretta, Lakeview parent).

In part, this sense of community was created by the stance adopted by the workshop organizers and participating teachers that everyone would participate in the activities as learners and parents. As a participant observer, my field notes are filled with examples of my own emotional responses to many of the activities. For instance, during the first workshop we were all asked to share a memory of a positive or negative school experience from the past. I quote from my field notes of the workshop:

I shared a negative experience from my senior year in high school when my Spanish teacher threatened to fail me during my last semester and I would

> not have enough credits to graduate. I explained to the group how I thought it was a power trip by the teacher and how angry I felt (several heads nodded). I vowed as a teacher I would never do that to a student. During the dialogue time, Michelle, a young mother sitting next to me, responded that she thought it was a positive experience. By influencing my teaching practice, a negative experience for me had become a positive experience for my students. I felt grateful for her insight, as if a weight had been lifted. (Lauri, Field Notes)

In an exercise called "Cutting an Issue" the facilitator described a good issue as one that is easy to understand, affects a lot of people, and has a reasonable chance of achieving positive results quickly. When asked what issue they would be willing to organize around, parents identified two issues involving the lunchroom: some of the meals were nearly universally detested. Macaroni and cheese was one such meal. It wasn't that the children and teachers didn't like macaroni and cheese—they didn't like *that* macaroni and cheese. Secondly, children who qualified for free lunch (most of the children in the school) were required to pay for chocolate milk most days, and parents were aware that at some other schools chocolate milk was free every day.

When we talk about this episode with colleagues, a frequent reaction is "Macaroni and cheese? Chocolate milk? Are these the most important problems facing Lakeview Elementary School?" Of course they are not, but experienced organizers know that the first issues parents organize around tend to be less profound than you might expect, but that's good from an organizing point of view. When the issue is low test scores, for example, parents are intimidated by their lack of knowledge and specialized vocabulary, but parents feel entitled to their opinions about macaroni and cheese and free milk. Organizing around such issues allows them to enter their first negotiations on familiar turf, and success here gives parents the experience and confidence to address more significant issues.

With very little advice from the facilitators, the parents formed a committee and made an appointment with the lunchroom manager. The first meeting was a huge success. The lunchroom manager said if they didn't want macaroni and cheese, she wouldn't order it any more. Parents also learned that a previous principal believed chocolate milk was not good for children and had decided it would be included with free lunches only one day a week. The next day it was announced that chocolate milk could be included with the free lunch every day and there would be no more macaroni and cheese.

The parents who met with the lunchroom manager were elated. They then requested a meeting with the food supervisor for the district, got a list of all the meals available, and conducted a survey among upper-grade children regarding their likes and dislikes. They planned to take the results to the lunchroom manager, so she could consider this information in menu planning. During the course of the project parents began to address two other issues: that children had only ten minutes to eat the free breakfast at school; and they had no recess. Our project ended before these issues were resolved, but we continued to meet parents in the roles of organizers when they asked.

Observer's Notebook: As workshop participants took up the issue of changing the school lunch program, they began to speak up and feel more empowered as parents. Sarah noted that others had begun to listen to what she had to say:

> I would normally just let my kid go to school, meet the teacher, she's passing her, OK. But now ... I'm jotting down meetings and ... my voice does count, and I can, you know, it might not be right, but at least I can get in there and share my views ... it just made me feel really good. (Sarah, Lakeview parent)

Jan, a young Native American woman who had attended Lakeview School as a child, describes how speaking up in the school can make a difference:

> I learned quite a bit in the workshop. I learned that voicing your opinions in a positive way can help maybe change things that you take an interest in, as far as your children's education. ... How to address your concerns, your points, to teachers or principals. (Jan, Lakeview parent)

Sonia also acknowledged the power of parents. As a result of her involvement in the Powerful Literacy workshops, she was invited by VOICE Buffalo to attend a community organizing conference in Chicago. In her words:

> The meetings [in Chicago] were very informative. I found out what people can do when they get together . . . some of the things I found out I would never have thought that we as a people had that kind of power. . . there's a lot of issues that parents don't realize they can change. We probably think we can't, but we can, we just don't know about it. (Sonia, Lakeview parent)

The teachers who participated in the workshops also noticed a change in the parents. As Deborah stated it:

> The thing I liked most was seeing the parents interact and seeing them become empowered as the weeks went on. . . . And just the way they expressed themselves. Sitting up straighter in their chair and making more eye contact and you could just see a growth in self-esteem. . . . More people are being involved now with the school and making changes. Like with the lunches, that's a big thing. I mean people have complained for a couple of years about that and nothing has ever been done. . . . So to see the parents go, hey, I can talk about this is wonderful. (Deborah, Lakeview teacher)

THE AFTERMATH

Following successes by organizations like the Industrial Areas Foundation and VOICE Buffalo, we had planned to continue to build so that parents would take on bigger and bigger issues like the school curriculum, teaching methods, the school budget, discipline, and parents' role in school governance, but this was not to be. The school board announced that several schools would have to be closed because of shrinking student numbers and budget considerations. Lakeview Elementary School was one of the schools that was closed, but not before a small number of parents from our workshops organized themselves, got two thousand names on a petition and turned out one hundred parents for a meeting with the superintendent and some school board members. The decision, of course, had been irrevocable before it was announced. So much for the rhetoric of shared decision making that the school board had espoused during the previous five years. Lakeview Elementary School was closed, its students and teachers scattered across the city in a new "choice" program adopted by the district.

Observer's Notebook: I talked with Mary about her experiences collecting signatures in the neighborhood to protest the school's closing. Not wanting to appear before the board members at the public hearing alone, Mary asked her "timid" neighbor, Marisol, to go with her. As Mary described the scene, Marisol walked forward with her up to the microphone in front of the superintendent, the school board, and assembled neighborhood residents. In Mary's words, "She didn't say anything, but she put her arm on my shoulder and stood with me while I read off the petitions."

The fact that Lakeview Elementary School was closed was a terrible blow, but we learned some useful things about parent power and literacy and our roles. Participants overcame their isolation and came together as a community. Parents learned about the benefits of progressive methods of improving literacy and formed new relationships with their children around literacy. They were exposed to new attitudes toward authority and learned how to replace authoritarian styles of exercising authority with negotiated styles. They experienced some success in exercising their newfound, legitimate power.

WHAT THE COLLABORATORS LEARNED

One of the most striking lessons for the three of us was, not surprisingly, the differences in what Lauri, the participant observer, saw happening and what Patrick and Mary, the facilitators, thought was going on. All three wrote the proposal to fund the workshops and we talked frequently over the two years of the project about how different activities and exercises were received, but Patrick and Mary planned the agendas and conducted the workshops together, as Lauri moved between her role as parent and her role as researcher. So while Patrick and Mary developed exercises to strengthen parents' use of explicit language as a tool in negotiating to get their needs met (among other goals), Lauri experienced with the parents the sense of community and trust that developed from sharing personal stories about their own and their children's school experiences.

When Lauri read the first draft of the Finns' part of this chapter several months ago, she was surprised to learn that Patrick and Mary had been thinking about Basil Bernstein's work. There had been nothing about his work in the proposal and his name never came up in the workshops; nor was there any discussion of the impact of social class on language habits, authority modes, or feelings of power or isolation. Ironically, because Bernstein's ideas had been such an integral part of Patrick and Mary's years of teaching and working and living together, in this instance they had implicitly understood that it was inevitable these ideas would play a key role in any parent workshops they developed.

As Patrick says,

Whether we're teaching, conducting workshops, or organizing we're guided by beliefs about society, politics, language, and effective social change. Sometimes this is very conscious and sometimes it's just the context we've constructed for ourselves. We've been doing workshops and using the workshop format in our classrooms for a long time. I can't say the name 'Bernstein' ever came up while we were planning these workshops, but we have very explicitly discussed the connection between him and our way of working on community in classes and workshops many times in the past.

As facilitators, Patrick and Mary felt that the workshops gave parents experiences that could help them develop and use the literacy skills and relationships that could contribute to their being more powerful advocates for their children and themselves. Reviewing Lauri's participant data seemed to confirm their views. Evidence suggested that what had been planned and implemented had succeeded in its three objectives: building community, fostering parent involvement in their children's literacy, and empowering parents. Nevertheless, the next time they do a class or a workshop, they intend to be more explicit in discussing their beliefs and objectives with the participants.

Although the tone of the workshops had been democratic and participatory in atmosphere, post-workshop conversations about the facilitators' underlying theoretical assumptions led Lauri to question: If Patrick and Mary held certain assumptions about the nature of the parents' "working class" language, did they intend to "uplift" them out of a sense that the parents were deficient in some way? She wondered aloud if there had been an "agenda" on the part of the facilitators that she was unaware of.

Lauri's sense of disquiet, and her openness and trust in raising it with Patrick and Mary, indicates the importance of not only examining underlying assumptions in work with parents, but in making them *explicit* to everyone. If Patrick had prepared activities on Bernstein for the parents as he used to do for his graduate classes with teachers, the idea of social class and structural barriers to equity in educational outcomes could have been very profitably discussed in the workshops. And such discussion could have occurred without disrupting the trust and community that had been built in a group of parents, teachers, and university faculty because both Patrick and Mary are clear in their own minds that the goal of their work is *not* to make poor people middle-class. While they see facility with the dominant (middle-class) discourse in schools and society as very useful, even necessary, for everyone who seeks the power and resources to get their needs met, there is much that is associated with middle-class culture (e.g., materialism, individualism) that makes it less than ideal.

In the end, however, it is important to emphasize that different people get different things out of the same or shared experiences—what Lauri and other parents and teachers took from the workshops was not necessarily what Patrick and Mary thought they were giving. For Patrick, it was a matter of selling people on the idea of being more powerful working-class people, and giving them the tools and experiences that help them achieve that status. For Mary, it was a matter of giving as much as you get because being part of such a community, even on a short -term basis, is so personally satisfying and rewarding. For Lauri, it was about the participants struggling to create their own meaning, find their collective voices, and establish a space for everyone in the school community.

NOTES

1. Working with parents, teachers, and community members, the Urban Education committee at the University at Buffalo established a community-wide Coalition for Urban Education (CUE) and held five "Stakeholder Dialogues" to discuss urban school reform (see Johnson, p. 157). At one of the CUE meetings a parent said, "O.K., we've dialogued about the problems in the Buffalo schools. When are we going to DO something?" The conversation turned to parent involvement in the schools and resulted in the Powerful Literacy Project.

2. Observations and data collection of participant responses to the Powerful Literacy Project were conducted over a two-year period and included recording field notes during workshop activities and interviews with thirteen parents after the completion of each phase of the workshops. These interviews inquired about their involvement with the school, their ongoing literacy activities with their children, and their responses to workshop activities. All parents also filled out short anonymous evaluation forms at the end of each workshop series. In-depth interviews were also conducted with four teachers who participated regularly in the workshops. Parents' journal writings, samples

of curriculum activities, and photographs of workshop sessions were also collected. Interviews and field notes were transcribed, coded, and major conceptual themes were identified in the data through a constant comparative approach (Glasser and Strauss, 1999). Pseudonyms were used for all place names and participants who are quoted throughout this chapter.

3. The concept of levels of literacy has been discussed by Gordon Wells (1991), James Gee (1991), and Patrick Finn (1999). The three levels referred to here are adapted from their classifications.

4. "Ideal schools" are schools that employ the "Basic Teaching Paradigm" (Willis 1977) where students generally cooperate and the curriculum consists of high-status knowledge (not business arithmetic but calculus; not contemporary adolescent novels but Shakespeare).

5. Anyon (1981) identified four kinds of schools in terms of the parents' income. In working-class schools parents' incomes were below the 50th percentile; in middle-class schools parents' income were between the 50th and 90th percentile; in affluent professional parents' incomes were between the 90th and 98th percentile; in executive elite schools parents' incomes were above the 98th percentile.

6. For more information on the workshops, contact Patrick Finn at pjfinn@acsu.buffalo.edu.

7. Our workshop structure bears a close resemblance to those developed by Freirean "popular educators" working with union organizers. See Lisa Delp et al. (2002).

8. Information about "Ask the Right Question Project, Inc." can be found at http://www.rightquestion.org.

REFERENCES

Anyon, J. (1981). Social class and school knowledge. *Curriculum Inquiry 11*(1), 3–42.

AVP (Alternatives to Violence Project, Inc.). *Manual—Basic Course*, 15 Rutherford Place, New York, NY 10003, 1986. See Web site: http://www.avpusa.org.

Bernstein, B. (1971). *Theoretical studies towards a sociology of education*. London: Routledge and Kegan Paul.

Bernstein, B. (1973a). *Applied studies towards a sociology of education*. London: Routledge and Kegan Paul.

Bernstein, B. (1973b). *Towards a theory of educational transmission*. London: Routledge and Kegan Paul.

Delp, L., Outman-Kramer, M., Schurman, S., & Wong, K. (2002). *Teaching for change: Popular education and the labor movement*. Los Angeles: UCLA Center for Labor Research and Education.

Finn, P. (1999). *Literacy with an attitude: Educating working-class children in their own self-interest*. Albany, NY: State University of New York Press.

Gee, J. P. (1991). What is literacy? In C. Mitchell & K. Weiler (Eds.), *Rewriting literacy: Culture and the discourse of the other* (pp. 3–11). New York: Bergin & Garvey.

Givon, T. (1979). *On understanding grammar*. New York: Academic Press.

Glaser, B. G., & Strauss, A. L. (1999). *The discovery of grounded theory: Strategies for qualitative research*. Hawthorne: Gryter.

Lopez, G., Scribner, J., & Mahitivanichcha, K. (2001). Redefining parental involvement: Lessons from high-performing migrant-impacted schools. *American Educational Research Journal, 38*, 253–288.

Vopat, J. (1994). *The parent project: A workshop approach to parent involvement*. Portland, ME: Stenhouse Publishers.

Wells, G. C. (1991). Apprenticeship in literacy. In C. E. Walsh (Ed.), *Language as praxis: Culture, language and pedagogy* (pp. 51–57). Norwood, NJ: Ablex Publishing.

Willis, P. E. (1977). *Learning to labor: How working class kids get working class jobs*. Westmead, England: Saxon House.

Contributors

ARNOLD APRILL is the Executive Director of the Chicago Arts Partnerships in Education (CAPE).

SUZANNE BOROWICZ is a doctoral candidate in the Department of Learning and Instruction at the State University of New York at Buffalo.

DENNIS CARLSON is Professor and Director of the Center for Education and Cultural Studies at Miami University of Ohio. He is the author of *Leaving Safe Harbors: Toward a New Progressivism in American Education and Public Life* (Routledge, 2002).

GREG FARRELL is President and CEO of Expeditionary Learning/Outward Bound USA.

MARY E. FINN is the former director of the Urban Education Institute in the Graduate School of Education at the State University of New York at Buffalo.

PATRICK J. FINN is Associate Professor Emeritus in the Department of Learning and Instruction at the State University of New York at Buffalo. He is the author of *Literacy with an Attitude: Educating Working-Class Students in Their Own Self-Interest* (SUNY Press, 1999).

MARY H. GRESHAM is the Dean of the Graduate School of Education and Vice President for Public Service and Urban Affairs at the State University of New York at Buffalo.

ANN MARIE LAURICELLA is a doctoral candidate in the Department of Learning and Instruction at the State University of New York at Buffalo.

LAURI JOHNSON is an Assistant Professor in the Department of Educational Leadership and Policy at the State University of New York at Buffalo and the co-author of *Dealing with Diversity Through Multicultural Fiction: Library-Classroom Partnerships* (American Library Association, 1993).

REBECCA LEWIS is NCATE (National Council for Accreditation of Teacher Education) Coordinator at the State University of New York College at Geneseo.

MICHAEL J. MCCARTHY is the principal of King Middle School in Portland, Maine.

SUZANNE M. MILLER is an Associate Professor in the Department of Learning and Instruction at the State University of New York at Buffalo and Project Coordinator for the City Voices, City Visions Project. She is the co-editor of *Multicultural Literature and Literacies: Making Space for Difference* (SUNY Press, 1993).

PEDRO NOGUERA is Professor in The Steinhardt School of Education and the Executive Director of the Metropolitan Center for Urban Education at New York University. He is the author of *City Schools and the American Dream: Reclaiming the Promise of Public Education* (Teachers College Press, 2003).

JEANNIE OAKES is Presidential Professor and Director of the Institute for Democracy, Education, and Access (IDEA) at the University of California, Los Angeles (UCLA). Her most recent book is *Teaching to Change the World (second ed.,* McGraw-Hill, 2002).

MICHAEL A. REBELL is Executive Director and Counsel of the Campaign for Fiscal Equity (CFE). He is the co-author of *Equality and Education: Federal Civil Rights Enforcement in the New York City School System* (Princeton University Press, 1985).

GILLIAN S. RICHARDSON is an Assistant Professor in the Education Department at Canisius College in Buffalo, New York.

MATHIAS J. SCHERGEN is an art educator at the Jenner Academy of the Arts in the Chicago Public Schools.

DENNIS SHIRLEY is Professor and Chair of the Department of Teacher Education, Special Education, and Curriculum and Instruction at Boston College. His most recent book is *Valley Interfaith and School Reform: Organizing for Power in South Texas* (University of Texas Press, 2002).

HENRY LOUIS TAYLOR JR. is Professor and Director of the Center for Urban Studies at the State University of New York at Buffalo. His most recent book is *Historical Roots of the Urban Crisis: African Americans in the Industrial City, 1900–1950* (Garland, 2000).

Index